NATIONAL HEALTH CARE

The Editor

RAY H. ELLING is Professor of Sociology and Head of the Social Science Division, Department of Clinical Medicine and Health Care, School of Medicine, University of Connecticut Health Center. He received a diploma from the Sorbonne, his M.A. from the University of Chicago, and his Ph.D. from Yale University. A specialist in the study of organization–environment relations, Professor Elling has published articles in professional journals and contributed to several books. He has served as secretary–treasurer of the Medical Sociology Section of the American Sociological Association and is a member of the Committee for Equal Health Rights of the Medical Care Section of the American Public Health Association. He is currently on leave of absence as chief of the Behavioral Sciences Unit, Division of Research in Epidemiology and Communications Sciences, W.H.O., Geneva.

National

EDITED BY

Health Care

ISSUES AND PROBLEMS IN
SOCIALIZED MEDICINE

Ray H. Elling

University of Connecticut

Aldine • Atherton

Chicago/New York

This work is dedicated to:
Margit, Ronald, Gerard
and Martin

National Health Care: Issues and Problems in Socialized Medicine
Edited by Ray H. Elling
Copyright © 1971 by Aldine · Atherton, Inc.

First published 1971 by
Aldine · Atherton, Inc.
529 South Wabash Avenue
Chicago, Illinois 60605

Library of Congress Catalog Number 77-159602
ISBN 0-202-30232-6, cloth; 0-202-30233-4, paper

Printed in the United States of America
DESIGNED BY LORETTA LI

Contents

NATIONAL HEALTH CARE

Introduction

With the passage of Medicare (Title XVIII of the Social Security Amendments of 1965), the United States became the last industrialized nation of the world to adopt a compulsory health insurance program. In the long political process of developing and passing legislation in this field the term *socialized medicine,* has often served as an ideological rallying point for conservative forces opposing new health insurance and other social legislation bearing upon the provision and experience of health services.[1] Rather than clarifying issues, the term has often clouded them.

The real issues are many and complex, though they can be starkly stated.

1. The place of health and health care in the hierarchy of values of the society. (Does health deserve higher or lower priority than education or the military?)

2. Alternative ways of financing health care. (Should this be

1

done through universal, tax-supported, compulsory insurance or through voluntary, self payment?)

3. The evaluation of care and determination of its even or uneven distribution to all citizens. (Are these assessments to be made by independent professionals, by experts working for government, or by some combination of experts and consumers?)

4. The preparation of health workers and the division of labor. (Will primary, first-line care continue to be given by some type of physician or will physicians all become specialists and leave primary care to some new group such as nurse-practitioners or master's level, primary care providers?)

5. The boundaries of the health worker's role. (Should physicians concern themselves only with treatment of illness in the body and mind of the patient, or should their efforts extend to preventive work on pathogenic aspects of the environment and the social, economic, cultural, and political orders?)

6. Alternative ways of rewarding health workers. (How are physicians and other health workers best motivated to serve society, when they get a fee for each service or when they receive a salary for their total efforts?)

7. The appropriate organizational units. (Considering only front-line, primary care, is this best rendered through a group practice, solo practice, hospital clinics, neighborhood health centers, or some as yet undiscovered form of organization?)

8. The interrelations among health agencies and programs. (Should hospitals build beds and develop expensive service programs in response to a coordinated plan or should they respond through individual initiative and competition to a health services market?)

9. Alternative structures and processes in planning and administering health services on a national, regional, and local basis. (Should health services programs be planned and administered by governmental or private agencies?)

These are live issues. The prospect of a national health care system of some kind being adopted in this country in the next few years is very real.[2] There are more than half a dozen proposals before the U.S. Congress at this writing, all have major sponsors and all are designed to bring about more universal, comprehensive financial coverage of health care costs with use of federal funds to some extent. What is more surprising, since one cannot imagine this having happened a few years ago, two of the proposals stem from two of the major conservative forces in medical care—the AMA and the private insurance industry.

But this degree of common thrust does not mean that controversy over national health care is at an end. Instead, we might see this as a period of reassessment and definition of positions following a few years' experience with Medicare and Medicaid.[3] The reassessment is almost over. While there is broad agreement on the necessity of some form of national health care, the stage has only been set for major controversy over the more enduring issues such as those identified above.[4] In fact, the many proposals now before the Congress differ as to general approach (degree of government financing and direction and extent to which coverage is compulsory or voluntary), coverage of all or some of the population, comprehensiveness of benefits, administrative structures, method of payment to physicians and other providers, sources of financing, and cost.

> The five [main] proposals may be described, broadly speaking, as based on an insurance concept and may be classified according to plans based primarily on social insurance principles and plans that emphasize maximum use of private insurance. The Griffiths and Committee for National Health Insurance proposals follow in the tradition of social insurance programs in that they are essentially universal for the groups covered, with the programs administered by government agencies and financed at least in part by social insurance contributions.
>
> The AMA Medicredit and the Pettengill–Aetna proposals are based primarily on private insurance with coverage available on a voluntary basis, administration largely in the hands of private insurance carriers (supervised by government) and financing from private sources and governmental general revenues. The Javits bill incorporates elements of both these approaches. It provides for a universal Federal program based on social insurance financing, but offers the alternative of "electing out" of the basic program by securing approved private insurance coverage.[5]

I intend to provide in this book some context for the better understanding of the many and complex issues around which the controversy over national health care will swirl. If there is one fundamental point to make, it is that financing, insurance, payment—the money aspects of national health care—cannot solve our health care problems without provision for the motivational and organizational arrangements that will prove to be adequate to an attack on the key and general health problems of our people. If a system of national payment for comprehensive health care were put in force tomorrow, without change in the numbers and arrangement of health manpower, without change in the payment and motivational structure to bring about greater attention to preventive and rehabilitative measures, without planning structures adequate to the task of interorganizational and interprofessional coordination, and without other organizational changes, we would face greater chaos than we do today.

And today our health care system is no bargain. The United States spends more of its total resources for health than any other country. Yet it falls short of many other countries on certain primary indexes of health. As now deployed, there is a growing shortage of physicians. Medical care is unevenly distributed among the rich and poor, majority and minority groups, and urban and rural dwellers. And health-care costs are sky rocketing.

No doubt the growing pressure for some form of national health care is due in part to the fact that all groups—majority as well as minority—are beginning to experience the inadequacies of our system.

> The poor have known for years that medical care was expensive, hard to get and uneven in quality. So has much of rural and small-town America. Now the urban middle class, which must receive its care from the same poorly organized system, is learning all this, too. Although high costs have hit harder than any other problem so far, the American middle class is beginning to understand that poor organization also can result in death or disability. . . .
> If cost were any indication of quality, then America would be the healthiest nation in recorded history. We spend more money on health and medical care than any other people in the world: $63 billion a year, 6.7 per cent of our Gross National Product, $294 per person. No other country can match any of these figures.
> But a dozen nations, each of which spends less per country and per person, can match us and do a better job of preventing infant deaths. Twelve nations also have a lower maternal mortality rate.

In seventeen countries, men live longer than in the United States. Women have a better chance of surviving in ten other countries. And the percentage of men who will die between the ages of forty and fifty is less in seventeen other nations. Obviously, we are not the healthiest nation in the world. We are not even close.[6]

The health of a people is a complex matter involving biological inheritance, education, income, physical environment, and cultural ways. But the medical care system remains an important concern in this picture. Yet the United States lacks a national health policy. Without a policy there are no goals and no strategies or organizational structures for pursuing them. "This is what we have today, and the result is that medical care, instead of being a public responsibility, is a private business. It is operated more for the convenience of its practitioners than according to the needs of the sick."[7]

If our health is not adequate and if our health care system is in part at fault, and if money to pay for care is only part of the answer, then it is very important how national health care is to be organized. Broadly, and starkly stated, the controversy is joined around public responsibility versus private business; the health interests of the people versus the professional autonomy of the practitioners.

To provide some of the context for better understanding this controversy, this book is organized into five parts. In the first, some fundamental alternatives in social philosophy are presented, and some of the historical background is covered against which the controversy in its present form can be seen. In the second part, the inadequacies of the present system in terms of the health of the black American are detailed. It includes a defense of the present system that serves as a position against which proposals for change in subsequent parts can be weighed. The third section deals with national health insurance proposals; and methods of payment to physicians are dealt with in Part III. In Part IV we take up questions of manpower and organization—group versus solo practice. Finally, we are concerned with relations between health agencies and planning of health services.

The introduction to each part is meant to highlight the controversy. At the end of each section a bibliography is included to enable the reader to pursue the issues further on his own. In addition, most chapters include a useful set of references.

It has frankly been difficult to locate adequate statements of the conservative position covering specific aspects of national health care. Somehow, the conservative position, when it is well stated, and not simply a matter of bombast and ideological labels (something that occurs on both sides) is generally broad-ranging, dealing with most aspects of the controversy. While the article by Spencer serves as a fundamental statement of conservative social philosophy, it is dated and mainly of historical interest. Thus the excellent article by Halberstam is included as a general defense of the current U.S. health system, albeit with recognition of the need for moderate change. Halberstam's chapter can be seen as a challenge to the points made in each of the following pieces that urge significant change and deal more with specific aspects of national health care. In addition, as editor concerned with controversy, I have attempted to outline the conservative argument in introductory comments or editorial footnotes when the position is not represented by included articles.

NOTES

1. Richard Harris, *A Sacred Trust* (New York, New American Library, 1966) includes a blow-by-blow account of the history and passage of the Medicare legislation.
2. "Health Care Drive, Broad National Plan to Pay Medical Bills Gains Growing Support," *The Wall Street Journal* (April 1, 1970), p. 1. "Health Care, Rx for Change," *Saturday Review,* A special issue, with articles by Senator Abraham Ribicoff, Dr. John H. Knowles, Carl M. Cobb and Rashi Fein, (August 22, 1970).
3. "Medicare and Medicaid, Problems, Issues and Alternatives," Report of the Staff to the Committee on Finance, United States Senate, February 9, 1970. Wilbur Cohen, "National Health Insurance—Problems and Prospects," The 1970 Michael M. Davis Lecture, Center for Health Administration Studies, University of Chicago.
4. "National Health Care, The Gathering Storm," *American Medical News,* (October 27, 1969), pp. 1, 8.
5. Saul Waldman and Evelyn Peel, "National Health Insurance: A Comparison of Five Proposals," Research and Statistics Note, Social Security Administration, Office of Research and Statistics, Note No. 12—1970, July 23, 1970. See also, Martin E. Segal Company "1970 Proposals for National Health Insurance," *Newsletter* 14 (July, 1970).
6. Abraham Ribicoff, "The 'Healthiest Nation' Myth," *Saturday Review, op. cit.,* p. 19.
7. *Ibid.,* p. 20.

I History and Social Philosophy

The full background of man's attempts to provide for his own and his brothers' health would extend to all human societies at all times. Every society has some institutionalized means of seeking to prevent and alleviate personal misfortune and illness. But it was only in the last century, after the discovery of the germ theory of disease and its application in asepsis and antisepsis gave the average hospital patient a better-than-even chance of surviving, that public demand for medical care entered significantly into the sphere of political controversy. Before the effectiveness of scientific medical care was recognized, concern for protection against industrial accidents and other aspects of health was part of a broader picture of social security in the face of the ravages of the industrial revolution.

As early as 1849, in reaction to the abortive revolutionary attempts of 1848, Bismark said, "The social insecurity of the worker is the real cause of their being a peril to the state"[1] But it was not until he became chancellor of all Germany and sought to

undercut a new tide of social revolution that the first national
health insurance was passed. On June 15, 1883, after Liberals
fought for the sacred principles of individualism and laissez-faire
"and called Bismark a socialist—Bismark who was out to destroy the socialist movement,"[2] the first compulsory national
"Sickness Insurance Act" became law.

> Bismark, of course, would have liked to have a uniform, cen-
> tralized sickness insurance organization. Realizing that such a
> scheme would never obtain a parliamentary majority, he compro-
> mised and the bill permitted that use be made of the infinite
> variety of existing private sickness benefit societies. The only
> conditions were that these funds would provide minimum bene-
> fits set by law, that they would present annual reports, and
> would invest their funds in accordance with certain regulations.

> The Act required workers engaged in limited occupations to be
> insured with one of the existing funds or one to be created for
> the purpose. Two-thirds of the premiums were contributed by the
> employers, and the funds were administered by both groups
> in proportion to the contributions made. The benefits included
> medical care and sickness money in case of illness and also in
> case of accident during the first 13 weeks; i.e., before accident
> insurance became effective, and in addition maternity and funeral
> benefits.[3]

Even governmental development of broad environmental and
mass public health measures was opposed by the classical Liberals before personal medical care became an issue. Spencer, one
of the leading social and political philosophers of the period, offered some of the more enduring arguments against government
"intervention" in the health field in his statement of 1850 (with
notes from 1890 added in this edited version). Under "the law
of equal freedom," government was not to abridge the rights of
one person in favor of another. For government to set standards
and thereby prop up "the priesthood" of medicine was to show
favoritism. Also, the principles of social Darwinism dictated that
if the ignorant and the less fit patronized quacks and other less
effective practitioners, they should be left to survive or not as
best they could. Natural forces were at work; these were good;

they should not be tampered with unduly. So would man evolve to a higher, more fit sort of being. The proper approach to problems was for enterprise to turn a profit in attacking and solving them.

Although this sounds extreme today, these views of individual liberty, enterprise, and suspicion of government originated in the work of John Locke and others whose ideas and phrases contributed to our Constitution. Social Darwinism as reflected in Spencer's writing only bolstered a hands-off policy in the face of human wastage generated by the industrial revolution.

Although dated and curious in some respects (our knowledge base has changed; we no longer pursue public health programs for reasons of bad humors, though some portion of our current "scientifically based" programs may turn out to be equally curious), the basic arguments and sentiments in Spencer's chapter run deep, even in our current political thought and controversy.

The summary principle of this philosophy of government, is "that government is best which governs least." The purest expression of this philosophy is perhaps found in John Stuart Mill's *Essay on Liberty* (1859) in which the primary purpose of government was to secure the individual's liberty, interpreted narrowly as freedom from restraint. Exceptions to the policy of confining governmental activity to the narrowest limits were viewed as possibly necessary and unavoidable, but unfortunate.[4]

In quite an opposite vein from Spencer, Sigerist, writing in 1938, even views the thousands of "perfectly useless" members of society as "unfortunate fellow citizens" for whom humanitarian motives dictate that we must provide medical care in the hope that ways will be found to reduce their numbers or make them contributing members of society. Adequate health care is seen as a basic human right of all members of society. Sigerist goes beyond the label "socialized medicine," to describe an ideal health care program. Here goals and composition of the program are what are essential, rather than the source of financing. Yet financing, payment, and governmental responsibility relate to motivation and organization. Sigerist takes up several classic arguments against socialized medicine and attempts to refute each: it will lead to regimentation of doctor and patient; salaried employment will destroy incentives and lead to professional neglect;

free choice of physician and the patient's related confidence in his doctor will be harmed; quality will be lowered through routine; and government control will mean decisions based on politics rather than merit. His concluding call for systems of care that will bring our medical knowledge to bear on behalf of all the people has a very modern ring to it.

Glaser provides a more current view of socialized medicine in several countries. His examination offers two major lessons: first, there are considerable variations in national health care systems; second, regardless of the form the system takes, the physician continues to stand high in prestige, authority, and rewards.

The additional readings at the end of this part are divided into general works; those dealing with developments in Britain, the United States, and other countries and cross-national comparisons. Much in the way of valuable contemporary history and social philosophy is available in the recently developed approach of systematically comparing health systems of different countries. A selection of these works is included in the last section of the additional readings.[5]

NOTES

1. As quoted by Henry E. Sigerist, "From Bismark to Beveridge, Developments and Trends in Social Security Legislation," *Bulletin of the History of Medicine* 13 (April, 1943), pp. 365–388; quote and source, p. 376.
2. *Ibid.*, p. 380.
3. *Ibid.*
4. W. J. Shepard, "History and Theory of Government," *Encyclopedia of the Social Sciences,* (New York, Macmillan, 1932), V. 7, pp. 8–15.
5. See especially the special issue of *Medical Care* (May–June, 1971) made up of the Asilomar Conference papers on the cross-national study of medical care systems.

1 Sanitary Supervision

HERBERT SPENCER*

The current ideas respecting legislative interference in sanitary matters, do not seem to have taken the form of a definite theory. The Eastern Medical Association of Scotland does indeed hold "that it is the duty of the State to adopt measures for protecting the health as well as the property of its subjects;" and *The Times* lately asserted that "the Privy Council is chargeable with the health of the Empire;"** but no considerable political party has adopted either of these dogmas by way of a distinct confession of faith.

That it comes within the proper sphere of government to repress nuisances is evident. He who contaminates the atmosphere breathed by his neighbour, is infringing his neighbour's rights.

---

* 1820–1903. English social philosopher. His views of man and society were supported by a belief in natural selection and the "wise severity of natural laws." *Social Statics* first appeared in 1850. The present selection is from *Social Statistics, Abridged and Revised* (New York, D. Appleton & Co., 1892).
** See *The Times,* October 17, 1848

11

Men having equal claims to the free use of the elements, and having that exercise more or less limited by whatever makes the elements more or less unusable, are obviously trespassed against by any one who unnecessarily vitiates the elements, and renders them detrimental to health, or disagreeable to the senses; and in the discharge of its function as protector, a government is called upon to afford redress to those so trespassed against.

Beyond this, however, it cannot lawfully go. As already shown in several kindred cases, for a government to take from a citizen more property than is needful for the efficient defence of that citizen's rights, is to infringe his rights. And hence all taxation for sanitary superintendence coming, as it does, within this category, must be condemned.

The theory which Boards of Health and the like imply, is not only inconsistent with our definition of State-duty, but is open to strictures similar to those made in analogous cases. If, by saying "that it is the duty of the State to adopt measures for protecting the health of its subjects," it is meant (as it *is* meant by the majority of the medical profession) that the State should interpose between quacks and those who patronize them, or between the druggist and the artizan who wants a remedy for his cold—if it is meant that to guard people against empirical treatment, the State should forbid all unlicensed persons from prescribing; then the reply is, that to do so is directly to violate the moral law. Men's rights are infringed by these, as much as by all other, trade-interferences. The invalid is at liberty to buy medicine and advice from whomsoever he pleases; the unlicensed practitioner is at liberty to sell these to whosoever will buy. On no pretext can a barrier be set up between the two, without the law of equal freedom being broken; and least of all may the Government, whose office it is to uphold that law, become a transgressor of it.

Moreover this doctrine, that it is the duty of the State to protect the health of its subjects, cannot be established, for the same reason that its kindred doctrines cannot, namely, the impossibility of saying how far the alleged duty shall be carried. Health depends on the fulfilment of numerous conditions—can be "protected" only by insuring that fulfilment. If, therefore, it is the duty of the State to protect the health of its subjects, it is its duty to see that all the conditions to heatlh are fulfilled by them. The legislature must prescribe so many meals a day for each individual; fix the quantities and qualities of food for men, women and children; state the proportion of fluids, when to be taken, and of what kind; specify the amount of exercise, and define its character; describe the clothing to be employed; determine the hours of sleep; and to enforce these regulations it must employ officials to oversee every one's domestic arrangements. If, on the other hand, a universal supervision of private conduct is not meant, then there comes the question—Where, between this and no supervision at all, lies the boundary up to which supervision is a duty?

There is a manifest analogy between committing to Government-guardianship the physical health of the people, and committing to it their moral health. If the welfare of men's souls can be fitly dealt with by acts of parliament, why then the welfare of their bodies can be fitly dealt with likewise. The disinfecting society from vice may naturally be cited as a precedent for disinfecting it from pestilence. Purifying the haunts of men from noxious vapours may be held quite as legitimate as purifying their moral atmosphere. The fear that false doctrines may be instilled by unauthorized preachers, has its analogue in the fear that unauthorized practitioners may give deleterious medicines or advice. And the prosecutions once committed to prevent the one evil, countenance the penalties used to put down the other. Contrariwise, the arguments employed by the dissenter to show that the moral sanity of the people is not a matter for State-superintendence, are applicable, with a slight change of terms, to their physical sanity also.

Let no one think this analogy imaginary. The two notions are not only theoretically related; we have facts proving that they tend to embody themselves in similar institutions. There is an inclination on the part of the medical profession to get itself organized after the fashion of the clergy. Little do the public at large know how actively professional publications are agitating for State-appointed overseers of the public health. Take up the *Lancet,* and you will find articles written to show the necessity of making poor-law medical officers independent of Boards of Guardians, by appointing them for life, holding them responsible only to central authority, and giving them handsome salaries from the Consolidated Fund. The *Journal of Public Health* proposes that "every house on becoming vacant be examined by a competent person as to its being in a condition adapted for the safe dwelling in of the future tenants;" and to this end would raise by fees, chargeable on the landlords, "a revenue adequate to pay a sufficient staff of inspectors four or five hundred pounds a year each." A non-professional publication, echoing the appeal, says—"No reasonable men can doubt that if a proper system of ventilation were rendered imperative upon landlords, not only would the cholera and other epidemic diseases be checked, but the general standard of health would be raised." While the *Medical Times* shows its leanings by announcing, with marked approbation, that "the Ottoman Government has recently published a decree for the appointment of physicians to be paid by the State," who "are bound to treat gratuitously all—both rich and poor—who shall demand advice."

The most specious excuse for not extending to medical advice the principles of free trade, is the same as that given for not leaving education to be diffused under them; namely, that the judgment of the consumer is not a sufficient guarantee for the goodness of the commodity. The intolerance shown by orthodox surgeons and physicians towards unordained followers of their calling, is to be understood as arising from a desire to defend the public against quackery. Ignorant people, say they, cannot distinguish good treatment from bad, or skilful advisers from unskilful ones: hence it is needful that the choice should be made for them. And then, following in the track of priesthoods, for whose persecutions a similar defense has always been set up, they agitate for more stringent regulations against unlicensed practitioners, and descant upon the dangers to which men are exposed by an unrestricted system. . . . Let it be conceded that very many of the poorer class *are* injured by druggists' prescriptions and quack medicines.* The allegation having been thus, for argument's sake, admitted in full, let us now consider whether it constitutes a sufficient plea for legal interference.

Inconvenience, suffering, and death, are the penalties attached by Nature to ignorance, as well as to incompetence—are also the means of remedying these. Partly by weeding out those

---

* The infliction of such injuries is not peculiar to quacks. During the last four years (I add this note in 1890) I have had occasion to consult seven medical men, and six out of the seven did me harm!

of lowest development, and partly by subjecting those who remain to the never-ceasing discipline of experience, Nature secures the growth of a race who shall both understand the conditions of existence, and be able to act up to them. It is impossible in any degree to suspend this discipline by stepping in between ignorance and its consequences, without, to a corresponding degree, suspending the progress. If to be ignorant were as safe as to be wise, no one would become wise. And all measures which tend to put ignorance upon a par with wisdom, inevitably check the growth of wisdom. Acts of parliament to save silly people from the evils which putting faith in empirics may entail on them, do this, and are therefore bad. It is best to let the foolish man suffer the penalty of his foolishness. For the pain—he must bear it as well as he can: for the experience—he must treasure it up, and act more rationally in future. To others as well as to himself will his case be a warning. And by multiplication of such warnings, there cannot fail to be generated a caution corresponding to the danger to be shunned.

A sad population of imbeciles would our schemers fill the world with, could their plans last. A sorry kind of human constitution would they make for us—a constitution continually going wrong, and needing to be set right again—a constitution ever tending to self-destruction. Why the whole effort of Nature is to get rid of such—to clear the world of them, and make room for better. Mark how the diseased are dealt with. Consumptive patients, with lungs incompetent to perform the duties of lungs, people with digestive organs that will not take up enough nutriment, people with defective hearts which break down under effort, people with any constitutional flaw preventing due fulfilment of the conditions of life, are continually dying out, and leaving behind those fit for the climate, food, and habits to which they are born. Even the less-imperfectly organized who, under ordinary circumstances, manage to live with comfort, are still the first to be carried off by adverse influences; and only such as are robust enough to resist these—that is, only such as are tolerably well adapted to both the usual and incidental necessities of existence, remain. And thus is the race kept free from vitiation. Of course this statement is in substance a truism; for no other arrangement of things is conceivable. But it is a truism to which most men pay little regard. And if they commonly overlook its application to body, still less do they note its bearing upon mind. Yet it is equally true here. Nature just as much insists on fitness between mental character and circumstances, as between physical character and circumstances; and radical defects are as much causes of death in the one case as in the other. He on whom his own stupidity, or vice, or idleness, entails loss of life, must, in the generalizations of philosophy, be classed with the victims of weak viscera or malformed limbs. In his case, as in the others, there exists a fatal non-adaptation; and it matters not in the abstract whether it be a moral, an intellectual, or a corporeal one. Beings thus imperfect are Nature's failures, and are recalled by her when found to be such. Along with the rest they are put upon trial. If they are sufficiently complete to live, they *do* live, and it is well they should live. If they are not sufficiently complete to live, they die, and it is best they should die. And however irregular the action of this law may appear—however it may seem that much chaff is left behind which should be winnowed out, and that much grain is taken away which should be left behind; yet due consideration must satisfy every one that the *average* effect is to purify society from those who are, *in some respect or other,* essentially faulty.

Of course, in so far as the severity of this process is mitigated by the spontaneous sympathy of men for one another, it is proper that it should be mitigated: albeit there is unquestionably harm done when sympathy is shown, without any regard to ultimate results. But the drawbacks hence arising are nothing like commensurate with the benefits otherwise conferred. Only when this sympathy prompts to a breach of equity—only when it originates an interference forbidden by the law of equal freedom— only when, by so doing, it suspends in some particular department of life the relationship between constitution and conditions, does it work pure evil. Then, however, it defeats its own end. It favours the multiplication of those worst fitted for existence, and, by consequence, hinders the multiplication of those best fitted for existence—leaving, as it does, less room for them. It tends to fill the world with those to whom life will bring most pain, and tends to keep out of it those to whom life will bring most pleasure. It inflicts positive misery, and prevents positive happiness.

Turning now to consider these impatiently-agitated schemes for improving our sanitary condition by act of parliament, the first criticism to be passed on them is that they are needless, inasmuch as there are already efficient influences at work gradually accomplishing every desideratum. . . .

We have had a multitude of blue-books, Board of Health reports, leading articles, pamphlets, and lectures, descriptive of bad drainage, overflowing cesspools, festering graveyards, impure water, and the filthiness and humidity of low lodging houses. The facts thus published are thought to warrant, or rather to demand, legislative interference. It seems never to be asked, whether any corrective process is going on. Although the rate of mortality has been gradually decreasing, and the value of life is higher in England than elsewhere—although the cleanliness of our towns is greater now than ever before, and our spontaneously-grown sanitary arrangements are far better than those existing on the Continent, where the stinks of Cologne, the uncovered drains of Paris, the water-tubs of Berlin,* and the miserable footways of the German towns, show what State-management effects; yet it is perversely assumed that by State-management only can the remaining impediments to public health be removed. Surely the causes which have brought the sewage, the paving and lighting, and the water-supply of our towns, to the present state, have not suddenly ceased. Surely that amelioration which has been taking place in the condition of London for these two or three centuries, may be expected to continue. Surely the public spirit which has carried out so many urban improvements since the Municipal Corporations Act gave greater facilities, can carry out other improvements. One would have thought that less excuse for meddling existed now than ever. Now that so much has been effected; now that the laws of health are beginning to be generally studied; now that people are reforming their habits of living; now that the use of baths is spreading; now that temperance, and ventilation, and due exercise are getting thought about—to interfere *now,* of all times, is surely as rash and uncalled-for a step as was ever taken. . . .

* For putting out fires in Berlin they depend on open tubs of water that stand about the city at certain points, ready to be dragged where they are wanted. [Since 1850 an English firm has changed all this.]

Even could State-agency compass for our towns the most perfect salubrity, it would be in the end better to remain as we are, rather than obtain such a benefit by such means. It is quite possible to give too much even for a great desideratum. However valuable good bodily health may be, it is dearly purchased when mental health goes in exchange. Whoso thinks that Government can supply sanitary advantages for nothing, or at the cost of more taxes only, is woefully mistaken. They must be paid for with character as well as with taxes.

Let it be again remembered that men cannot *make* force. All they can do is to avail themselves of force already existing, and employ it for working out this or that purpose. They cannot increase it; they cannot get from it more than its due effect; and as much as they expend of it for doing one thing, must they lack of it for doing other things. Thus it is now becoming a received doctrine, that what we call chemical affinity, heat, light, electricity, magnetism, and motion, are all manifestations of the same primordial force—that they are convertible into one another; and, as a corollary, that it is impossible to obtain in any one form of this force more than its equivalent in the previous form. Now this is equally true of the agencies acting in society. It is quite possible to divert the power at present working out one result, to the working out of some other result. But you cannot make more of it, and you cannot have it for nothing. Just as much better as this particular thing is done, so much worse must another thing be done

Or, changing the illustration, and regarding society as an organism, we may say that it is impossible artificially to use up social vitality for the more active performance of one function, without diminishing the activity with which other functions are performed. So long as society is let alone, its various structures will go on developing in due subordination to one another. If some of them are very imperfect, and make no appreciable progress towards efficiency, it is because still more important organs are equally imperfect, and because the growth of these involves cessation of growth elsewhere. Be sure, also, that whenever there arises a special necessity for the better performance of any one function, or for the establishment of some new function, Nature will respond. Instance, in proof of this, the increase of particular

manufacturing towns and sea-ports, or the formation of incorporated companies. Is there a rising demand for some commodity
of general consumption? Immediately the organ secreting that
commodity becomes more active, absorbs more people, begins to
enlarge, and secretes in greater abundance. To interfere with this
process by producing premature development in any particular
direction, is inevitably to disturb the due balance of organization,
by causing somewhere else a corresponding atrophy. At any
given time the amount of a society's vital force is fixed. Dependent as is that vital force on the extent to which men have ac-
quired fitness for a co-operative life—upon the efficiency with
which they can combine as elements of the social organism, we
may be quite certain that, while their characters remain constant,
nothing can increase its total quantity. We may be also certain
that this total quantity can produce only its equivalent of results;
and that no legislators can get more from it, although by wasting
it they may get less.

Already, in treating of Poor-Laws and National Education, we
have examined in detail the reactions by which these attempts at
a multiplication of results are defeated. In the case of sanitary
administrations, a similar reaction may be traced; showing itself,
among other ways, in the checking of social improvements which
demand popular enterprise. . . .

One apparent difficulty accompanying the doctrine now con-
tended for remains to be noticed. If sanitary administration by
the State be wrong, because it implies a deduction from the citizen's property greater than is needful for maintaining his rights,
then is sanitary administration by municipal authorities wrong
also for the same reason. Be it by general government or by local
government, the levying of compulsory rates for drainage, and
for paving and lighting, is inadmissible, as indirectly making legislative protection more costly than necessary, or, in other words,
turning it into aggression; and if so, it follows that neither the
past, present, nor proposed methods of securing the health of
towns are equitable.

This seems an awkward conclusion; nevertheless, as deducible
from our general principle, we have no alternative but to accept
it. How streets and courts are rightly to be kept in order remains
to be considered. Respecting sewage there would be no difficulty.

20 : HERBERT SPENCER

Houses might readily be drained on the same mercantile principle that they are now supplied with water. It is probable that in
the hands of a private company, the resulting manure would not
only pay the cost of collection, but would yield a considerable
profit. But if not, the return on the invested capital would be
made up by charges to those whose houses were drained: the alternative of having their connexions with the main sewer
stopped, being as good a security for payment as the analogous
ones possessed by water and gas companies.*

To the objection that the perversity of individual landlords
and the desire of some to take unfair advantage of the rest,
would render such an arrangement impracticable, the reply is
that in new suburban streets, not yet taken to by the authorities,
such an arrangement is, to a considerable extent, already carried
out, and would be much better carried out but for the consciousness that it is merely temporary. Moreover, no adverse inference
could be drawn, were it even shown that for the present such an
arrangement *is* impracticable. So, also, was personal freedom
once. So once was representative government, and is still with
many nations. As repeatedly pointed out, the practicability of
recognizing men's rights is proportionate to the degree in which
men have become moral. That an organization dictated by the
law of equal freedom cannot yet be fully realized, is no proof of
its imperfection: is proof only of *our* imperfection. And as, by
diminishing this, the process of adaptation has already fitted us
for institutions which were once too good for us, so will it go on
to fit us for others that may be too good for us now.

* At the time this was written (1850) I was not aware that a con-
clusive illustration existed. Six years afterwards I learnt from the sur-
veyor of Cheltenham (then Mr. H. Dangerfield) that before that town
was incorporated there had been formed a company by which the place
was drained; and this company paid 7 per cent. on its capital!

2 Socialized Medicine

HENRY E. SIGERIST*

In a report published last year by the American Foundation, a professor of medicine in a grade A medical school in the Middle West, member of the Association of American Physicians, wrote: "I do not believe that a patient is entitled to free medical service any more than he is entitled to free housing, free clothing, and free feeding." In other words: if a society is unable to provide work for all its members, it is perfectly normal for the unemployed to be evicted from his home and to run around naked, sick, and starving. Such a view is not only barbaric but it is utterly foolish. Nobody seriously believes that any group of unemployed American workers would sit down quietly and wait for death to relieve them. They would kick before they

Reprinted by permission of the publisher from *The Yale Review*, (Spring, 1938), pp. 463–81. © Yale University.
* M.D., 1891–1957. Held many important positions, including Professor of the History of Medicine, University of Leipzig, and Director of the Institute of the History of Medicine, Johns Hopkins University.

starved, and any government that shared the professor's view would be overthrown at the first major economic crisis.

If our professor's statement represented the general view of American society, there would be no reason for discussing our present system of medical care. Medical service then would be a commodity sold on the market to whoever could afford to purchase it. American society, however, like any other civilized society feels differently in the matter. It has come to realize that a highly specialized modern industrial nation cannot function normally if its members are sick and that it is a wasteful burden to carry a large number of sick and half sick people. The propertied class, moreover, knows very well that a diseased working class is a menace to its own health. Tuberculosis to-day is largely confined to the low income groups, but venereal diseases have not yet learned to respect class barriers.

Most people agree that it is in the interest of society to fight disease and to provide medical care for the whole population regardless of the economic status of the individual. This is, to begin with, a purely practical and utilitarian consideration. Our attitude, however, is also influenced by humanitarian motives. After all, some of the humanitarian ideals of the nineteenth century are still alive. Every society has many thousands of perfectly useless members, mostly feeble-minded and mentally diseased people who will never be able to work and will never contribute anything to society. And yet we do not destroy them. We consider them unfortunate fellow citizens. We feed them, nurse them, try to provide tolerable living conditions for them, hoping that science, some day, will give us sufficient data to allow us to reduce their number.

There are people to-day—their number is increasing—who think that man has a right to health. The chief cause of disease is poverty. If we are unable to provide work for everybody and to guarantee a decent standard of living to every individual willing to work, whatever his intelligence may be, we are collectively responsible for the chief cause of disease. The least we can do is to make provisions for the protection and restoration of the people's health. They have an undeniable right to such provisions.

Once we accept the principle that medical care must be available to all, we must examine whether the people actually receive the services they need, under the present system. There are still doctors who pretend quite ingenuously that there is not one man in the United States who could not get medical care in case of illness if he took the trouble to ask for it. They point out proudly that our hospitals have charity wards and that the medical profession, conscious of its humanitarian traditions, has always been ready to help the poor without remuneration.

Nobody will deny the good will and idealism of the medical profession. It has made desperate efforts to remain a liberal profession and has refused steadily but in vain to be dragged into business, into a competitive world that is ruled by iron economic necessities. The doctors are not responsible for the fact that the social and economic structure of society has changed. They did the best they could and kept to the job under increasingly adverse conditions. Their good will and idealism are still wanted, more than ever before; not for charity services, however, but to enable them to face the present conditions with an open mind and courageously, and to cooperate in their readjustment.

Long before the depression, it was felt that medicine had infinitely more to give than the people actually received. At the height of prosperity, in 1928, the Committee on the Costs of Medical Care was appointed to survey conditions. Whoever looked around without prejudice saw people, many people, who had not sufficient medical care. We all knew families whose budget was wrecked by a sudden illness, and we all had friends who hesitated to enter a hospital or to undergo certain treatments because they could not afford them. The many reports of the Committee on the Costs of Medical Care gave us facts and figures for what we vaguely knew, and demonstrated unmistakably that large sections of our population lacked adequate medical care.

If any doubts are left, they will be dispelled by the results of the National Health Survey that was undertaken by the United States Public Health Service as a W.P.A. project. From preliminary reports we already know that the lower a family's income is, the higher is the incidence of disease and the smaller the volume of medical care received. We know that hundreds of thousands of cases of illness are needless and could have been prevented, that many thousands of people die prematurely; and we also know that one-third of the population of this wealthy country is not only ill-fed, ill-housed, and ill-clothed, but also ill-cared for in sickness.

The facts that have become known as a result of the various surveys are so overwhelming that even the American Medical Association could not ignore them and had to admit recently that "a varying number of people may at times be insufficiently supplied with medical service."

The present conditions are not only most depressing and harmful to society but also unnecessary and stupid in a country that has such splendid medical equipment. No country in the world has a better standard of physicians, public health officers, nurses, and social workers; no country has better hospital or laboratory facilities. It is almost a miracle how the United States in less than half a century caught up with European medicine and surpassed it in many respects. Accumulated wealth and the wisdom of a group of medical leaders made it possible. And yet, one-third of the population has no medical service or not enough, and great possibilities of preventive medicine have not even been considered yet.

The cause of this maladjustment is easy to guess. Medical service, as a result of the progress of medicine, has become increasingly expensive. A hundred years ago a man with an indefinite pain in his belly went to see a doctor who asked a few questions, palpated the abdomen, and prescribed a laxative. The procedure did not cost much. Most people could afford the fee, or if they were totally indigent they were given the advice free of charge. In most such cases, the patient recovered as he probably would have done without consulting a doctor. In some cases, however, a tumor possibly developed from which the patient died.

The same type of patient consulting a doctor to-day has a series of X-ray pictures and a number of laboratory tests made which may lead to the early recognition of a disease at a time when successful treatment is still possible. It is obvious, however, that such an examination, not to mention the treatment, costs money, more than many people can afford to pay at the time.

In other words, it is not only difficult for the indigent to secure for himself adequate medical care, but for all families of moderate means, all those whose income does not exceed $3,000 or even more. This, however, means more than three-quarters of the entire population. The fee-for-service system may have worked—I doubt if it ever did—as long as medicine had little to give. Today it is impossible to protect the people's health effectively under any such system because there is too wide a gap between the scientific status of medicine and the economic status of the population. Therefore, if we think that the people's health is a major concern of society, we must necessarily devise some other system.

This has been widely recognized, particularly by the victims of the present system, namely, the patients; and since the Committee on the Costs of Medical Care began its work the discussion on the reorganization of medical service has never ceased. It has been and still is a heated and passionate discussion, in which emotional arguments are more frequently heard than rational ones. Many physicians are brilliant specialists in their field but extremely poor economists and sociologists—the natural result of a one-sided technical and scientific education. The discussion also suffered through the fact that many physicians operated with ill-defined concepts. Medical service under any but the traditional plan was indiscriminately called "socialized medicine," a vague term that few people took the trouble to define; a term that smelled of socialism or even bolshevism, and whatever its meaning might be certainly implied something utterly un-American.

While the discussion went on, experiments were undertaken to provide medical service for definite groups. Some of these schemes were sound, others futile. One mistake is frequently made in discussions and experiments, and particularly often in the plans recommended by medical organizations: the primary problem is not to devise a system that will enable the patient to pay the doctor's bill, be it on the installment plan, or through pre-payment, or under some insurance scheme. The economic consideration is secondary. (Our primary concern must be to find a system that will allow us to reach the people, and to give them the best possible medical service.) We know little enough in medicine, but we know something and infinitely more than we did fifty years ago. We now must learn to apply our knowledge without restrictions. And once we know what we must do and want to do, then we can discuss ways and means of financing such a system of medical service.

Let us be Utopian for a moment—knowing that more than once Utopian ideas have become reality—and let us visualize an ideal medical system, a system that would allow us to utilize all the present resources of medical science. (Everybody agrees that such a system must emphasize the preventive aspect of medicine). Every child knows that prevention is better than cure, and yet of every thirty dollars spent for medical care to-day, only one is spent in prevention and twenty-nine go for cure—one more evidence that the present system is unable to provide medical service in a sensible way. What, then, would the ideal plan be?

Let us take an administrative district as an example, a county, or a group of smaller counties. The first concern would be to establish a health centre consisting of a hospital, dispensary, tuberculosis station, anti-venereal station, pre-natal, maternity, and infant welfare station, bureau of physical education, bureau of health propaganda, laboratories, public health department, and whatever special institution the local conditions might require. An industrial region would call for a division for the prevention and treatment of industrial accidents and diseases. A malarial region would require other special provisions.

The health centre would be staffed with physicians representing all specialties, with public health officers, scientists, dentists, pharmacists, nurses, public health nurses, social workers, and technicians. It would be an organic medical unit, working as a team, ready to give complete medical service, preventive, diagnostic, and curative. Its function would be to protect the health of the inhabitants of the district by applying all the weapons that medical science has forged. The director of the centre would be the chief medical officer of the district, responsible for the people's health and accountable for it to the health department of the State.

Members of the health centre, general practitioners, would be placed in the various towns, as outposts of the centre. There should be at least two working together, an experienced practitioner and a younger man. There should be at least two, not only to increase the efficiency of the service but also to allow the individual doctor to have regular vacations, to attend post-graduate courses at regular intervals, and to do clinical work in the centre from time to time.

These doctors, aided by nurses and technicians, would form the local health station, the branch unit of the centre. They would work in close cooperation with the centre, referring difficult cases to it for examination, sending in patients to be hospitalized, receiving the specialists' help and advice whenever required. One of their most important functions would be to survey the health conditions of their region. They would find in one family that the mother had died of tuberculosis and that the children were menaced. Such a family would have to be watched very carefully. Its living conditions might have to be improved. The children would have to be examined regularly, and provisions made to have them spend their vacations in healthy environments, in the mountains or on the seashore. In another family the doctors would find that the father had died of arteriosclerosis, his brother of nephritis. They would know what the weak spot of this family was, and in what direction they would have to concentrate their attention.

Another function of the local doctors would be to enlighten the population in matters of health. They would organize a committee of citizens with which they could discuss the local health problems and on whose co-operation they could rely. They would also take the initiative in organizing a nursery, playgrounds for children, physical culture clubs, and similar institutions. And whatever they undertook they would always feel that they were strongly backed by the health centre. Regular conferences would bring the doctors together and give them a chance to discuss their experiences.

In the cities, health centres would be established in the various districts and in the larger enterprises, where the workers would be given entrance and periodic examinations, not in order to determine whether they should be employed or not, but in order to find out for what occupation they are best fitted. In a highly differentiated society like ours, there is a job for nearly every physical condition and grade of intelligence.

Sanatoria for the treatment of tuberculosis, hospitals and labor colonies for mental patients, and health resorts for the treatment of chronic diseases would be established at strategic points and would receive the patients assigned to them by the various health centres.

Under such a scheme the central health authorities, state and federal, would have a great task to fulfill. They would be responsible for the people's health. They would issue policies, would co-ordinate the efforts of the various local groups, would encourage research and work out methods for the application of the results of research on a nationwide scale.

If medical care is to be available to all, it must be free of charge like education. Physicians and other medical personnel would receive salaries, the amount of which would be determined by experience and responsibility.

I think there is no need to go into further details. Sketchy as this outline is, it has made clear what type of medicine I have in mind. It is socialized medicine, a system under which medical care is not sold to the population or given as a matter of charity. Medical care, under such a system has become a function of the state, a public service, to which every citizen is entitled. It is a system that allows the practice of preventive medicine on a large scale and makes it possible to apply all resources of medical science unrestrictedly.

Such a system may seem Utopian, but it is not. It actually is in operation in one-sixth of the inhabited earth, in the Soviet Union. Russia was the first country to establish a complete system of socialized medicine and did it under incredible difficulties, when the country was almost totally wrecked. In 1918 the Commissariat of Public Health was established and the work of construction began systematically. Hospitals, sanatoria, health centres were erected all over the country. New medical industries had to be created. The number of physicians was increased five times. New medical schools and new schools for the training of nurses and other personnel were built. The guiding principle of Soviet medicine is to create the best possible working and living conditions, to provide the best facilities for rest and recreation, and to protect people medically from the moment of conception to the moment of death.

The Soviet Union still needs 70,000 more doctors, hundreds of thousands more nurses, and a great deal of additional equipment, but the system of socialized medicine that has been applied is sound; it works, and in the short period from 1913 to 1936, it has produced remarkable results. According to figures given in official Soviet sources, the general death rate dropped from 30.2 to 11.2 for every 1,000 population; infant mortality was reduced by more than fifty per cent, while the death rate from pulmonary tuberculosis—still a serious problem in the U.S.S.R.—was reduced by one-half. Great progress was made in combatting venereal diseases. The incidence of primary syphilis decreased from 25.7 per 10,000 population to 1.8 in cities and from 2.66 to 0.62 in villages. Cholera, a dreaded scourge in tsarist days, has been almost overcome since 1927. Trachoma, a contagious eye disease that was very widespread among the national minorities and was responsible for thousands of cases of blindness, decreased considerably, and much progress was made in combatting malaria. In a country like Russia, such results would have been inconceivable under any other medical plan.

We must now discuss the question whether a system of socialized medicine could be developed in the United States, where the social and economic structure of society is so completely different from that in the Soviet Union. First of all, we must remember that today medical care is given to the people not only on a fee-for-service basis but under a variety of systems. There already is a large amount of state medicine in America. From modest beginnings in 1798, the Marine Hospital Service has grown into the United States Public Health Service, which together with the state and municipal services is constantly expanding. In former years, the task of the public health services was limited. It consisted mostly in protecting the country against communicable diseases that might invade it, in creating sanitary living conditions, and similar tasks The measures applied were meant to protect society as a whole.

In the last twenty years, the public health services showed a definite tendency to get closer to the individual and to perform not only preventive but curative functions as well. There were not enough charity wards in private hospitals to admit the mass of indigent patients. Public hospitals were erected in increasing number and today more than sixty per cent of all hospital beds are owned and operated by the government. Who else could have taken care of the thousands of tubercular and mental patients, the crippled, the blind, and otherwise handicapped people? And when new tasks became urgent, the government again had to step in and to establish services for pre-natal and maternity care, for the protection of infants and school children. Today only one-tenth of the work performed by the public health services is devoted to the traditional tasks such as control of water supplies, sewage systems, quarantine, and so on, and nine-tenths of the work consists of new tasks which private medicine was unable to fulfil. Why not continue in this direction and satisfy further and not less urgent needs? Why abandon the child when it leaves school? Doesn't the adolescent need medical advice more than anyone else? In Moscow and several other Russian cities every boy and girl on entering a higher school is given not only a physical but also a mental examination. The idea is to bring the young student in touch with a psychiatrist whom he can consult later should he ever be in trouble and require psychological advice.

Why should the public health services not go still further and extend their care to the adult men and women in their working places? New dangers menace their health once they have joined in the process of production, and private medicine can satisfy their needs only to a small extent.

Many of our medical schools are operated on public funds. Nobody can deny that schools such as those of the Universities of Wisconsin, Michigan, Minnesota, California, to mention only a few, compare very favorably with the best privately endowed institutions in the East. Medical research is carried out in these schools on public funds. The health departments of many States have become important centres of scientific investigations, and research has become an increasingly important function of the federal public health service. The National Health Institute has made many valuable contributions, and a new Cancer Research Institute is in process of organization.

The government has demonstrated that it is able to educate physicians, to carry out research, and to give efficacious preventive and curative services. Why not expand these functions gradually so as to reach ever wider groups of the population? The American Medical Association is perfectly willing to let government agencies care for the indigent sick so that the private practitioner would be relieved of charity work. We discussed before, however, that not only the totally indigent but all the low-income families need more and better services which they are unable to purchase. Why shouldn't public services reach this group also? Once this were done, the great majority of the population would be served by public agencies, and medicine then would actually be socialized.

The New York State Medical Society in its declaration of principles published last spring, stated emphatically that "the health of the people is a direct concern of government." This statement was repeated in the much-discussed manifesto of four hundred and thirty leading physicians issued last November. The government had accepted this view long before and had formulated it in a bill providing medical care to the unemployed. If the government is to be responsible for the people's health, it must necessarily be able to control health activities. Nobody can possibly be made responsible for matters that escape his control. The medical profession is afraid of government competition, justly so. Government services are co-ordinated and organized and therefore obviously more efficient.

It is generally felt that the health problems of the nation cannot be solved in a haphazard way, and there is a growing demand for a national health policy. Such a policy, however, requires centralized direction. Unity of command is necessary to win a war. If health work is to be planful, there must be a planning agency and an organization able to carry out plans once they have been accepted. No group, however, has such an organization except the government.

Would it be possible to finance a system of socialized medicine in this country? We know that the American people spends at least three and a half billion dollars each year for medical care, less than half of what it spends for automobiles and somewhat more than it spends for tobacco, confections, ice cream, and soft drinks. These three and a half billion dollars are spent in a haphazard and wasteful way with the result that one-third of the population has no, or not enough, medical care. If the same amount were spent rationally, little more would be required to provide adequate medical service for the whole population.

How could this money be collected so as to be distributed planfully? In various ways. At present, a large volume of medical care is financed through insurance as a result of the Workmen's Compensation Act. A system is conceivable under which public agencies would care for the totally indigent while the low-income group would finance its services through compulsory insurance. The five per cent of families with higher income would take care of themselves in the way they pleased.

Health insurance was the solution of the medical problem sought by the industrial countries of Europe. Towards the middle of last century the number of indigent sick had increased so considerably that it was impossible to give them medical service on the basis of charity. In Russia where the indigent population was mostly rural, a system of state medicine financed through taxation was introduced in the rural districts as early as 1864. This so-called *Zemstvo* medicine was inadequate in quantity and in quality, but it was a great step forward in the right direction and brought medical care to millions of people who had never seen a doctor before. In the Western European countries, where the indigent population was mostly industrial, compulsory health insurance for wage-earners was introduced, in Germany first in 1883, and then gradually in most other European countries.

Health insurance was not the ideal solution of the medical problem, but it contributed a great deal towards improving health conditions, and no European country could possibly afford to abandon it. All European systems, however, have very serious drawbacks. Mistakes were made which must be avoided if this country is to follow a similar policy. In Germany the doctors refused to be salaried employees of the Sickness Funds. They insisted on being remunerated on a fee-for-service basis. Therefore, not only the patients but the physicians had to be controlled by the Funds, which could not afford to pay for unnecessary services. The result was that the Sickness Funds were invaded by a heavy and wasteful bureaucracy. The English system, according to which the doctor is remunerated on a capitation basis, has led to a cheap type of bottle practice, and for the premium he pays, the insured patient receives only general medical care. In France the medical profession has succeeded in sabotaging health insurance so successfully that a terrific wastage resulted.

All European systems embrace only employees whose income does not exceed $1,000 or $1,200. In most countries the small independent farmer is not included as it obviously would be difficult to collect premiums from him. These various systems, therefore, do not solve the health problem of the middle class. If we were to adopt health insurance we would have to make it compulsory for all families whose income is less than $3,000 a year, or it would be still better to go so far as to include all income brackets up to $5,000. We all know how difficult it is even in these higher-income groups to budget the cost of illness. To include all families with incomes up to $5,000, however, would be to include the overwhelming majority of the population, and there is no reason in the world why, in such a case, insurance should not be extended to the entire population so that the wealthy would contribute to improving the people's health whether they use the services or not, just as they contribute towards education even when they send their children to private schools. Just as an educated population benefits the propertied class, so does a healthy population, and it is mere justice that all citizens should contribute to the common welfare according to their ability.

Health insurance, compulsory for the entire population, would necessarily lead to a complete system of socialized medicine, and it would make little difference whether we called the contributions to be paid by the individual families a premium or a tax. Taxation would seem the more logical way to finance medical service because in times of depression government would have to mobilize other sources of income anyway.

I know what the traditional objections to socialized medicine are. We frequently hear that such a system would lead to "regimentation," while the word that applies to it is "organization." Why should anybody feel regimented by having the possibility to budget the cost of illness and by having the privilege to receive all the medical care he needs? We do not feel regimented when we send our children to school, or when we appeal to a court to protect our rights and our honor, or when we call on a minister of the church for advice without paying him a fee. Nobody would be compelled to seek treatment, and if a man particularly enjoyed his arthritis he would retain the liberty of having it. Conditions are different in the case of communicable diseases where a sick man is a direct menace to his environment. This has been recognized long ago, and society has made provisions to isolate as much as possible the contaminated individual. In several countries, the spreading of venereal diseases is considered a criminal offense and is prosecuted by law. There is a duty to health because the sick man is useless to society and often a burden, but it is a moral, not a legal obligation. Gradually we come to recognize that health is much more than the absence of disease, that it is something positive, a joyful attitude towards life.

Another objection frequently heard is that doctors, if they were salaried and had not the incentive of making money, would neglect their duties. I think that such an assumption is an insult to the medical profession, and it is very queer that this objection is frequently made by medical organizations. The Code of Ethics of the American Medical Association explicitly states that "a profession has for its prime object the service it can render to humanity; reward or financial gain should be a subordinate consideration." Can a doctor wish for more than to be given complete social security and to be able to devote all his time and all his energy to his patients without being obstructed by economic barriers? I have not been in practice for a long time, but for seventeen years I have helped to train physicians and I have kept in close touch with many of my former students, who are now practicing in cities and in rural districts. More than once they have come to see me in despair because they were unable to practice the type of medicine they had been taught. Economic considerations compelled them to lower their standard and to compromise. Every young doctor knows of such conflicts, and many of the best minds go into public health service because they refuse to be dragged into business. If a man's ambition is to become rich, he should not enter the medical career—one of the most harassing professions, in which very few people ever became wealthy. Thousands of doctors work on salaries at present, and nobody can deny that they are doing a good job. And whenever a position is vacant, hundreds apply for it, so that the idea of being salaried cannot be quite unattractive. Under socialized medicine, there would be plenty of incentive for the doctor. He could rise to positions of greater responsibility, and his income would increase accordingly.

Many people are afraid that under socialized medicine the free choice of a physician would be somewhat limited. They insist that everybody should be able to select the one doctor in whom he has greatest confidence. There can be no doubt that confidence is an essential factor in the relation of doctor to patient. The elder Seneca said: "Nihil magis aegris prodest quam ab eo curari a quo volunt"—Nothing is more advantageous to invalids than to be cared for by the person they wish. We must not forget, however, that our present system allows only very few people to choose their own doctor. The dispensary patient has to accept whatever doctor happens to be there. In most rural districts, only one or possibly two physicians are available so that the patient has practically no choice; and even those patients who in the cities could make a wide selection very often call on the neighborhood doctor whoever he may be. It is very difficult for a layman to pass judgment on the competence of a physician. If medicine were socialized, the free choice of a doctor would possibly be somewhat more limited than it is today, but the physicians being members of an organization would be under a certain control. They would have ample opportunities for post-graduate training, and incompetent elements could be eliminated —which is practically impossible today. Medical science, moreover, has progressed so much and has developed so many objective methods of examination, and the general standard of the medical profession, on the other hand, has been raised so considerably in the last decades that a man need not be a genius to be a competent doctor.

Everybody agrees that the personal relationship between physician and patient must be preserved. The patient does not want to consult a committee when he is in trouble, nor can medicine be practised by a corporation. The patient will always call on one doctor and open up his heart to him, but the fact that this doctor is a member of an organized group from which he can seek help and advice does not spoil the relationship. What spoils it today is that the doctor has to charge a fee for each individual service and that the patient has to pay the bill. Once the money question is removed, the relationship between physician and patient becomes purely human. The value of a commodity can be estimated pretty accurately, while it is humanly impossible to estimate the value of a medical service in dollars and cents. Advice given by a doctor in a half hour's conversation may have tremendous repercussions in a man's life, while a major operation may be entirely worthless. If we remove the doctor from the economic struggle, we set him free and allow him to practise what medical science has taught him.

It is not enough to provide medical care for everybody. Not only the quantity but also the quality of service matters a great deal. Many people fear that socialized medicine would lower the standards by developing a certain routine. I cannot share these apprehensions. If we look around today we soon find that the quality of service given to most people is rather inferior, to put it mildly. Necessary examinations and treatments are not made because the patient cannot afford them. Post-graduate medical education is in its infancy. The highest type of service is given in hospitals, wherever the doctors are members of organized groups. This, however, is just what socialized medicine tends to develop. It endeavors to bridge the gap that exists to-day between individual and hospital practice by bringing the general practitioner into close contact with a health centre.

The most serious objection to the socialization of medicine in America is that government control would necessarily bring politics into the medical field. Political corruption has been observed more than once in the past, and it obviously would be a catastrophe if appointments were made not according to merit but according to political considerations. The whole system would be wrecked if entire staffs were dismissed and replaced whenever a new party came into power. Corruption may occur in certain government activities, but this does not mean that graft and administration are one. Political interference can be opposed by public opinion, and, as a matter of fact, has been opposed successfully more than once. Nobody can deny that our United States Public Health Service is clean and most competently and efficiently administered. More than one State and city have succeeded in keeping their health departments free of politics. In the period of transition in which we are living, government will have to take over many functions of society that could not be performed otherwise, and if the country wishes to progress in an evolutionary rather than in a revolutionary way it will by necessity have to amend its political manners. Graft and corruption discredit the democratic form of government and pave the way to fascism. To fight them relentlessly is to fight for the cause of democracy.

The average citizen is not vitally interested in the construction of highways and bridges, but he is highly concerned about his and his family's health. Political corruption in the medical field would not be tolerated; it would be opposed by public opinion in the strongest possible way. It is, therefore, quite conceivable that the socialization of medicine would not only bring health to the people but also improve our political conditions.

Fifty years ago American medicine hardly counted in the world. It has assumed a position of leadership to-day. Splendidly equipped technically, it is still backward socially, and it would be a tragedy to see medicine wrecked by its own progress. Millions of dollars are spent every year to increase our knowledge of disease. It is time that we learned to apply whatever knowledge we have. And this requires courageous and unprejudiced thinking. A new frontier has been opened up to the medical man, and pioneers are wanted.

3 "Socialized Medicine" in Practice

WILLIAM A. GLASER*

Long resisted albeit ambiguously defined, "socialized medicine" seems finally to have come in America. To its proponents, the Health Insurance for the Aged Act of 1965 promises to alleviate the anxieties and satisfy the health needs of the aged; to its critics, it threatens to create a massive bureaucracy that will permit politically-motivated laymen to dictate to doctors and hospitals. Who is right?

A close reading of the statute gives no clear answer. It reveals the Act to be a general framework rather than a specific plan. The Act provides that money shall be collected from taxes and paid for the medical care of the aged—but the precise administrative structure is left for future negotiation. Thus one cannot be certain whether the Medicare statute will achieve either the

Reprinted by permission from author and publisher from *The Public Interest,* 1 (Spring, 1966) 90–106. © National Affairs, Inc. 1966.

* Ph.D., Senior Research Associate, Bureau of Applied Social Research, Columbia University.

hopes that inspired it or the fears that it has provoked. One cannot even say, with precision, whether or not it truly establishes "socialized medicine" in America. At present, one can do no more than make informed guesses, based on knowledge of American conditions and on facts from other countries with extensive public schemes of medical care.

This article will report how publicly-sponsored systems of medical care actually operate abroad. From these generalizations about the workings of "socialized medicine" in practice, I will make inferences as to trends that might occur in American medicine, as a result of the Medicare program. I shall concentrate on the topics customarily emphasized in American discussions about the dangers and merits of "socialized medicine"—namely, the relationships between doctors and public agencies, and the effects of public programs on the performance of doctors. A fuller examination of "socialized medicine" would say considerably more about the effects on hospitals, private health insurance schemes, medical schools, and other medical institutions.

The article is based on my research into the organization of medical care in Europe, the Soviet bloc, and the Middle East. This research, extending over a period of a year and a half, involved visits to sixteen countries and interviews with officials in Ministries of Health, officials in health insurance programs, secretaries of medical associations, members of hospital medical staffs, private practitioners, and others.

KINDS OF SOCIALIZED MEDICINE

Extensive public systems for providing medical care are of two types: national health insurance and national health services. Most developed countries, particularly in Europe, have some type of national health insurance. Basically, this is simply a method of paying the doctor for care given subscribers, and the conditions of private office practice or of hospital in-patient care are changed very little. National health insurance usually evolves out of a long history of private health insurance sponsored by labor unions and cooperatives. It is based on employment: workers and their employers contribute to funds, and the funds pay for medical care for these workers, usually for their dependents, and also usually for retired workers. In order to ensure collections, to extend coverage, and to improve fiscal efficiency, these programs are almost invariably given a public character by statute, at some point in their history. Instead of relying on voluntary contributions by workers and employers, social security taxes are levied on both; and, further, instead of having to live within the limited income generated by social security taxes, insurance funds in many countries are given large grants by the Treasury from general tax revenues. Usually the insurance funds enjoy considerable administrative autonomy, within the limits of general policy laid down by legislatures. In many countries, the funds are supervised by the Ministry of Labor; elsewhere, they are governed by their own boards. It is common that the insurance system involves no newly-created government agencies, but is simply composed of the pre-existing private funds, now strengthened with legal authority and public subsidies.

Because an insurance principle is based on employment, most national insurance schemes cover only employed persons, their dependents, and some recently retired workers. In the most developed countries, about three-quarters of the population is so covered; in some of the less affluent countries along the Mediterranean, a quarter or half of the population is covered. The groups who are not covered usually are the unemployed, the unemployable, the elderly with no continuous work experience, businessmen and some of the wealthier classes. Only recently are the farmers being included. The sick fund will usually pay the doctor's fees directly to the doctor; in a few countries, it reimburses the patient after he has paid the doctor. The funds also pay the hospitalization costs of subscribers; in most countries the funds pay the full hospital bill, including the cost of all drugs.

When most Americans speak of "socialized medicine," however, they usually visualize, not a system of national health insurance, but a national health service. This is a nationwide administrative structure that dispenses medical care and that may be used *as a matter of right* by all citizens, regardless of their status as workers or taxpayers. Such a system is very rare among developed countries, and is adopted only because national health insurance is incomplete or cannot be financed adequately through payroll taxes. Great Britain created such a national health service after several decades of experience with national health insurance; there was a desire to expand coverage of the population; more money was required to pay for hospitalization and physicians' fees than was available in the insurance funds; and the hospitals needed to be reorganized and improved. The English system does not "bureaucratize" the doctors, in the sense of arranging them in a chain of command. Instead, the National Health Service is a loosely arranged hierarchy of committees composed of laymen and medical representatives, functioning according to general directives from the Ministry of Health, and acting primarily as the dispensers of money. British doctors have contracts with these committees, but are not their employees or subordinates.

National health services are found more commonly in underdeveloped countries. Usually the colonial government maintained a small corps of salaried doctors to give care to the general public in polyclinics and hospitals. After independence, the new government confronts a society that has poor health, few doctors and facilities, and too little private purchasing power to support private practice. Therefore the new government expands its salaried medical corps, most of the country's doctors join it, and all but the rich use it. In many such systems, the doctors are arranged in a hierarchy of ranks and are employees of the Ministry of Health. The Soviet Union has the moxt extensive system of this type today. With various modification, the pattern will become standard in Asia, Africa, and Latin America.

AMERICAN MEDICARE IN WORLD PERSPECTIVE

The Health Insurance for the Aged Act creates, not a national health service, but a national health insurance program of limited scope. All employed and self-employed persons are taxed, but only two categories are covered—the aged who are eligible for social security benefits and other aged persons who become voluntary subscribers. The program is simply a way of coping with hospital and doctors' bills; it does not specifically reorganize the working conditions of doctors.

In every country, a comprehensive system of national health insurance usually evolves out of modest beginnings. By starting coverage with one group, the American program is typical. But by beginning with a special program for the aged, the U.S. is unique. In other countries, coverage is first sought for industrial workers, and the aged are included later or never. In most countries where national health insurance does cover the aged, these persons usually must have built up eligibility during prior years as subscribers and users of the sick funds; thus, care for the aged is simply an extension of care for the economically active. Italy is one of the few countries with a special fund for the aged, while Holland and Sweden are among the few countries where large numbers of aged are covered by the general health insurance program, regardless of whether these persons were eligible for treatment through the same sick funds during their economically active years. Because the aged are so expensive to treat, care can be financed only if hospitals and doctors agree to accept lower fees (as in Italy) or only if the government subsidizes the sick funds from general taxation (as in Holland and Sweden).

Demands for national health insurance, or for a national health service, arise in any country when medical care is unavailable or too expensive for large segments of the population. If the pressures for national health insurance occurred first on behalf of the aged in America, and first on behalf of industrial workers elsewhere in the world, the different priorities reflect the numerous unique characteristics of this country. America's wealth means that many people are capable of paying doctors and hospitals, albeit with the complaints that accompany medical expenditures everywhere. The strength of labor unions has resulted in well-financed private health insurance programs paid for, in large part, by employers; such extensive private coverage of large categories of workers has never been achieved in any other country, because of the weakness of private collective bargaining. In order to head off socialized medicine in America, the medical and hospital associations themselves have created extensive hospitalization and medical insurance; medical societies abroad rarely sponsor health insurance. In most countries, a program is either wholly public or wholly private, but America has a tradition of government grants to supplement inadequate private finances, and thus private hospitals, medical schools, and research centers have been able to survive and flourish with government help.

Thus the problems in America are selective gaps in coverage (rather than large deficits in care), high prices, and the control of undue hospitalization and drug costs. These problems have not been sufficiently acute and widespread to generate demands for a sweeping reorganization of American health insurance and medical care—unlike the critical situations that have led to general changes abroad. Inadequate insurance coverage and high medical costs for the aged have been one of the special and persistent problems in America, and consequently national health insurance in America has begun at a point where it started nowhere else. In other countries, coverage spread by subsequent amendments to the original legislation; but there is no assurance that America will follow the same evolution, unless a general breakdown in medical care unexpectedly occurs.

THE POWER OF THE MEDICAL PROFESSION

One might think that "socialized medicine" potentially could transfer power over medical services from the doctors to the laymen—especially the laymen in strategic government posts. But in practice abroad, national health insurance and national health services are dominated by doctors. It would be very surprising if the same were not true of the actual administration of Medicare in America.

A fundamental reason for domination by the doctors, of course, is lay deference to professional expertise. In practice, most medical work is technical and naturally gravitates into the hands of the persons with the special training to do it. In most of the world, laymen greatly respect medicine and doctors, and the lay administrators in socialized medical systems invariably treat the doctors with much deference. Consequently, in most administrative decisions made by mixed committees with lay and professional members, the doctors exercise weight beyond their numbers; and in decisons made by lay administrators in the health services, the laymen often act on professional advice.

The Health Insurance for the Aged Act creates many openings for such domination by the doctors. It establishes all-medical or mixed medical-lay advisory committees in several key areas of decision-making, such as the approval of participating hospitals, the definition of reasonable charges, and the review of utilization. The statute requires the Department of Health, Education, and Welfare to consult associations representing doctors and hospitals. In practice—just as occurs in other countries—the Department will probably make no decisions unacceptable to the doctors on these committees or to the professional associations. Other clauses offer even greater potential scope for professional authority in the administration of the act: the insurance of medical fees (as distinct from hospitalization fees) is supposed to be conducted wherever possible through existing carriers, and thus the Blue Shield Plans sponsored by medical societies might take over this portion of Medicare. Only in Holland did a large proportion of the officially recognized sick funds evolve out of private funds originally created by the doctors themselves, and the Dutch evolution ensured a dominant voice for the doctors in the administration of national health insurance. American Medicare may well develop similarly.

Usually socialized medical institutions are not created abroad unless they have been made acceptable to the medical profession. If the scheme is national health insurance or a national health service enacted by a democratic legislature, the conservative political parties are usually strong enough to delay passage until the medical association's principal objections are met. Whether the government is authoritarian or democratic, the cooperation of the doctors is necessary to make the system work successfully, and therefore the officials modify the scheme to please them. Almost never is any new medical system adopted over the opposition of the doctors; in the rare cases when that happens—as in Belgium and Saskatchewan during recent years—the government usually is forced to make changes in subsequent negotiations. The American Medicare statute bears much evidence of caution and a desire to avoid confrontations with the doctors.

There are several concessions that the medical association seeks and usually obtains abroad. It demands and usually succeeds in getting a stipulation that all licensed physicians shall have the right to treat patients under health insurance or to join the health service. Such language appears at the beginning of the American Medicare statute.

In some countries the doctors fear the adoption of payment systems that will restrict their income and freedom, and they usually successfully insist that a traditional form of payment will be used in the official system. For example, fears that their governments would make them salaried employees led the English general practitioners to insist on a fixed payment per patient each year ("capitation fees") while Swedish doctors practicing under national health insurance preserved payment for each act ("fee-for-service"); fears that the government would control their fees by direct payments led the French doctors to press for a reimbursement system, by which the patient pays the doctor and then is repaid by the sick fund. The American Medicare program attempts to avoid involvement in the explosive subject of doctors' pay: bills in earlier years covered only hospitalization and not payment for care by doctors; the bill in 1965 finally included the payment of doctors but delegated the compensation formulae to private insurance carriers, which presumably will negotiate agreements acceptable to the doctors. So that doctors' incomes do not decline relative to the rest of the economy, the profession in foreign systems usually obtains some negotiating machinery that regularly reviews and increases fees and salaries.

Lest all medical care be given through the socialized medical system and lest all doctors' incomes be controlled by it, the medical society usually obtains guarantees that every doctor has the right not to join, and that every participant may conduct a part-time private practice. In many European countries, medical associations have induced sick funds to pledge that they will never create polyclinics but will always allow their subscribers to be treated in the doctors' private offices. Also in Europe, the medical associations have secured various formulas to give doctors statuses different from the ordinary employees of the governments: in the British National Health Service and in most of the continental hospitals, the doctor has a contract to give time and services, and thus can still retain the aura of a free professional; the salaried district medical officers who care for the poor and

rural inhabitants of Sweden are the only local government func-
tionaries who are technically appointees of the King; hospital
specialists in England are classified as "officers" of the Regional
Hospital Boards, while all other hospital staff members are employees of local hospital committees; after many years of com-
plaint about the power of the sick funds, the German medical
profession obtained a new arrangement whereby the funds would
deal only with a collective organization of the entire profession,
and this organization alone would pay and discipline individual
doctors.

THE CRUCIAL LINK

Usually doctors occupy all the jobs where controls can be exerted over other doctors. In the bureaucratized national health
services maintained by the Soviet Union and underdeveloped
countries, usually all the administrative posts—often including
the position of Minister of Health—are occupied by physicians.
In national health insurance schemes, the sick funds employ physicians who conduct nearly all the contacts with the doctors
treating insured persons. These physicians handle the particularly sensitive task of judging whether certain doctors are doing
medically unjustified work in order to earn extra money from the
funds, and they alone confer with such miscreants. Instead of
identifying themselves with laymen in the government and trade
unions, these doctors seem to feel a sense of professional solidar-
ity with the practitioners; for example, during my interviews, the
physicians in sick funds and Ministries of Health repeatedly referred to the rest of the medical profession as "we" and referred
to their fellow officials as "they" or "the government."

The medical association becomes a crucial link between the
medical profession and any "socialized" medical system, and it
becomes an important element in the administration of the system. In the past, medical associations in most countries were
mere pressure groups for the doctors, but they always grew in
importance and power after creation of national health insurance
or a national health service. Usually, regular consultative meetings are held with the sick funds and with the Ministry of Health.

The medical association usually becomes the bargaining agent for the doctors in all questions of pay and working conditions. In England and in some other countries, the national health service establishes committees of doctors to discipline those who violate their contracts, and these committees in practice are branches of the medical association. Doubtless the serveral advisory committees created by the American Medicare statute will also be filled by representatives of the medical and hospital associations; and the legislative requirement that the Secretary of Health, Education, and Welfare regularly consult with the professional associations will further cement their interlocking relationship with the health insurance structure.

The requirement of responsible participation in a "socialized" medical system has usually transformed the leaderships of medical associations abroad; before such a change, the leaders are militant representatives of the private office practitioners; afterwards, they are replaced by new leaders who are favorable to the new system and who are skilled in negotiation and in administration rather than in the techniques of pressure group warfare. The decision of the American Medical Association convention in 1965 to negotiate with the Johnson Administration for a satisfactory administrative structure, rather than to boycott Medicare, foreshadows a similar taming of the medical association's mutinous impulses in America.

Because of the concessions obtained from the system, "socialized medicine" often works to the benefit of the doctors. Unpaid bills cease. The right of private practice enables many to earn a considerable income from high private fees, in addition to the fees and salaries earned under the official scheme. In most countries, doctors are eager to get this mixture of public and private practice, since their incomes and economic security surpass those of full-time private practitioners. In countries with many doctors and a low-income population, such as Italy and India, few doctors can survive financially without a part-time public appointment. In countries with few doctors and heavy demand, such as Sweden, the medical association can press successfully for high salaries, high fees, and therefore very high incomes. In most of the world, the greatest ambition of a doctor is to become a professor of medicine in a public medical school or chief of service in a public hospital; with this certificate of eminence, the physician enjoys high prestige and a large income from private practice. Although the professors and service chiefs are powerful and prosperous everywhere, "socialized medicine" does not always guarantee contentment for other doctors; in countries with many doctors and low national incomes, fees and salaries may be low and doctors are often angry—although they still may earn more money than if "socialized medicine" did not exist.

THE LIMITS OF LAY DOMINATION

One of the great fears of American critics of "socialized medicine" is that the doctors will be controlled by laymen and that technical medical problems will be decided by political criteria. Laymen always play an important role in the establishment of national health insurance or of a national health service. Complaints about the distribution, maintenance, or costs of pre-existing private medical services come primarily from the trade unions and from the political parties of the Left. "Socialized medicine" sometimes is enacted by democratic legislatures with the votes of these groups; or it sometimes is decreed by dictatorships either to please these groups or to swing public support from these groups to the dictatorship itself. Once national health insurance or a national health service is adopted, the trade unions and the political parties of the Left remain to criticize any general deficiencies in the services rendered, but the details of daily work almost always are turned over to the doctors and medical administrators. In some countries, the governing committees of health insurance or the health service contain representatives from the trade unions and political parties, but usually these committes meet only occasionally, they are concerned with general policies, and they leave specific matters to their staffs.

In practice, the medical services are insulated from politics because politicians, trade union leaders, and most other pressure group leaders have little interest in medicine and little knowledge of medical services. This is true whether the government is totalitarian, authoritarian, or democratic. A totalitarian government is supposed to try to mobilize all social institutions, but in practice its leaders are preoccupied with matters far removed from medicine, such as foreign policy, industrialization, and the military. Even unusually energetic dictators such as Josef Stalin take notice of the medical services only if there are drastic breakdowns or if too much money is requested during the annual preparation of the national budget.

If any of these programs are induced to make certain decisions on non-medical grounds, it involves the location of hospitals and clinics. Occasionally, influential members of parliaments and of governing committees secure facilities for their home communities in order to please their political constituents, when rational planning might locate them elsewhere. But instead of being peculiar to "socialized medicine", the wasteful distribution of facilities can occur in all systems. For example, the United States has many small hospitals that were established from community pride or from a voluntary association's desire to have its own facilities, when economy might have dictated fewer and larger installations arranged according to regional plans.

One might expect considerable political interference with the appointment of doctors to key posts, such as professorships in medical schools and the jobs of chiefs of service in hospitals. And one might expect such pressures to be greatest in totalitarian and authoritarian governments; totalitarian regimes are dedicated to transforming and mobilizing the society, while authoritarian governments distribute the spoils among the ruling cliques. Much less of this occurs than one thinks. Very few doctors belong to totalitarian parties, authoritarian parties, or democratic political machines, and thus few are available for such patronage. For example, the proportion of doctors belonging to the Nazi and Communist Parties was much lower than the membership rates of other occupations, and thus the Nazi and Soviet governments always had to fill the great majority of posts with doctors who cared little about politics. At the early stages of their existence, totalitarian and authoritarian governments often try to install some "more acceptable" doctors in place of professors and chiefs of service who were closely identified with the old regime; but after a few years, such political appointments cease. In most countries, the professors and chiefs of service are screened and selected by committees on which doctors hold most of the seats, and in practice the members resent outside interference from the politicians, from the Church, or from other laymen. (In practice, of course, the factional influences within the medical profession are thereby allowed to replace lay politics in determining selections.) Conforming to this tradition, the American Medicare statute explicitly guarantees that health insurance is a payment mechanism without leverage to affect appointments; in one of the law's several concessions to the doctors and hospital administrators, an introductory clause says that no "Federal officer or employee [shall] exercise any supervision or control . . . over the selection, tenure, or compensation of any officer or employee of any institution, agency, or person providing health services."

There is one type of lay government official who wields considerable authority over "socialized" medical services: he is not a powerhungry ideologue but the humdrum budget officer. Left to their own discretion, doctors would modernize all the hospitals and clinics, increase staffs, order more drugs, charge higher fees, and cause spectacular increases in costs. Under privately organized medical care, they are inhibited by patients' inability to pay too much. In some wealthy countries, such as the United States, doctors and hospitals are able to give steadily more expensive care because of the population's wealth and because of the steadily increasing premiums that private health insurance schemes can collect from their subscribers. But under national health insurance, mounting costs would require an increase in social security payroll taxes and in Treasury subsidies. Under a national health service, higher medical costs would require higher income and excise taxes. Meanwhile, other government agencies are also seeking more funds. Thus, in the annual battle of the budget, the Treasury men tend to view the doctors as one of many special agencies that are trying to spend too much money on the basis of fancy claims. In order to maintain the fiscal integrity of the social security system, to prevent higher taxes, to prevent national deficits and the decline of the currency in international trade, and to give priority to other expenditures —such as national defense—the budget officers exercise considerable power over the functions of the medical services and over the pay of doctors.

Just as rapidly rising costs are troublesome in private American medical care, so rising costs will doubtless beset Medicare in the future. And just as conflicts between budget officers and the medical services wrack health schemes abroad, so they may torment American Medicare. The potential pressures on the sick funds are obvious: hospital costs are very high and rise steadily because of the lavish use of laboratory tests and drugs, heavy staffing, and numerous amenities for patients; doctors are accustomed to high incomes and freedom in setting their fees. The drafters of the Medicare statute appeared to anticipate trouble: the insurance funds are supposed to pay the "reasonable costs" of hospitalization and the "reasonable charges" for physicians' care; extensive research and negotiation are prescribed to fix the "reasonable costs" of hospitalization; the sensitive problem of deciding what medical fees are "resonable charges" and can be paid from social security funds is handed over gingerly to the private health insurance carriers who will receive social security money and who will pay the doctors.

But the still vaguely defined system is full of potential conflicts that could be exacerbated by each group's single-minded preoccupation with its own ideas, although—as Holland's experience shows—wisdom and cooperation can avoid trouble. If the less commendable precedent of several other countries is followed, any of the following could occur: the budget officers of the sick funds and the hospitals could fight over payments, with the fiscal officers trying to keep within the resources of the social security taxes and with the hospitals trying to raise their services and salaries; the sick funds and hospitals could agree on "reasonable costs" exceeding the resources of the sick funds and could become involved in disputes with the Treasury over the need for supplementary grants from general tax funds; the public agency that pays the private medical insurance carriers for physicians' care might contend that the carriers are not controlling fees sufficiently to keep within the budget, while the carriers and medical societies could claim that some of the ambiguous wording of the statute gives them exclusive power to make such judgments, regardless of the budgetary consequences; the Department of Health, Education, and Welfare might claim that it has the responsibility to protect its insured from overcharging by doctors, while the medical association replies that such bargains are a private matter between doctors and patients.

DOCTOR AND PATIENT

One of the fears of critics of "socialized medicine" is change in doctor-patient relations, particularly by the entry of lay officials into medical questions. Such a possibility worries the medical association in each country, and as a result it insists that "socialized medicine" change pre-existing doctor-patient relations as little as possible. As a result, socialized medicine tends to freeze the pre-existing working conditions of doctors and simply changes the way they are paid. The Medicare statute is even more forceful than other national health insurance laws in drawing the line. Its introductory words say that "Nothing in this title shall be construed to authorize any Federal officer or employee to exercise any supervision or control over the practice of medicine or the manner in which medical services are provided."

The sites of doctor-patient contacts that are paid for under the official systems abroad are usually the traditional sites. In most countries—the United States is one of the few exceptions in this respect—general practitioners traditionally do not treat patients in hospitals, and "socialized medicine" simply perpetuates this custom. Where general practitioners customarily have seen patients in their private offices and in the patients' homes (as in most of Europe), the insurance scheme or health service continues to pay for home and office visits; where private insurance funds and the government traditionally provided polyclinics for participating general practitioners (as in Eastern Europe, the U.S.S.R., and many underdeveloped countries), "socialized medicine" builds more polyclinics. Where specialists customarily have seen patients in the hospital (as in England, Holland, or Sweden), the insurance schemes and health services pay the specialists by methods tending to restrict treatment to the inpatient or outpatient facilities of hospitals; where some specialists traditionally worked in hospitals while other specialists had full-time or part-time private office practices (as in France and Germany), national health insurance usually pays specialists' fees for both hospital care and office care.

Under all European schemes, the patient may see any general practitioner who will accept him. There are the usual limitations found under private practice: if a doctor is very busy, he will be unable to accept new patients who present no emergencies, and getting an early appointment with a general practitioner is particularly difficult in countries with few physicians, such as Sweden. A few limitations arise out of the organization of certain programs: in order to guarantee that doctors give conscientious care and do not build up long lists of patients for mercenary reasons, England and Holland limit the number of patients for whom a G.P. will be paid under the official system, but any number of other patients may be taken privately; official schemes will not pay for patients who "shop around" among doctors for multiple opinions, although such patients may still enjoy this luxury by paying privately. In those European countries that pay fees to specialists for office visits, the patient may select any specialist of his own choice.

In several important ways, some patients may lack freedom of choice—but this tends to arise from traditional practices. In several countries with national health services—for example, in the U.S.S.R., in Poland, and in the rural areas of underdeveloped countries—all persons living in a district are automatically assigned to a general practitioner appointed for that district. When a patient is hospitalized under national health insurance or under a national health service, he is treated by whichever specialists are assigned by the chief of service, and the patient and general practitioner usually have no say in designating the particular doctor. Similarly, when a patient seeks a specialist's care in the outpatient clinic of a hospital or in a community polyclinic, he must see whatever specialist is on duty at the time of his visit, although some countries allow him to schedule an appointment with a particular member of the duty rota.

The desire for the freedom to choose one's own specialist is one of the principal reasons for the survival of private practice in countries with "socialized medicine." In order to be treated by the chief of service and not by one of his young assistants, the patient must see the chief privately and pay personally. In order to avoid the crowded and unpleasant wards of public hospitals in Latin Europe and in underdeveloped countries, the patient must pay for one of the private rooms in the chief's public hospital or he may enter a private clinic where the chief has admitting privileges. In countries with "socialized medicine," private practice is less common among general practitioners than among specialists, but it survives for similar reasons. If paid privately, a G.P. may accept a patient whom he would be unable or unwilling to add to an already long list of insured patients. The private patient will get an appointment sooner and may get from the doctor more time and more emotional support.

The presence of private practice is one of the sources of conflict between the medical profession and the administrators of national health insurance and of national health services. Common accusations of the administrators are that doctors give more time and attention to their private patients, minimize time spent in the hospital and in other official work sites, and divert profitable patients from their public practices into their private practices. These complaints are particularly serious in Latin Europe and in underdeveloped countries, where low national incomes and poor tax collection result in low salaries for the public hospital doctors. Until salaries can be raised, the administrators and the medical association can do little except deplore neglect.

In practice, the sick funds and national health services have little say in the matter of how doctors treat patients. But the budgets of sick funds must be protected against the possibiltiy that a few doctors may do medically unnecessary work for money. Detecting and disciplining such doctors is one of the more controversial problems of national health insurance. The sick funds get bills covering all patients, and statistical records of work norms are calculated. The funds become suspicious of a doctor's practice only if he performs far more acts than do all other physicians, a comparison also commonly made by American private health insurance firms when controlling abuse. Only if a doctor is flagrantly out of line will the sick funds send one of their employed physicians to discuss the problem. Usually the only sanction is a refusal to pay all the doctor's bills, but this is possible only in systems where the funds pay the doctor directly. The patients and the public almost never hear of any disputes between doctors and funds. The European funds no longer reexamine individual patients in order to evaluate a doctor's practice, since the medical association would react explosively, as it did in France during the 1930's.

One of the drawbacks of "socialized medicine" is that it freezes the existing structure of medical insitutions and of doctor-patient relations. Improvements can be introduced only with difficulty. For example, the traditional practice of not allowing general practitioners to treat hospital inpatients is made permanent and is extended throughout the country by payment systems that give hospitalization fees or salaries only to members of hospital staffs. The establishment of the National Health Service in England widened this split by creating permanent staffs in numerous hospitals where local G.P.'s had practiced part of each day. Many reformers now urge that G.P.'s continue to see their patients during hospitalization in order to ensure continuity of care and provide the patient with a familiar face, but any such change would require revisions of the payment system, appeasement of the hospital specialists, and reorganization of the general practitioners' work schedules. It is equally difficult to modify the system of territorial assignment of general practitioners in Eastern Europe in order to give patients more free choice among doctors, since this would require changes in payment procedure, changes in work schedules, more personnel, better transportation, and more money. Alterations of any large structure usually raise the specter of higher costs and resistance by those doctors who are pleased by the *status quo;* administrators, therefore, usually let sleeping dogs lie.

THE QUANTITY AND QUALITY OF CARE

National health insurance or a national health service is sought because large social classes cannot afford medical care or because large regions of the country lack medical facilities. The result is always a mixture of successes and disappointments. "Socialized medicine" enables the poor to get medical care more easily, since financial barriers are reduced, but the quantity and quality of care are never altered as much as its creators had hoped.

The biggest difference is visible in underdeveloped countries, where governments build hospitals and clinics in rural areas and in urban slums that never had them before. The Soviet Union is the best example of a formerly underdeveloped country whose extensive medical services could not have been created without government planning and financing. However, adequate nationwide expansion of a government health service is limited by several factors: underdeveloped countries lack the tax resources to satisfy all needs; few doctors and nurses are willing to work outside the largest cities, and no government is willing or able to force them.

The effects on medical care in the somewhat more developed countries are more modest. Where quality depends on facilities, "socialized medicine" can lead to improvement because of the investment of public funds. In public hands, the hospitals for the poor may be financed far better than if private owners alone paid for buildings and equipment: improved financing was the principal motive for nationalization of private hospitals in Italy and in several other countries in recent centuries. National health insurance funds have built polyclinics in Spain, Italy, and Greece and have allowed participating doctors to see insured patients there, thus giving the doctors access to equipment that they could not afford to buy for their private offices.

In the highly-developed countries, the quality of the private office practitioner's work is affected very little. The sick funds and the Ministries of Health leave the problem of quality primarily to the medical schools, to the profession as a whole, and to the consciences of individual doctors. The medical association would fight any close scrutiny of the work of doctors by these public bodies, which are perceived solely as agencies for the payment of medical care. The quality of office care has probably improved since the introduction of national health insurance and of national health services in Europe—but in large part the change is due to the universal tendency for medicine to improve over time. Perhaps better collection of bills has enabled some doctors to buy equipment that they could not have afforded under completely private conditions. A few sick funds affect the quality of care slightly by paying higher fees for professionally approved as opposed to professionally disapproved procedures; for example, surgical reduction of hernia is paid for under French national health insurance while hand reduction is not covered. A few funds affect quality by refusing to pay for the acts of a specialty, such as surgical operations, unless they are done by a fully qualified specialist. In general, superior performance is not rewarded, except by appointment to the better posts and by referral of many private patients—forms of recognition that occur in all public and private systems. England's National Health Service awards higher salaries to specialists whose distinction is recognized by a committee of doctors, and leading Russian physicians receive medals and extra pay; but otherwise "socialized medicine" is compelled by the medical profession itself not to evaluate and discriminate among its members.

If the quality of medical care is not improved as much as one might expect, the same is true of the quantity. "Socialized medicine" probably reduces the number of people who would otherwise be inhibited by financial considerations from seeking medical care. But comparisons of statistics over time, and some recent surveys, suggest that the increased number of such patients is small. Some recent health surveys in England and elsewhere have turned up a surprising number of people who fail to take their medical problems to freely available health services, because of apathy or ignorance.

Thus, Americans should not expect spectacular increases in the quality and quantity of medical care under the new statute. The language of the law—previously quoted—prevents the government from regulating the quality of care directly (even assuming it were competent to do so), and American doctors are already so well equipped on the average that increased public spending will not materially improve their facilities. Many of the aged are already heavy users of medical care through private payments, private health insurance, and charity. Medicare's principal effects may be economic and psychological: it will enable the aged to spend their money on other things, and it will enable some of the aged to get care without applying as indigents. Among the principal effects of Medicare may be small increases in the incomes of doctors and hospitals, as in the case of national health insurance abroad: doctors and hospitals will collect full payment for some aged patients who might otherwise have been charged little or nothing, particularly for long-term care.

"SOCIALIZED MEDICINE" THROUGH HARMONIOUS EVOLUTION

After medical care for the aged is included under social security in the United States, probably there will be no immediate pressures for enactment of a more comprehensive national health insurance scheme or a national health service. The trade unions —the principal force behind "socialized medicine" abroad—are, for the most part, satisfied with the private arrangements secured through collective bargaining here. However, a mixture of public and private solutions eventually may be sought for the problems of incomplete benefits, mounting premiums, and unstable financing of the present mélange of private insurance and public assistance programs. Perhaps some form of standardization may develop by voluntary agreement among all these programs, with the use of federal taxation to collect insurance premiums, with legal standards, with federal subsidies, all under a representative council possessing statutory authority. Thus national health insurance may ultimately come to America by evolution—not by government fiat but by the private parties themselves using government procedures and sanctions to carry out their public mission. This pattern occurred in Holland, and the harmony and efficiency of that country's health services recommend it as a model.

Such a harmonious collaboration between government and private health agencies seems far removed from the usual rhetoric about "socialized medicine" in America. But development of such a system already seems well under way in the United States. Despite the occasional political controversies that catch headlines, daily relations between medical organizations and government have long been harmonious in America. And in many activities, government already provides medical services or assists private efforts with subsidies and sanctions. For example, few voluntary hospitals, and private medical schools could be constructed today without public grants; most of the funds for clinical research in America come from the federal Treasury; most medical students attend state-supported schools and many of the others are subsidized by government scholarships; the private practice of the health professions depends on government licensure administered by members of the professions; public hospitals owned by municipalities, states, the Veterans' Administration, and the United States Public Health Service relieve the voluntary and proprietary hospitals of much of the heavy burden of caring for the chronically ill and medically indigent. Thus the real issue in America—as in all other countries—is not *whether* government shall play a central role in medical care but *what* that role should be.

For Further Reading

GENERAL

Able-Smith, Brian, *The Hospitals, 1800–1948*. London, Heineman, 1964.

Ackeerkncht, Erwin, *Beitraege zur Geschichte der Medizinalreform von 1848, Sudhoff's Archiv fuer Geschichte der Medizin,* 25 (1932).

Anderson, Odin, *Health Services and the Dream of Equality: The United States Sweden and England.* New York, Appleton-Century-Crofts, 1971.

Davis, Michael M., and A. R. Warner, *Dispensaries, Their Management and Development.* New York, Macmillan, 1918.

Frank, Johann Peter, "The People's Misery: Mother of Diseases," Translated from the Latin, with an Introduction by H. E. Sigerist, *Bulletin of the History of Medicine,* 9 (January, 1941), 81–100.

Hayek, F. A., *The Constitution of Liberty.* Chicago, The University of Chicago Press, 1960.

Mill, John Stuart, *Essay on Liberty,* 1859. London, New York, Everyman's Library, 1931.

Newsholme, Arthur, *Medicine and the State.* London, Allen and Unwin, 1932.

Rivers, W. H. R., *Medicine, Magic, and Religion.* New York, Harcourt, Brace, 1924.

Rosen, George, *A History of Public Health*. New York, M. D. Publications, 1958.

————, "Provision of Medical Care; History, Sociology, Innovation," *Public Health Reports*, 74 (March, 1959), 199–209.

————, "The Hospital: Historical Sociology of a Community Institution," in E. Freidson ed., *The Hospital in Modern Society*. New York, Macmillan (Free Press), 1963, pp. 1–36.

Rumsey, Henry W., *Essays on State Medicine*. London, John Churchill, 1856.

Sand, Rene, *Health and Human Progress*. New York, Macmillan, 1936.

Shryock, Richard H., *The Development of Modern Medicine*. Philadelphia, University of Pennsylvania Press, 1936.

Stern, Bernhard V., *Social Factors in Medical Progress*. New York, Columbia University Press, 1927.

Marti-Ibanez, Felix, *Henry E. Sigerist on the History of Medicine*. New York, M.D. Publications, 1960.

Roemer, Milton I., *Henry E. Sigerist on the Sociology of Medicine*. New York, M. D. Publications, 1960.

Webb, Sidney and Beatrice, *The State and the Doctor*. London, Longmans, Green, 1910.

BRITAIN

Beveridge, William, *Social Insurance and Allied Services*. New York, Macmillan, 1942.

Eckstein, Harry, *The English Health Service, Its Origins, Structure, and Achievements*. Cambridge, Harvard University Press, 1964.

Frazer, W. M., *A History of English Public Health, 1834–1939*. London, Findall and Cox, 1950.

Gemmill, Paul F., *Britain's Search for Health: The First Decade of the National Health Service*. Philadelphia, University of Pennsylvania Press, 1960.

Hardy, Horatio Nelson, *The State of the Medical Profession in Great Britain and Ireland in 1900*. Dublin, Fannin, 1901.

Jewkes, John and Sylvia, *The Genesis of the British National Health Service*. Oxford, Basil Blackwell, 1961.

Lindsey, Almont, *Socialized Medicine in England and Wales*. Chapel Hill, University of North Carolina Press, 1962.

McLochlan, Gordon (ed.) *Problems and Progress in Medical Care*, London, New York, Oxford Univ. Press, 1971.

Mencher, Samuel, *British Private Medical Practice and the National Health Service*. Pittsburgh, University of Pittsburgh Press, 1968.

Stevens, Rosemary, *Medical Practice in Modern England*. New Haven, Yale University Press, 1966.

Stewart, William H., and Philip E. Enterline, "Effects of the National Health Service on Physician Utilization and Health in England and Wales," *New England Jrl. of Med.*, 265 (Dec. 14, 1961), 1187–1194.

More recently (1970) there is the "white paper" and the "white paper with green edges" both dealing with suggested reorganization of the national Health Service—available from Her Majesty's Stationery Office, London.

United States

Medical Care for the American People, The Final Report of the Committee on the Costs of Medical Care. Chicago, University of Chicago Press, 1932.

"The Committee on the Costs of Medical Care—25 Years of Progress," *American Jrl. of Pub. Health,* 48 (August, 1958).

American Medical Association, Bureau of Medical Economics, "A Critical Analysis of Sickness Insurance" *American Medical Association Bulletin,* 29 (April, 1934), 49–80.

"The Pill that Could Change America," American Medical Association, Chicago, 1959.

"Report of Committee on Planning and Development," American Medical Association, Chicago, 1969.

Anderson, Odin W., *The Uneasy Equilibrium.* New Haven, College and University Press, 1968.

Arnold, Thurman, *The Folklore of Capitalism.* New Haven, Yale University Press, 1937.

Backman, George W., and Lewis Meriam, *The Issue of Compulsory Health Insurance.* Washington, D.C., The Brookings Institution, 1948.

Burrow, James G., *AMA, Voice of American Medicine.* Baltimore, The Johns Hopkins Press, 1963.

Colombotos, John, "Physicians and Medicare: A Before–After Study of the Effects of Legislation on Attitudes," *American Sociological Rev.,* 34 (May, 1969), 318–334.

Davis, Michael M., *Medical Care for Tomorrow.* New York, Harper and Brothers, 1955.

Dingell, John D., "The AMA and the Health of the American People," *Congressional Record* 107 (April 10, 1961), A2357–2358 (daily ed.).

Duffy, John, *Rudolph Matas History of Medicine in Louisiana.* 2 vols. Baton Rouge, Louisiana State University Press, 1961.

Falk, I. S., "Medical Care Insurance: Lessons from Voluntary and Compulsory Plans," *American Jrl. of Pub. Health* 41 (May, 1951), 553–559.

Feingold, Eugene, *Medicare: Policy and Politics.* San Francisco, Chandler, 1966.

Morris Fishbein, "Health Security for the American People," American Medical Association Bulletin 31 (1936) 40–42.

Follman, V. F., Jr., *Medical Care and Health Insurance: A Study in Social Progress.* Homewood, Ill., Richard D. Irwin, 1963.

Hall, Durward G., "In Defense of the AMA." *Congressional Record,* 108 (June 5, 1962), A4299–4300 (daily ed.).

Harris, Richard, *A Sacred Trust.* New York, New American Library, 1966.

Moore, Harry H., *American Medicine and the People's Health.* New York, D. Appleton, 1927.

Rayack, Elton, *Professional Power and American Medicine, The Economics of the American Medical Association.* Cleveland, The World Publishing Co., 1967.

Wilbur, Dwight L., "Medicine as the Leader of Change," *The Bulletin of the American College of Physicians,* 9 (October, 1968), 426–431.

Yale Law Journal, The Editors, "The American Medical Association: Power, Purpose, and Politics in Organized Medicine," *Yale Law Journal,* 63 (1954), 937–1022.

OTHER COUNTRIES AND CROSS-NATIONAL COMPARISONS

Abel-Smith, Brian, *An International Study of Health Expenditure and Its Relevance for Health Planning,* Public Health Papers No. 32. Geneva, World Health Organization, 1967.

Anderson, Odin W., "Health Service Systems in the United States and Other Countries—Critical Comparisons," in L. J. De Grott, ed., *Medical Care: Social and Organizational Aspects.* Springfield, Ill., Charles C. Thomas, 1966, pp. 213–233.

Badgley, Robin F., and Samuel Wolfe, *Doctor's Strike: Medical Care and Conflict In Saskatchewan.* New York, Atherton, 1967.

Bjork, Gunnar, "Trends in Medical Care in Sweden," *Medical Care,* 2:3 (1969), 156–163.

Chen, William Y., "Medicine and Public Health in China Today," *Public Health Reports,* 76 (August, 1961), 699–711.

Evang, Karl, D. S. Murray and W. J. Lear, *Medical Care and Family Security Norway, England, U.S.A.* Englewood Cliffs, N.J., Prentice-Hall, 1963.

Field, Mark, *Soviet Socialized Medicine—An Introduction.* New York, Free Press, 1967.

Grant, John B., "International Trends in Health Care," *Amer. Jrl. of Pub. Health,* 38 (March, 1948) 381–397.

Halevi, M. S., "Health Services in Israel: Their Organization, Utilization and Financing," *Medical Care,* 2 (Oct.–Dec., 1964), 231–242.

Last, John M., "The Organization and Economics of Medical Care in Australia," *New Eng. Jrl. of Med.,* 272 (Feb. 11, 1965), 293–297.

Maybry, Jack, ed., *Cross-National Comparisons of Medical Care Systems,* special issue of *Medical Care* (May–June, 1971).

Mechanic, David, "Some Notes on Medical Care Systems: Contrasts in Medical Organization between the United States and Great Britain," in *Medical Sociology, A Selective View,* New York, The Free Press, 1968, pp. 325–365.

Mountain, J. W., and G. St. J. Perrott, "Health Insurance Programs and Plans of Western Europe," *Public Health Reports,* 62 (March 14, 1947), 369–399.

Roemer, Milton I., *Medical Care in Latin America.* Washington, D.C., Pan American Union, 1963, (processed).

Seham, Max, "An American Doctor Looks at 11 Foreign Health Systems," *Social Science and Medicine,* 3 (1969), 65–81.

Weinerman, E. Richard and Shirley, *Social Medicine in Eastern Europe.* Cambridge, Harvard University Press, 1969.

White, Kerr L., et al., "International Comparisons of Medical Care Utilization," *New England Journal of Medicine,* 277 (September 7, 1967), 516–522.

II The Current System

The social class system of a society results in a differential distribution of rewards, including health and health care. Proponents of socialized medicine have sought to establish publicly controlled systems to cover all the people with adequate preventive, therapeutic, and rehabilitative care and thereby equalize the burdens of the "five Ds" (disability, disease, physical discomfort, emotional distress, and premature death). Opponents of such broadly defined health care programs have emphasized individual enterprise and initiative and raised the specter of unnecessarily harsh and restrictive governments hindering the contribution that "free" professionals would naturally make on their own to the health of individuals and the society.

In the United States, the wealthiest nation of all time, there are still large numbers of persons who lack the basic means to maintain life. This is largely a class related phenomenon. Thus the large numbers of poor lower class whites show higher indexes of infant mortality and other preventable diseases and deaths than do wealthier middle and upper class whites. But the prob-

65

lem is deepened by the racist strains of our society.[1] Thus blacks, American Indians, Mexican Americans, Puerto Ricans, and other lower class minority groups experience especially serious deprivation when it comes to health and health care relative to the white middle and upper classes.[2]

A recent assessment of health differences between deprived Americans and those reasonably well off summarizes the situation this way:

> Heart disease, hypertension, arthritis, mental disease, visual impairment and orthopedic disability are all more common among the poor. Death rates from tuberculosis, syphilis, influenza, pneumonia and vascular lesions of the central nervous system are twice as high among nonwhites as among whites. With proper adjustment for age, heart disease, stroke and cancer are all more frequent in the ghetto.
>
> For the poor, the risk of dying under the age of 25 is four times the national average. Life expectancy among the nonwhite population is 63.6 years as compared to 70.2 years in the white population. The maternal mortality rate among nonwhites is 90.2 per 100,000 as compared to 22.4 per 100,000 in whites. The infant mortality rates of nonwhites in 1940 was 70 per cent greater than that of whites. In 1962, 22 years later, it was 90 percent greater; according to the United States Children's Bureau, infant mortality rises as family income decreases. Fifty per cent of poor children are incompletely immunized against smallpox or measles. Sixty per cent of poor children have never seen a dentist. If they are poor and if they are black, Jonathan Kozol's Death at an Early Age literally applies.[3]

In his article, Falk details the extent to which Blacks in our Society suffer more and die younger than do their white brothers. The article is a few years old, but it presents a picture that is still sadly true, if not worse. In the face of such disparities, a number of organizations have grown up to affect change. Falk goes into some of the background and development of the Medical Committee for Human Rights (MCHR) one of several "movement" organizations seeking to right the wrongs of our class-structured, racist society.[4] The MCHR now has active chapters in some 30 urban centers across the country.

Differential health and health care is a complex phenomenon involving problems of payment for care, availability of personnel and facilities, understanding of health problems and what to do about them, differences in culture and living conditions, and genetic differences, as well as subtle and not so subtle social psychological factors such as discrimination. Some of the suggested additional readings go into these conditions. It is worth special note that we often ignore money and power and resort to "more comfortable" psychological and cultural explanations of class differences in care.[5]

Halberstam rests his defense of the present system of medical care on many of these conditions. He focuses heavily on broad cultural, social, economic, genetic, and environmental conditions as the major factors influencing "the five Ds." Thus, if there are disparities, the medical care system, as traditionally conceived, can not be blamed. Halberstam cautions against medicine taking on the broader social ills that bring suffering patients to the physician—not because he is against prevention, but because he doubts medicine's ability to deliver and fears that it will be properly subject to blame if it promises in these broader areas and can't deliver.

There is an important inconsistency in Halberstam's general argument. If medicine is of little or no value in affecting the health of the people, how can he argue for the importance of keeping the organization of medical practice more or less as it is?

This inconsistency aside, the article is one of the most spirited, well stated defenses of the present medical care system. In it, the author challenges the thought that other types of health manpower can solve the shortage of physicians by taking the physician's place in primary care; he supports fee-for-service arrangements instead of a salary; he points out some advantages of solo practice as opposed to group practice; physician satisfaction in terms of good income and professional autonomy are defended; and universal health insurance is supported, but with a mix of private and government sponsorship and control.

Halberstam's article deserves careful reading, for it offers arguments counter to many of those supporting specific suggestions for change found in articles of subsequent sections.

NOTES

1. *Report of the National Advisory Commission on Civil Disorders* (New York, Bantam Books, 1968).
2. Lester Breslow and Paul Cornely, *Health Crisis in America* (New York, American Public Health Association, 1970). Also H. C. Chase, "White-Nonwhite Mortality Differentials in the United States," *Health, Education, and Welfare Indicators* (February–October, 1965) 16.
3. Charles R. Greene, "Medical Care for Underprivileged Populations," *The New England Journal of Medicine,* 282 (May 21, 1970) 1187–88.

   While there is little doubt that higher levels of disease, disability, discomfort, distress and death are found in the lower classes than in upper classes, the reader should be aware of an ongoing controversy over the extent and changing nature of these relationships. One investigator assembles data suggesting that differences in actual morbidity and mortality disappear as society moves into the "post industrial" era of generally higher living standards. At the same time, this author maintains that the lower classes continue to "feel" sicker or show more concern for illness (see Charles Kadushin, "Social Class and the Experience of Ill Health," *Sociological Inquiry,* 34 (1964) 67–80). Others document the continuing disparity between classes in our society in terms of life and death. (See Aaron Antonovsky, "Social Class, Life Expectancy and Overall Mortality," *The Milbank Memorial Fund Quarterly,* 45 (1967) 31–73). Summarizing Monroe Lerner's close examination of evidence with regard to physical illness and Marc Fried's coverage of mental illness, the editors of *Poverty and Health* conclude that there are still marked differences by class in level of disease and death, though the gaps may be declining. (See John Kosa, Aaron Antonovsky and Irving K. Zola, *Poverty and Health, A Sociological Analysis.* (Cambridge, Harvard University Press, 1969), p. 320. A health survey that the editor of this volume has been doing with research colleagues in the "North End" of Hartford, a largely black, Puerto Rican, lower class ghetto, found striking differences in disease and death in this area as compared with the rest of the city. For example, depending on which measure was used, infant mortality was between two and three times what it was in the rest of the city! At the same time, there was a mixed picture with respect to level of health concern by social class. The "lowest" class (Category V of the "Hollingshead Index of Social Position," [New Haven, Yale, 1957, mimeographed]) showed less concern for things like "blood in your bowel movement," "swelling of ankles," and "shortness of breath on climbing stairs." But these same "lower" class respondents showed significantly more concern about "a toothache" and "a headcold." A summary interpretation offered here is that the lower classes do indeed suffer more illness and live a shorter time. When it comes to health concern, they are more concerned about illness experiences that interrupt their essential immediate activities such as eating sleeping and working, while they are less concerned about symptoms that, in professional terms, are seen as having possibly dire consequences for the future (See R. Elling, R. Martin, R. Wintrob, and K. Greenwald, *Health and Health Services in Hartford's "North End,"* (Univ. of Conn. Health Center, 1970, reproduced).

4. *Rights in Conflict,* Report to the National Commission on the Causes and Prevention of Violence with an introduction by Max Frankel (New York, Bantam Books, 1968).
5. William Ryan, *Blaming the Victim* (New York, Random House [Pantheon] 1970).

4 The Negro American's Health and the Medical Committee for Human Rights

LESLIE A. FALK*

The purpose of this article is to convey some insight into the Negro American's health problems—and a few efforts by health professionals to assist in their solution.

The Negro in the United States is the victim of a deep-seated discrimination-poverty syndrome.[1] The south typifies the problems of poverty, discrimination, and segregation most clearly. But, both the north and the south have had a "closed society." And the northern city's segregated ghetto seethes with unrest, just as does the more rural south.

Both regions illustrate in different ways the unwillingness of the Negro American to continue to accept his persecution. The Negro has embarked on a heightened course of social struggle in which he has been joined by many white allies. He has now

Reprinted by permission of the author and publisher from *Medical Care*, 4 (July–September, 1966), 171–177.

* M.D., Professor and Chairman, Department of Family and Community Medicine, Meharry Medical College, Nashville, Tennessee.

struggled to his knees and is forcing a social revolution. The civil rights movement represents perhaps the most active social justice cause the United States has seen since the abolition of slavery a hundred years ago.[2]

Among the allies are many health professionals, some of them constituted as the Medical Committee for Human Rights.[3]

BRIEF HISTORY OF THE NEGRO IN THE U.S.

The Negro came first to the American colonies on a basis not unlike white servants, but subsequent events debased him to the unequal status he has had to bear ever since.[4] Slavery, of course, was not invented in the United States. Many of the European powers had entered the African slave trade up to the seventeenth century.[5] For example, in 1555, a London merchant brought the first of many Negro slaves to London, and by 1771 there were some 15,000 slaves in England.[6] But slavery declined in England, while it thrived in the American colonies, and even more so *after* the American Revolution.

A Dutch man-of-war had brought the first 20 of the many Negro slaves to the colonies in 1619. In that century, Negro and white indentured servants worked side by side, and the Negro earned his freedom after a period of years, just as did the white. It took until the eighteenth century for *chattel* slavery, colour prejudice, and the caste system to be adopted into colonial custom and law. The plantation system preceded the Negro, but he became a plantation *slave* more and more typically as time progressed.

Attempts by some colonists to restrict the slave trade failed to win the support of the English government, and the young republic did no better. It is true that following the American Revolution many of the new states prohibited the slave trade, but neither the Declaration of Independence nor the new Constitution ended "the peculiar institution," as the southerners themselves called slavery. Federal law did forbid the importation of further slaves in 1809. However, illegal importation, combined with "natural" population increase (to which the white plantation owner contributed sizeably) quadrupled the Negro population between then and 1860. By the time of the Civil War

(1861–65) there were four million slaves and some 400,000 "free" Negroes in the United States.

Cotton plantation slave labour was highly profitable. It is estimated that a slave in the south cost a master an average of only 19 dollars a year to maintain, while his productivity was many times that amount.[7] No wonder, then, that lavish expenditures went toward seeking to recapture escaped slaves through rewards, posses, bribery, and kidnapping. By 1860, the price of the average slave had increased eight-fold over that of the beginning of the century. This price was high enough that only a minority of the whites could afford a slave. But, tragically, a majority of whites, doomed to a lasting "poor white" status, *could* adopt anti-Negro prejudice only at the price of their own degradation.

Among the 1843 apologists for slavery was Dr Samuel Cartwright, a Natchez, Mississippi, physician who alleged that nothing but arbitrary power. . .can restrain the excesses of his (i.e. the slave's) mental nature."[8] This capacity of the white to project his own excesses on to the Negro has, of course, been a continuing fact. It has deluged the printed page with racial drivel. It has resulted in the vast proliferation of the anti-Negro "dirty joke," with its sterotypes if alleged stupidity and oversexed promiscuity.

The Emancipation Proclamation of 1863 freed the Negro slave. The victory of the Union gave him (temporarily) the franchise, land, and a budding educational system. For eight years Negro and poor white progressed.[9] There were Negro U.S. Senators, Congressmen, and judges—and a promising social welfare program. However, the unremitting efforts of the ex-plantation owners to recapture their profitable labor culminated in an agreement with the North which led to the virtual re-enslavement of the Negro in the south. His land was retaken by the "share-cropper" system, his vote was removed by "law," and his education was systematically debased or prevented. The whole system was made possible by widespread use of force and violence (murder, lynching, beating, burning. . .) by hooded hoodlums, the Ku Klux Klan, and by a cultural license of the white southerner to use violence on any 'uppity' Negro.

The badly betrayed Negro began to gather the strength to regain his rights in the early twentieth century. The "Niagara Movement" was founded and became the National Association for the Advancement of Colored People. The Second World War saw significant gains for the Negro. But, his post Second World War economic situation became *worse,* in comparison to the white man, than it had been previously due to the poorer education of *de facto* segregated schools, the adverse home environment of the segregated Negro ghetto, and the almost complete exclusion of the Negro from apprenticeship in the skilled trades. The period embodied a very mixed pattern: opportunities for the educated Negro, but the abyss of unemployment for the typical Negro—be he unskilled laborer, farmer, or a youth.

There was a temporary lull in action during the "McCarthyite Period" but then a startled nation rubbed its eyes and attuned its ears to new sights and phrases as the 1950s came. Most amazingly of all, the public had to recognize that a "Negro Revolution" was occurring. Led by Southern Negro students, joined by some whites, "sit-ins" and "freedom rides" began.[10] "We Shall Overcome" became a new nationally known song—one of courage, dignity, faith, and hope.

The adults acted too, led by Mrs. Rosalie Parks, the Reverend Dr. Martin Luther King, and many others, using the peaceful social weapons of civil disobedience, of boycott, prayer, vigil, and of mass demonstrations. The white power structure refused to grant almost every demand voluntarily, but the "freedom movement" achieved a whole series of judicial, legislative, economic, and public-opinion victories, and change did occur.

However, improvements came most in the south, and automation devastated the Negro's job market in the north. The Harlem and the Watts riots typify the warning signs of the growing urban city slum unrest. Thus, the northern city Negro population also comes to life, a major social revolution unfolds and expresses itself in all aspects of American life.

THE HEALTH OF THE U.S. NEGRO

How do health and medical care fit into this scheme of things? First, let us review some of an extensive literature on the Negro's health status.[11-18]

Mortality statistics are almost universally adverse when Negro and white rates are compared. The average U.S. Negro dies seven years earlier than the average U.S. white.* In the South, a Negro male has a particularly short life expectancy—only 50 years, compared with 67 for the white male.

A Negro woman is four times more likely to die in childbirth than a white woman. Prematurity is 50 per cent more frequent among the Negro, with a higher incidence of mental retardation and congenital malformation. A Negro infant is twice as likely to die as a white infant. Negro children die at a much higher rate than do white children. For example, whooping cough mortality of Negro children was six times that of white children in 1949–51.

Tuberculosis deaths are four times as high among the Negro as among the white. The problem is greatest, of course, in the urban Negro ghetto, due to overcrowding, inadequate nutrition, and too little case-finding. Syphilis is a serious and a resurgent problem; death rates are seven times higher among Negroes, while incidence rates are even greater.

The Negro has a higher mortality rate than whites for the three main U.S. killers—heart disease, cancer, and cerebral vascular accidents. He is also a homicide victim more often than is the white as measured by rates.

Morbidity

Morbidity data show similar trends. Diabetes is found more often among Negro women than white women. Hypertensive heart disease exacts a great toll. Cancer of the uterine cervix is twice as frequent among Negro women as white women. The data show a clear social-class progression.

Pasamanick reviews the adverse mental disorder prevalence among Negroes, refuting in some detail anti-Negro articles on the subject, and pointing to 'class and caste' causes instead.[19] The Mental health problems caused by segregation are thor-

---

* Recent data will be treated in the present tense to avoid the boring detail of exactly which year was involved in which study. The principles remain the same, but the number should not be taken too literally as representing the exact current fact.

oughly discussed in a series of articles,[20] including the adverse effects of school segregation.[21]

The main known disease of genetic origin among the Negro is sickle-cell anaemia. This has made it an entity dear to the hearts of the racists, but they omit mention, of course, of the fact that intermarriage decreases its incidence (as it does for most genetic diseases of whites).

Health Services

The health services received by the Negro from doctors, hospitals, and dentists are of poorer quality and less frequent than those received by the whites. They have also been permeated with the results of anti-Negro prejudice and segregationist practices.[22,23] Segregation in hospitals,[24] health departments,[25] and in doctor's offices [26] has led to unavailability and debasement of services. Refusal of emergency care to Negroes has been a particularly vicious practice, leading to unnecessary deaths of many Negroes, among them the blood-bank pioneer, Professor Charles Drew. [27,28]

Public health services were found to be *less* available to Negroes than to whites in the south, despite the greater need, in an authoritative study by a leading U.S. public health expert. Such crucial services as pre-natal and well-baby care, tuberculosis clinics, and dental care showed "alarming neglect."[29]

Uncorrected lesions of various kinds occur more frequently among the Negro, e.g. visual, hearing, and dental defects. Be this due to segregated hospital care, anti-Negro prejudice or ignorance of Negro needs on the part of many white health professionals, or to financial or educational factors, the results are striking.

Not many Negroes have been offered the opportunity to become health professionals. The number of Negro doctors, dentists, and nurses is low, and is not increasing significantly at present.[30,32]

Negro Health in Mississippi

Mississippi[33] may be taken as a specific example to illustrate these general problems.

Mississippi's some 2,300,000 population included approximately 950,000 Negroes in 1964.[34] In 1960, Negro Mississippians had an average annual income of only $606, while whites averaged over three times as much—$2,023. One can predict from this fact much of what will be described below.

Illiteracy is rampant. Only 42 per cent of Negro Mississippians over age 25 had completed high school up to 1960. And even some of these are hardly literate, since the quality of education offered the Negro child can only be described as abominably deficient.

Housing is unhealthful and deficient. Of the 207,611 housing units inhabited by Negroes, 111,138 had no water piped into them, 137,881 had no toilet facilities, and 160,413 had no bathtub (or shower).[34] It seems hardly surprising, therefore, that there were estimated to be 32,810 persons with intestinal parasite infestation (hookworm, ascariasis, strongyloides, etc.) in the state in 1961–62.[35]

Other examples of adverse Negro health indexes are: reported deaths (Table 1), life expectancy (Table 2), maternal deaths (Tables 3 and 4), and infant mortality (Tables 5 and 6). This information is adapted primarily from State Board of Health and U.S. reports collated by Alfred Kogon, M.D., M.P.H., a Medical Committee for Human Rights Volunteer in August 1964, working with Miss Rachel Brown,[36] a volunteer for C.O.F.O., an organization described below.

The information indicates—
that a Negro Mississippian could expect many fewer years of life than could a white Mississippian (Table 2); that Negro mothers in Mississippi die in child-birth more than three times as frequently as do white mothers (Table 3); that the most common specific causes of these maternal deaths were toxaemia and hae-

TABLE 1: *Reported deaths per 1000 population, 1960 by race.* (Source: U. S. Statistical Abstract, 1963)

	Total	Negro	White
Missippi	10.0	11.4	8.4
United States	9.5	10.1	9.5

TABLE 2: *Life expectancy at birth in Mississippi, 1960*

	Years of life expected	
Sex	Negro	White
Male	62	68
Female	66	75

morrhage and infection, all known as preventable or "reducible" causes (Table 4).

The Chairman of the Mississippi State Medical Association's committee on Maternal and Child Health (who is also Chairman of the Department of Obstetrics and Gynecology at the University of Mississippi Medical Centre) writes that 74 per cent of the deaths in 1960 were avoidable.[37] Both physician and patient factors were involved in most of the cases, the failure to seek prenatal care being, as usual, the most common patient problem. Physician faults are not specified.

Midwife home deliveries constituted almost *half* the Negro births in 1961, contrasted with less than one per cent of the white deliveries (Table 5). Training and supervision of midwives

TABLE 3: *Maternal deaths per 10,000 live births.*

Negro	White
12.5	3.3

TABLE 4: *Reported maternal deaths by cause and race, 1961: Deaths per 10,000 live births.*
(Adapted from 43rd Biennial Report of the Mississippi State Board of Health, 1963, p. 102.)

Cause of Death	Non-white	White
All causes	12.5	3.3
Toxaemia	5.0	0.7
Haemorrhage	4.0	0.4
Sepsis	1.2	0.7
Abortion	0.9	0.8

78 : LESLIE A. FALK

TABLE 5: *Live births by attendant and race—1961.*
Per cent
(Source: 43rd Biennial Report of the Mississippi State Board of Health, 1963, p. 103)

	Non-white	White
Total	100.0	100.0
Physician—in hospital	51.0	99.2
Physician—in home	4.4	0.3
Midwife	44.3	0.4
Other	0.3	0.1

leaves much to be desired. (European readers should not confuse the poorly trained southern midwife with their own nurse-midwives.)

Perinatal mortality in Mississippi is over twice as high for the Negro baby as for the white baby (Table 6).

Health Personnel

Severe shortages of heatlh care personnel exist (Tables 7 and 8), and extremely few professionals are Negroes.

The University of Mississippi Medical School in Jackson is now a four-year medical school, but it has accepted no Negro medical students, interns, or residents to date. State money has been used to train a few Negro doctors and nurses outside the state, but the result has been minimal.

Negro physicians have not been allowed membership in medical societies. Negro dentists, few as they are, are not admitted to the dental societies.

TABLE 6: *Reported infant mortality—1961.*
Deaths per 1,000 live births

Place	Non-white	White
Mississippi	49.9	23.6
United States	40.7	23.4

TABLE 7: *Health personnel, Mississippi and U.S.*
Physicians and dentists per 100,000 population, 1960

	U.S.	Mississippi
Physicians	142	77
Dentists	56	28

Services

Services for the Negro Mississippian are deficient in many
ways. Discrimination has led to his being seen last in the doctor's
office and in the hospital. The poverty of the state severely limits
its social program. In 1964, hospitalization for Old Age Assistance recipients was the only medical care provision of the public
assistance program. Voluntary nonprofit charity services existed,
of course, but their scope was very limited. Out-patient service
and chronic disease beds are extremely scarce.

THE MEDICAL COMMITTEE FOR HUMAN RIGHTS

Bearing these grim facts in mind, let us turn our attention to a
new health-care group which was formed to provide special
focus on the Negroes' health needs within the context of the civil
rights revolution. This new organization of health personnel in
the U.S. and Canada originated, in June 1964, in response
to a request for assistance from a group of civil rights organizations concerned with the great 1964 Mississippi Summer

TABLE 8: *Health personnel and population of Mississippi, by race—
1960.*

	White	Negro	Other
Physicians, surgeons	1,411	59	4
Dentists	428	37	0
Professional nurses	4,069	376	0
Student nurses	348	25	0
All professionals	6,256	497	4
Population	1,257,546	920,595	2

Project.[38,40] It has since grown to work in many southern communities and in the northern city slums. Attempts are made to serve and maintain working relationships with all the civil rights groups—SNCC (The Student Non-Violent Coordinating Committee), CORE (The Congress of Racial Equality), the NAACP (National Association for the Advancement of Colored People), SCLC (Dr. Martin Luther King's group—the Southern Christian Leadership Conference), as well as professional groups such as the National Medical and Dental Associations (the only associations open to Negro doctors and dentists in many southern counties).

The initial request stressed the emergency need for a "medical presence" in Mississippi, and called attention to the murder of the three young civil rights volunteers—James Chaney, Andrew Goodman, and Michael Schwerner. It indicated that "outside" health professionals were necessary to help the few licensed Negro doctors and to put the white professionals on their good behaviour.

Drs Robert Coles and Joseph Brenner, psychiatrists from Cambridge, Massachusetts, had been at a week-long briefing of the student summer volunteers.[41] They felt compelled to write a letter to all Mississippi physicians urging them to provide the best of medical care to the civil rights workers, no matter how much they might disagree with the civil rights workers' presence, with obviously implied concern that some would let prejudice interfere with medical care. This made them *persona non grata* with the Mississippi medical profession, although it probably helped assure more humanitarian medical behaviour in some instances. The need for other health professionals to become as concerned as Drs Coles and Brenner was clear.

A fact-finding group of four arrived in Jackson, Mississippi, on 5th July 1964. The writer was one of these. A definitive meeting was held with Negro and white civil rights leaders in medical, religious, and legal circles. As might be expected from Mississippi's 'closed society,' no white Mississippi doctor was present. Several Negro doctors were.

The July meeting resulted in agreement on the following initial program:

1. Recruiting of health volunteers to assist licensed practitioners by:

(a) providing civil rights workers with information on how to seek health care services from local health personnel;

(b) arranging for consultations and referrals with qualified practitioners and hospitals;

(c) visiting and counselling with civil rights workers;

(d) performing "Good Samaritan" functions, if no local practitioner was available, especially for life-saving purposes.

2. Arranging payment for medical care on behalf of civil rights workers and preparing for medical care insurance coverage by their sponsoring organizations.

3. Helping to prepare health-care project proposals and requests for financing grants for the resident Negro populations— for consideration by foundations and public agencies.

4. Assisting in correcting discriminatory and segregationist patterns in health services, for example in submitting documented reports and affidavits to the Civil Rights Commission and other appropriate bodies.

Many dozens of short-term health volunteers and a few long-term representatives (especially public health nurses) gave their time, money, and efforts throughout the year.

Several professional nurses were found among the summer volunteers, and some became long-term staff members, as contributions began to build a financial basis for the Medical Committee to employ them.

When the murdered civil rights workers' bodies were found, the Medical Committee for Human Rights sponsored an autopsy by a distinguished pathologist,[42] and helped the truth to be discovered and known.

Much of the work of the civil rights workers involved founding community centers and "Freedom Schools," mostly for teenagers. The latter included giving courses on Negro history, literature and civil rights. Health education teaching, including basic sex education and family planning (birth control) information, came naturally to the foreground.

The local Negro doctors and dentists were consulted on all steps. Discussions with white doctors were also initiated to create fuller understanding and to attempt to reach mutual agreement. Attitudes varied, of course, but by and large, professional and humanitarian bridges were built.

Physicians, nurses, dentists, clinical psychologists, and professionals of many other health disciplines, as well as health students, contributed their 'presence' and brought to bear their knowledge and skills as events allowed.

A group of distinguished sponsors was found, including Drs. Benjamin Spock, Paul Dudley White, Walsh McDermott, Alan Guttmacher, Joseph Stokes, Jr., Paul Cornely, Kenneth Clement, Leo Davidoff, and Louis Lasagna.

Soon, the actual health problems among civil rights workers began to come into focus. Injuries inflicted on civil rights workers for their activities were seen—lacerations, cattle-prod burns, contusions, and worse. In addition, of course, the usual host of diseases and problems of the human condition under trying circumstances was seen. At the other end of the scale, psychological tension states were found which required advice and attention, even though, as Coles and Brenner state, "we found in these youths a remarkable capacity for psychological stability in the face of threats, arrests, jailings, and violence."[43]

A "rest and recreation" program was initiated to attempt to minimize the problems, and steps were introduced to provide health examinations and to complete indicated but unobtained immunizations and other preventive services. A training session at Tougaloo College (10 miles north of Jackson, Miss.) gave an opportunity to initiate such a planned health programme.

HEALTH ACTION BY THE POPULATION

Having responded to the emergency needs of the civil rights influx, attention could soon be focused on the health needs of the community, especially on the health needs of the socially deprived, and, most of all, those of the Negro. A basic stance toward community health was taken. Participation of the local people in formulating their own health needs came to be the primary focus, and was fostered through home visits, utilizing a health questionnaire as a tool.

Having expressed their views on their own health needs, these were then perfected by a dialogue with the health professionals. Several "Health Improvement Associations," a term used for community health councils, were founded. Health education, sex education, infant care and feeding, and birth-control information received major attention. How to stimulate use and growth of health departments and other programs began to be worked at.

A "health mobile" was provided through the Delta Ministry, an entity of the National Council of Churches (Protestant denominations), with which the Medical Committee has cooperated closely and from which it has received generous financial support.

Some similar patterns were found for work in the northern city ghettoes. The health councils founded have tended to represent a new force in health affairs in these communities.

1965[43]

Participation in the Selma to Montgomery, Alabama march and the events relating to it was another key episode in the "involvement" of the Medical Committee along with other civil rights forces. A major "medical presence" operation was conducted and then a long-term health program left behind in Alabama.

Bogolusa, Louisiana became another site of joint activity as it became a crucial civil rights center, and activity in that state increased.

A number of health students (especially medical and nursing students) worked under the Medical Committee for Human Rights auspices in Mississippi during the summer of 1965, under the direction of a Southern field director, a young Negro psychiatrist.

Nationally, a publication, *Health Rights*, was established, as well as a more organizational monthly, *The Torch*.

Efforts were made to move the American Medical Association to end the racial exclusion practices of its affiliates in all state and county medical societies (many "deep south" county medical societies still exclude doctors because of race). More success, so far, was achieved with the American Dental Association.

The Civil Rights Act of 1964 has made it possible to attempt abolition of all racial discriminatory patterns in hospitals, health departments, mental health facilities, even doctors' and dentists' offices. Some 38 affidavits were submitted from one county alone by the Medical Committee to document the existing racial segregation patterns. Such activities have helped substantially in reducing such discriminatory practices, but many remain.

The Federal "poverty program" and other new national programs have opened up new opportunities for use of public money to reduce some of the many problems described. A major national effort by public and voluntary forces is thus under way to tackle the most serious blight in US life—Negro ill-health and discrimination because of race.

Thus, a great social revolution continues in ways which will deeply influence our lives. As the great Negro leader Frederick Douglass said, "The whole history of the progress of human liberty shows that all concessions yet made to her august claims have been born of earnest struggle. . .If there is no struggle there is no progress."[44]

SUMMARY

1. The Negro in the United States is the victim of a deep-seated discrimination-poverty syndrome.
2. A Negro revolution is under way.
3. A brief social history of the Negro in the United States is presented.
4. Adverse statistics on mortality, morbidity and availability of health services are reviewed.
5. The State of Mississippi is presented as a specific example.
6. The history and function of the Medical Committee for human Rights are reviewed.

NOTES

An effort is made to guide the reader first to some bibliographies, books, and reviews, due to the vastness of the literature and the breadth of the subject covered. References 1–3 thus give several sources in their general category.
1. *Historical*
   Aptheker, H. (1951) *A Documentary History of the Negro People in the United States* (New York: Citadel Press), 942 pp.

Douglass, F. (1845) *Narrative of the Life of Frederick Douglass an American Slave, with a preface by William Lloyd Garrison.* Reprinted by Dolphin Books (New York: Doubleday & Co., 1963), 124 pp.

Duberman, M. B. (1903) *In White America: A Documentary Play* (New York: Signet Books), 126 pp. Includes an appendix of sample documents.

DuBois, W. E. B. (1896) *The Suppression of the African Slave Trade to America.* Harvard Historical Studies.

————. (1903) *The Souls of Black Folk.* A. C. McClurg & Co. Reprinted by Blue Havon Press, N.Y. 1953.

Elkins, S. M. (1963) *Slavery.* Paperback Universal Library Edition (New York: Grossett & Dunlap) 248 pp.

Franklin, J. H. (1956) *From Slavery to Freedom* (New York: Knopf).

Griffin, J. H. (1960) *Black Like Me* (New York: Signet Books), 157 pp.

Myrdal, G. (1944) *An American Dilemma: The Negro Problem and Modern Democracy* (New York: Harper & Row), 2 vols.

Woodward, C. V. (1957) *The Strange Cancer of Jim Crow* (London: Oxford Univ. Press), 183 pp. *See* its "Suggested Readings."

2. *The Negro Revolution*

Baldwin, J. (1961) *Nobody Knows My Name* (New York: Dial Press), 241 pp.

Carr, R. K. (Ed.) (1951) "Civil Rights in America." *The Annals of the American Academy of Political and Social Science,* 275, May, pp. 1–160.

Clark, K. B. (1953) "Desegregation." *J. Soc. Issues,* 9, 4.

Hansberry, L. (1964) *The Movement* (New York: Simon & Schuster), 127 pp.

King, M. L. (1958) *Stride Toward Freedom* (New York: Ballantine Books), 190 pp.; (1963) *Why We Can't Wait* (New York: Harper & Row), 178 pp.

Lomax, L. (1963) *The Negro Revolt* (New York: Signet Books), 288 pp. Silberman, C. *Crisis in Black and White* (New York: Random House).

3. *The Medical Committee for Human Rights*

Falk, L. A. (1965) "Involvement of the Health Professional in the Civil Rights Movement." *United Mental Hlth. News* (Pittsburgh, Pa.), 6, No. 3, pp. 3–4.

Medical Committee for Human Rights, *Health Rights* (1965–66), Nos. 1 and 2; Medical Committee for Human Rights, 211 W. 56th St. New York.

Orris, L., Gold, H. M. and Sager, R. (1965) "Physicians in Mississippi." *Bull. Physicians' Forum,* 2, pp. 13–19.

Sachar, E. J. (1964) "Now is the Summer of Our Discontent." *Harvard Alumni Bull.,* pp. 10–15.

"Standby in Mississippi, Volunteer Medical Aid for Civil Rights Workers" (1964) *MD Publication* 8, No. 11, pp. 133–136.

Wells, A. O. (1964) "Journey to Understanding: The Doctor." *The Nation.* Dec. 28, pp. 515–516.

4. Elkins, *op. cit.,* pp. 37–52.

5. Stampp, K. H. (1956) *The Peculiar Institution, Slavery in the Ante Bellum South* (New York: Knopf) p. 17.

6. Skone, J. F. (1957) "The Coloured Worker." Paper read at a Sessional Meeting at West Bromwich, 28th Feb. 1957. *J. Roy Soc. Hlth.*

7. DuBois, W. E. B. (1935) *Black Reconstruction in America,* 1860–1880. Harbor Scholar Classics Edition (1956). (New York: S. A. Russell), p. 9.

8. Deutsch, A. (1949) "The First U.S. Census of the Insane and Its Use as Pro-Slavery Propaganda." *Bull. hist. Med.,* 15, 469–482.

9. Franklin, J. H. (1961) *Reconstruction: After the Civil War* (Chicago: Univ. of Chicago Press), 258 pp.

10. Zinn, H. (1964) *SNCC, the New Abolitionists* (Boston: Beacon Press); *Ibid.* "The Southern Mystique."

11. Pettigrew, A. H. (1965) Chapter 4, pp. 72–79 on "Negro American Health," in Pettigrew, T. *"Profile of the American Negro.* References pp. 202–235. (Princeton, N.J.: Van Nostrand). This is a major review of the literature.

12. Young, W. M., Jr. (1964) "To Be Equal." Chapter 7, *Poor Health in the Richest Nation* (New York: McGraw-Hill), pp. 182–211. The National Urban League, of which Mr Young is the executive, is also on the verge of issuing an annotated bibliography on "Health and the Negro."

13. Cobb, M. (1947) "Medical Care and the Plight of the Negro," *The Crisis,* 54, 201–211. Reprinted in expanded form as special pamphlet by the N.A.A.C.P., 38 pp., 1947. Reproduced in Congressional Record, 94, No. 84, pp. 5,717–5,721; (1948) "Progress and Portents for the Negro in Medicine." *The Crisis,* 55, 107–122, 125–126. Amplified and reprinted as N.A.A.C.P. pamphlet, 53 pp.; (1951) "Medical Care for Minority Groups." (In symposium on *Medical Care for Americans) Ann. Amer. Acad. Pol. Soc. Sci.,* 273, pp. 169–175.

14. Cornely, P. (1955) "Problems in Health and Medical Care for Negroes." Urban League, Pittsburgh, Pa. Mimeographed, 4 pp.; Editorial. (1965) "Health and Ethnic Minorities in the Sixties." *Amer. J. Pub. Hlth.,* 55, pp. 495–498.

15. Goldstein, M. S. (1954) "Longevity and Health Status of Whites and Non-Whites in the United States." *J. nat. med. Ass.,* 46, pp. 83–104.

16. Health Information Foundation (1958) "The Health of the Non-White Population." *Prog. in Hlth. Services,* 7, 6 pp.

17. Tomasson, R. F. (1960) "Patterns in Negro-White Differential Mortality, 1930–1957." *The Milbank Memorial Fund Quart.* (New York: Milbank Memorial Fund) 38, No. 4, pp. 362–386.

18. Brailey, M. E. (1958) *Tuberculosis in White and Negro Children* (New Haven: Harvard Univ. Press), 2 vols.

19. Pasamanick, B. (1964) "Myths Regarding Prevalence of Mental Disease in the American Negro; A Century of Misuse of Mental Hospital Data and Some New Findings." *J. nat. med. Ass.,* 56, pp. 6–17.

20. *Mental Health and Segregation* (1963) M. M. Grossack (ed.) (New York: Springer) 247 pp. (includes 187 references); *see also* Cannon, J. A. (1964) "The Psycho-Social Aspects of Segregation." *J. nat. med. Ass.,* 56, pp. 160–163.

21. Group for the Advancement of Psychiatry No. 37. (1957) *Psychiatric Aspects of School Desegregation.*
22. Clement, K. (1965) "America's Health—Here, Too—Discrimination." *Agenda* (Indust. Union Dept. AFL–CIO, 815 16th St., N.W., Washington, D.C. 20006). 1, pp. 16–20.
23. Editorial (1960) "Medical Care and Racial Discrimination." *Amer. J. Pub. Hlth.,* 52, pp. 1749–50.
24. Seham, M. (1964) "Discrimination Against Negroes in Hospitals." *New England J. Med.,* 271, pp. 940–943.
25. Cornely, P. B. (1955) "Segregation and Discrimination in Medical Care in the United States." *Amer. J. Pub. Hlth.,* 46, pp. 1074–1081.
26. Smith, E. B. (1961) "Discrimination in Medicine." *Interracial Rev.,* pp. 312–313.
27. Maund, A. (ca. 1950) *The Untouchables.* Southern Conference Educational Fund. Illustrated by Ben Shahn, 32 pp.
28. Editorial. "Hospital Discrimination Must End." *J. nat. med. Ass.,* 45, 284–286; Editorial (1947) "Old Clothes to Sam: The Negro's Hospital Dilemma." *Bull. medico-chir. Soc. District of Columbia,* 4, No. 2.
29. Cornely, P. B. (1942) "Comparison of Certain Health Services Available for Negroes and White Persons." *Amer. J. Pub. Hlth.,* 32, pp. 1117–1124.
30. National Medical Fellowships (1962) "New Opportunities for Negroes in Medicine." pp. 9–10.
31. Smith, E. B. (1965) "The Disappearing Pittsburgh Physician." *J. nat. med. Ass.,* 57, p. 229.
32. Ibid. and Falk, L. A. (1963) "Medical Care and the Negro in Allegheny County." *J. nat. med. Ass.,* 55, pp. 322–325.
33. Silver, J. W. (1964) *Mississipi: The Closed Society* (New York: Harcourt Brace & World), 250 pp.; Wharton, V L. (1947) *The Negro in Mississippi* 1865–1890 (Univ. of North Carolina Press: Harper Torchbook Edition 1965), 298 pp.
34. "Statistical Abstract of the United States." Nat. Center Hlth. Statist., Annual Editions, Government Printing Office, Washington, D.C.
35. "Vital Statistics Mississippi, 1962." Public Health Statistics, Mississippi State Board of Health, Jackson, Mississippi, A. L. Gray, MD, Executive Office, 139 pp. Mimeographed.
36. Brown, R. (1964) "Medical Care and the Mississippi Negro," COFO Publication 12. Mimeographed, 18 pp.
37. Newton, M. (1964) "Maternal Mortality in Mississippi During 1960." *J. Mississippi State med. Assoc.,* pp. 61–62.
38. Clement, K. W. (1964) "Dr Clement Finds 'Unhealthy' Medical Treatment in Mississippi." *The Call and Post,* Cleveland, Ohio, July 18.
39. Sutherland, E. (1965) "Letters from Mississippi." (New York: McGraw-Hill) A selection of volunteer student civil rights letters with editor's comments, 234 pp.
40. A Unitarian Universalist Presence in Mississippi, Reports and Recommendations of a Denominational Team (1965), 25 Beacon Street, Boston, Mass., 20 pp.

41. Coles, R. and Brenner, J. (1965) "American Youth in a Social Struggle: The Mississippi Summer Project." *Amer. J. Orthopsychiatry*, 35, pp. 909–926.
42. Spain, D. (1964) "Mississippi Eyewitness." *Ramparts* (Magazine, 1182 Chestnut Street, Menlo Park, California) pp. 43–49. *See also* Huie, W. B. (1965) *Three Lives for Mississippi*. WCC Books (New York Herald Tribune), 252 pp.
43. Auster, S. L. and Levine, T. (1965) "Special Reports on Selma." *Amer. J. Orthopsychiatry*, 35, pp. 972–980.
44. West India Emancipation Speech (1857) Quoted in Foner, P. S. *Frederick Douglass* (1964) (New York: Citadel Press), 444 pp.

5 *In Defense of the System*

MICHAEL HALBERSTAM*

The doctors in the hospital dining room sit around munching cheese sandwiches, comparing patients and grousing about the public and the bureaucrats. A surgeon complains about the dubious malpractice case in which academic physicians from the Health Department testified against a practicing doctor, while the courtroom drank it all in—"See what bastards doctors are!" An internist replies that physicians have to be disciplined, just like anyone else. A woman doctor interjects that the clinic case load is so high that she doesn't have enough time with each patient. The surgeon replies sardonically that the Health Department has a cure for this—"We don't do enough about our doctors' social consciousness." Pretty soon one of the doctors will

Reprinted by permission of the author and the publisher from THE NEW YORK TIMES MAGAZINE (November 9, 1969). © 1969 by The New York Times Company. Originally published under the title "The M.D. Should Not Try to Cure Society."
* M. D. in private practice of internal medicine, Washington, D.C.

finish eating, nod to his friends, and excuse himself, saying, "I'd like to talk more, but I've got to go and save some lives."

The scene is Tashkent, U.S.S.R., in Aleksandr Solzhenitsyn's "Cancer Ward," but it could just as well be a hospital dining room in America. The foot soldiers of medicine, of whom I am one, bitch contentedly about an unappreciative public and an insensitive bureaucracy. The complaints of the Soviet physicians seem a bit more pointed than those of most of the doctors I know personally, more akin to those American doctors who saw Medicare as the death of private practice. Yet there is no doubt that all of us—the Soviet physicians in the cancer ward, the small-town private practitioner in Arizona, and the big-city internist—have more in common with one another than we have with the medical administrators or academic physicians of our own countries. We are bound by the half-proud, half-put-upon feeling of those who do the real fighting while the armchair generals sip sherry in their tents.

This dichotomy between practicing and nonpracticing academic physicians came home to me as I thought about American medicine today. The bitterest critics of medicine have usually been physicians themselves. It's nice to belong to a profession which constantly examines itself, but at times one has the feeling it is overdone.

For, as I started to research this article by pulling out my file labeled "Medicine, Criticism," and sorting out the articles, clippings and reprints, I soon began to despair of the task. How could one encompass all the problems in American medicine today? Quotations and headlines rushed through my mind: "Medicine is a pushcart industry" (the dean of Harvard Medical School, echoed by Dr. Leona Baumgartner), "Medicine is a cottage industry" (Drs. Ivan Bennet of Johns Hopkins, David Rutstein of Harvard, Martin Cherkasky of Montefiore), "Health Crisis in America," "American Infant Mortality Rate High," "All Concerned Are Castigated for Ghetto Care 'Nonsystem,'" "Impersonal Care Denounced."

It wasn't that, as a practicing physician, I felt impelled to answer all this criticism (I had made some of it myself), but that it was too broad even to consider. I felt as I sometimes do when backed into a corner at a social gathering and denounced by some friendly lawyer or reporter who knows exactly what's the matter with medicine. One has a tendency in those circumstances to react a bit snappishly, to point out that every American institution from the Metropolitan Opera to the Supreme Court is under attack these days, that medicine is under attack in other nations, and that even before Daumier, Molière and Shaw, people were caustic about their healers.

I write as one who loves his profession and is loyal to it, warts and all. I want the warts off, but I love it still. One can be wary of physicians, who, while professing devotion to some mystic ideal of medicine, spend most of their energies attacking their field before the press and Congressional committees. The political conservatism of most of my colleagues annoys me at times, but does not depress me. I have noticed that the most "liberal" wings of the profession, the psychiatrists and the academic physicians, have until the last three years been the most laggard in actually treating or doing anything else for the poor. This deficiency is being made up, but the irony escapes neither me nor the conservative G.P. who treats 50 patients a day.

Certain facts about American medicine are incontestable. At a meeting of doctors in Washington last year, I sat next to a man who had practiced in the area for 35 years. I asked him what was different about practice now compared with when he had started.

"There aren't any bad doctors," he said. I raised my eyebrows a bit, and he stopped me. "Sure, you might be able to think of a few that you think aren't so good, but when I started there were dozens of doctors around who had gone to unaccredited schools, who were drunks and dope addicts, who never read a book or went to a meeting or a hospital since they left medical school. You can't believe the difference. You can take competence for granted nowadays."

The more I thought about it, the more sense it made. When Abraham Flexner was commissioned to do a report on medical education in 1909, the United States had 125 medical schools, some of them operating like mail-order diploma mills. Twenty years later, mainly because of Flexner's report, the dreadful schools were gone—but their graduates lingered on. They practiced through the nineteen-twenties and thirties and early forties, an era when the specialty boards and hospital committees that now do most of the enforcing on quality of care were either non-existent or just developing.

Today one practices with the assumption that one's colleagues are competent. For example, I give away no trade secret by saying that most physicians are little better than the average layman in judging the ability of another doctor. In small or medium-sized towns, perhaps, an internist can have long enough contact with the other physicians to get a firsthand idea of how good they are, but in a growing suburb or big city he may have solid knowledge of only a small percentage of his colleagues, most of them in his own specialty. Like the public at large, he operates on trust. When my son had an ear infection, my wife took him to an ear-nose-and-throat man recommended by his pediatrician. When surgery eventually became necessary, the E.N.T. man operated—and I had never checked on him or even met him. He operated at a good hospital, he was recommended by a good pediatrician, and so I assumed competence.

If, in fact, I had wanted to check on him, there would have been no good way save for me to take an E.N.T. residency myself. Even the surgical box score, as once proposed by Russell Baker, would have been of no help, for the doctor with a 20 per cent complication rate may operate on older or sicker patients than the one with 10 per cent. Detailed examination of each serious complication by a jury of his peers—which is done in all good hospitals—is the only way a physician's competence can be maintained.

If we're so smart, then how come we're so sick? Our infant mortality rate is poor and even middle-aged white men in the United States have a higher death rate than those in other Western nations. Dr. John Knowles of Massachusetts General Hospital says that on a trip to Saigon he found medical conditions which resembled those "in certain parts of Boston."

By "certain parts of Boston," Dr. Knowles meant the black slums. The infant mortality rate for Negroes in this country is twice that of whites. Even our white infant mortality rate is higher than that of many countries, but some of this can be attributed to pure geography. We will always be hard put to achieve the kind of infant-care statistics of compact, relatively homogenous countries like Denmark and Holland. Even with a private airplane, the prosperous rancher's wife in Wyoming is at a disadvantage if she has an obstetrical emergency.

But our mortality figures reflect convincingly the fact that most Americans die of excess rather than neglect or poverty. This is shown by the comparative life expectancies for men and women. Writing in The New England Journal of Medicine, William Forbes has pointed out that not only do American women live longer than American men, they live longer compared with women of most other countries while our men do poorly compared with men elsewhere. Since distribution, financing and quality of care is certainly equal for men and women in the U.S., Forbes infers that it is not medical care which accounts for the poor showing of American white men, but rather "cultural patterns."

These patterns are quite obvious—in every one of our national excesses, men are more excessive than women. They smoke more (and get more lung cancer and emphysema), they drink more (and get more cirrhosis and infection), they drive faster (and get into more accidents), and they eat more (and get more heart attacks). The cold fact is that most of our preventable diseases are preventable, not by the doctor, but by the patient.

We know this, but few of us want to acknowledge it. I know that I am more likely to have an auto accident if I have two drinks at a cocktail party, but I go to parties all the time and never take a taxi home. I am convinced that for each steak I eat a little plaque of cholesterol is deposited in my anterior descending coronary artery, and yet I continue to eat steak. Perfectly rational humans come to me for a yearly check-up, get their yearly psychologic assault or entrapment, and yet continue to smoke two packs a day. We know what we should do for our health, but few of us are willing to do everything we should (which is reassuring, since the purpose of life, whatever it may be, is clearly not just to see who can live longest). Some, however, are unwilling to do anything.

In the face of these depressing realities, the good, liberal establishment calls for more preventive medicine. Financial analyst Sylvia Porter writes, "We must conserve doctors' services by far greater emphasis on preventive medicine and diagnostic screening." Senator Harrison Williams, Democrat of New Jersey, has introduced a bill which would provide nationwide centers in which blood could be taken and analyzed for various abnormalities, thereby nipping disease in the bud.

(The trouble with this approach is that many of the "diseases" so detected are untreatable, and many may not be diseases at all, but merely variations in blood levels of normal substances. In order to prove the latter, however, the patient must go on to submit to a progression of tests, some of them dangerous, all of them expensive. Uncritical acceptance of "multiphasic screening" would merely add to our health bills, not our health. In the medical literature such programs are still being evaluated and do not look very hopeful. Among politicians and economists, however, they look like a panacea.)

Some observers, acknowledging that social factors rather than "medical" ones lurk behind many of our problems, urge medicine to tackle these directly. Dr. Jack Geiger of Tufts, who has done pioneering work among the poor in Boston and Mississippi, has written that merely supplying care is not enough. "To provide health services for a concentration camp would not only be futile, it would be an act of profound cynicism. Our medical schools and teaching hospitals must find ways of bringing their resources to bear on the central social issues that underlie health. The urban crisis should get at least as much attention in teaching hospitals and medical schools as molecular biology."

Dr. Knowles, writing about alcoholism and its association with poverty and ignorance, noted that "it is a cruel paradox that medicine generally has had the least effect on these disease-provoking conditions and instead has restricted itself to traditional acute, curative, after-the-fact . . . functions. Prevention of disease through alteration and alleviation of those social conditions which generate disease has been left to others—the politicians, welfare workers, clergymen and struggling minority groups."

Now, I consider myself a member in fair standing of the Eastern Establishment, I have met Dr. Geiger and admire him, and I am sure that Dr. Knowles and I have many things in common and would get along well if we ever met. Yet when I read statements like this I realize I have more in common with the Birchite

G.P. seeing 50 patients a day in Kingman, Ariz., than I have with the nicest member of the Harvard medical faculty. What Dr. Knowles and Dr. Geiger and all my friends want of the medical profession is another marching phalanx to help solve social problems. This is a fine task. I would like to help solve social problems myself, but while I did, who'd be minding the store? If physicians are to be trained to "alter and alleviate" social conditions, why did I bother to study anatomy, which really was sort of a drag?

The "field" of medicine is certainly elastic. Medicine as a profession grew out of the individual's concern about his physical health; then during the 18th and 19th centuries the direct relationship between certain environmental conditions and certain diseases was recognized, and the field of public health was added to medicine. In the 19th century mental aberrations began to be acknowledged as an illness rather than a visitation from God or the devil, and the specialty of psychiatry developed. By the middle of the 20th century we designated alcoholism as an illness, and tried to get the drunkard out of the police lock-up and into therapy. Now we appear about to add poverty, ignorance, war and civil unrest to the doctor's responsibilities. And we are concerned about a physician shortage!

No one with a feeling for medicine's past and an appreciation of its present can fail to be amazed about the enormous number of problems which our society would like to unload on the profession. As we in America become less accustomed to taking the word of our minister or our elders on what used to be moral questions, we have sought authority somewhere else—and have frequently settled on medicine.

In the last five years, therefore, medical schools have been urged to devote more time to the following areas: computers, anthropology, sociology, sexual behavior, statistics, ecology, space medicine, learning techniques, and crowd psychology. Still, the deans are trying to knock a year or two off the whole curriculum.

My critics will argue that the profession's bailiwick is not laid out by divine law, but rather by usage and social pressure, and thus that areas now considered nonmedical should and will become medicine's. The province of any profession, however, is not arbitrary, but relates to a central core—in medicine, concern for the health of the individual. No other professional is granted access to our bodies and our thoughts as is the physician. The doctor is the only person who can put his finger in you and not get arrested.

Aspirants to the profession accept this central concern. A medical school dean, confronted by an applicant who says his goal in life is to end the misery of the slums, might well steer the applicant into law, city planning, politics, or a dozen other equally fine professions. Only the physician, doing his thing, has responsibility for the individual's health. I would guess and hope that my black patients care less about my social and political feelings than my ability to diagnose chest pain and my availability on a Sunday afternoon.

Medicine's concerns are not infinitely expandable nor is its body of knowledge infinitely dilutable. Each doctor testifying before Congress, writing articles, lobbying for gun control, marching for peace in Vietnam, or distributing petitions to abolish the Supreme Court is a doctor away from his patients or his research.

There are other pitfalls in urging greater social and political commitment on the part of physicians. The urgers usually assume that the commitment will take the direction that they themselves would prefer, but, given past evidence, this is hardly the case. How amused we in Boston in the nineteen-fifties used to be with the political activists in the profession, the small town docs who thought that an M.D. degree gave them an instant grasp of economics, political theory and sociology! Our scorn was unquestionably increased by the fact that the insight thus vouchsafed was always on what was then the conservative side, with strong emphasis on local control, welfare reform and participatory democracy. In those days Bostonians thought doctors should concentrate on what they knew best—medicine.

There is no doubt that activists of both left and right tend, if only unconsciously, to trade on the M.D. degree. Part of their effectiveness in political fights comes from the fact that physicians have traditionally been "above" partisan and nonmedical issues. The more they participate the more this special respect will fade. It will be damaged most, not by men like Benjamin

Spock, who asks no special favors and whose activism is honestly stated, but by youthful believers who want to do something—anything—to demonstrate their sympathy with *La Causa,* the grape-pickers' strike. The medical students who dressed up in white coats and red armbands and appointed themselves "physicians" to Columbia's striking students last spring were there primarily because they believed in the cause, secondarily they were healers. They had every right to believe in the cause and to work for it, but playing doctor was hardly the best way to do so.

Youthful activism can be appropriate. Recently the house staff of D.C. General Hospital, led by a determined resident named Martin Shargel, protested against inadequate staff and equipment in what is the capital's municipal hospital. The protest was forceful and determined, but rhetoric was minimal. The house staff was not demonstrating against global injustice, but about conditions in an institution that they knew better than any group in the city. They were listened to because they were articulate, accurate, polite and yet passionate. They made change occur.

Of course, there will be occasions when physicians will confront social disease directly. The doctor who works in a mining town should concern himself with mine safety and lung disease, the chest surgeon with cigarette smoking, the suburban psychiatrist with drug abuse. Doctors like I. A. Buff, Alton Ochsner and Donald Louria have provided valuable leadership in these fields, and they have been supported by many of their colleagues. Even here, however, the physician's involvement is tempered by his own personality and the demands of his primary responsibility.

Believing all this, I feel American medical education has failed to give students and young doctors an adequate preparation for the society in which they will practice. Medical students, internes and residents must be taught enough social anthropology and must experience enough diversity in life so that they can relate to all people, not just those of their own background. Unlike Dr. Knowles, I want students to feel and identify the diversities of our society, not so they may change that society, but so they may better help their patients. Some doctors may move to a concern for social ills, but all physicians should neither be expected nor encouraged to do so. All over the country there is an appalling lock-step in which high-school kids who are good in science enroll in "Pre-Med" at college, spend three years wrapped up in lab courses with an occasional survey view of World History or Elementary Psychology, get into medical school, work hard, and graduate with a combined A.B.-M.D. These are nice young people, but they are less physicians than they are Doctors of Engineering (Human). They can hardly be expected to be interested in how others live, having barely lived themselves.

This pattern is, I think, changing for the better. It was at its worst in the fifties and early sixties, when the God of Research dominated medical schools, where every student with brains or ambition hung around during the summer to work in some professor's lab, and where the desire to take care of actual humans was regarded as a faint disgrace to the school. At good hospitals, all the residents were expected to have a research interest. When I was an interne, I would see my residents lurking along the corridors at night, on their way to draw blood from some pet project. Although medical schools talked of "the care of the whole patient," this ideal was not pursued in practice. It was apparent to all that insensitivity, rudeness, or outright callousness would never hinder a bright interne's progress up the residency ladder so long as he knew the patient's biochemical data.

The craze for research at any price led many decent academic physicians into experimentation that bordered on the unethical. In this book "Human Guinea Pigs," the English physician M. H. Pappworth cited dozens of examples of questionable research in this country. The experiments cited were often not very serious or dangerous, but they were conducted in an atmosphere which led our best young doctors to believe that the patient's interest was secondary to that of Knowledge. A few more days in the hospital for the patient, a couple of extra pokes with a needle, a few more tubes in new places, all these could be justified if a scientific paper resulted.

It is today's students who have been changing all this. Rather than working in labs in the summer, they more and more want to get into the community, to learn about people, to see delivery of care firsthand. The change here cannot be separated from the growing disillusion with science for science's sake that we see in other fields. What we can do is no longer so important as whether we should do it. The medical schools and training programs here must catch up with the needs of their own students. It is only the occasional school that offers a course or even a lecture in medical sociology, and often such material is optional or nongraded. In schools where everything from anatomy to ophthalmology is required and graded on the basis of cutthroat exams, giving students an optional course in sociology is the equivalent of telling them it's unimportant.

While waiting for these new students to graduate, what can the country do to increase its medical services? Reform (or revolution) has been suggested involving (1) the use of nonphysician aides, (2) the use of computers and technology, and (3) the way in which physicians are organized to practice.

The economist Victor Fuchs notes that in medicine there are many people with a high-school or technical education (lab workers, etc.) and many with years of graduate study (physicians) and comparatively few in between. He and others feel that some of the shortage of services can be relieved by training "paramedical personnel" or physician aides to fill gaps in the system. Dr. Victor Sidel (now of Einstein Medical School) has studied the *"feldsher"* system of nonphysicians in Russia. Some critics see medicine and its allied professions as deliberately shutting out newcomers by a wall of diplomas.

There is no doubt that nonphysicians can render many of the services doctors traditionally perform in our culture. As Dr. James Feffer has noted, an ophthalmologist prescribing glasses is overtrained for this job—by about 12 years. Physicians know this, and have been using co-workers in offices and hospitals for years. I suspect, however, that as the use of physician assistants grows, the demand for physicians will continue unabated. How often, for example, has one heard a young mother complain, "I like our pediatrician, but he's got so many assistants running around weighing babies and giving shots and talking to mothers that you never have enough time to talk to *him*."

Many people coming to a doctor's office for treatment of a specific ailment have already consulted various paramedical people before deciding to see a physician. As the educational level of the country rises, and soon well over half of the adults will have attended college, one wonders how many people will be willing to accept the reassurances of a nonphysician with less, or little more, education than they have. Indeed, the trend of the country is to "trade up" in medical care—and we find people with headaches referring themselves to a neurologist and those with a rash consulting a dermatologist directly. How many pregnant American women will accept the care of a midwife rather than a doctor?

We may hope that we will be able to slow up this trend toward patient-directed oversophistication in care, but I doubt if we are going to reverse it—and the acceptance of nonphysicians for first-line care would be a reversal of great magnitude. Our non-white population, which is already suspicious about experimentation with its social needs, is not going to be much more receptive to the idea of nonphysician care. In fact, one might predict that Berkeley and Cambridge will welcome midwife delivery long before Watts and Roxbury.

Nonphysicians perhaps can be used more effectively in certain life-threatening situations than they can in routine or minor medical care. With the blessing of physicians, nurses and special technicians already provide most of the care in coronary units for acute heart-attack victims, and on the battlefield corpsmen provide life-saving measures for badly wounded men. There are few diagnostic possibilities or treatment alternatives in such crises, and therefore these workers do not need to know a great deal of medicine—they have to know one thing very well. On the other hand, such "trivial" complaints as headache or abdominal pain may signal any one of hundreds of conditions. Only someone with extensive theoretical knowledge and practical experience can sift through such patients and know whom to reassure, whom to prescribe for, and whom to admit instantly to the hospital. For most of us with a headache or belly pain, this someone is going to continue to be a physician. In many "minor" cases, a physician's reassurance is effective because he *is* a physician.

This country should, I think, establish five or ten more "hospital schools" of medicine. These schools would accept college graduates, give standard medical-school courses, and grant an M.D. degree, but neither their faculties nor students would be oriented toward research. Theory would not be ignored, but emphasis would be on the direct application of biochemistry and physiology to patient care. Students who show an interest in or talent for research could transfer to more theoretically oriented institutions after two years, but the bulk of graduates would go out to care for patients, as specialists or family physicians. There are difficulties with this plan—neither faculty nor students are in overabundance—but I suspect it will be more pertinent to the needs of the eighties than an attempt to train sub-physicians. But both should be tried.

Technology will aid both patient and doctor in the future, as it already is doing, but it is unlikely that there will be any quantum jumps in the quality of patient care. While computers have been programed to read electrocardiograms and perform other eso-teric tasks, some of the simplest and most time-consuming proce-dures in medicine seem to have been untouched by technology. A physician wanting to review his patient's X-rays must sort through a bulky folder containing dozens of slippery transparen-cies whose true nature is never known until they are held awk-wardkly up against a viewing box.

Hospital charts remain clumsy and unstandardized, never available when one needs them, and with a distressing tendency to fall apart. Finding a hospital bed or a consultant for an emer-gency patient still often involves a frustrating round of phone calls and delays, which a central registry would help eliminate.

Most academic critics of American medicine see as its main hope a rationalization of its organization. Dr. Baumgartner notes that medicine could learn much from big business. The ineffi-ciency of practice, with thousands of doctors working away in their own little offices, is a constant affront to Ph. D.'s trained to think in economies of scale. Most medical planners see great hope in group practice, as a way of increasing the efficiency of practicing doctors. In such group settings, they feel, doctors can gather the equipment and personnel necessary to work more effectively.

They particularly favor prepaid group practice. They cite studies which show that Americans who get their medicial care through traditional fee-for-service undergo more surgery and more hospitalization than those in prepaid groups. Dr. Caldwell Esselstyn, formerly of the Half Moon Clinic and now with the

New York State Health Department, has said, "fee-for-service was invented as an incentive to encourage the production of more services." Walter Reuther has suggested that physicians work on a piecework basis like garment workers, and Dr. Martin Cherkasky feels that private practice should be scrapped in favor of a salaried service at $80,000 per year.

Meantime, I continue to practice by myself, tucked away in a cozy office, and turning out patients like the Aran Islanders turn out sweaters—one by one. Since I am neither more callous nor more stupid than most, and since I wouldn't at all mind earning $80,000 a year, why do I (and many of the physicians I respect the most) persist in such an archaic method?

The reason is that medicine still often amounts to one man asking another for help. In many (but not all) fields of medicine, effectiveness depends on a deep and continuing personal relationship between healer and patient. By introducing additional physicians and personnel, "efficiency" may actually be counterproductive, just as mass-scale education and housing projects have been. Some of today's most perceptive social critics, such as Paul Goodman, see virtue in smaller, not larger, units of service.

Dr. Gilbert Farfel, a physician on the staff of the highly praised Permanente prepaid clinics in California, wrote in the January issue of Medical Economics that he was on "first call" for his group of 30 internists "once or twice a month." At Permanente, as in other good prepaid groups, a patient has his "own" physician for regular visits, but if the patient gets sick at night the odds are high against his speaking to his own doctor on the phone, much less being examined by him. Even during the day, emergency cases are often not seen by their own doctors in this group.

In smaller prepaid groups the odds in favor of seeing your own doctor when you are really sick are somewhat better, but even in these the physicians are rarely "on" much more than every fourth night and weekend. These groups advertise for doctors on the basis of how much they pay and how liberal they are with nights off call.

Now, like most doctors today I take a fair amount of time off from my practice, more than my physician father or uncle ever did. However, even with a week of medical meetings and three or four weeks of vaction, I am available to my patients nine out of ten nights, nine out of ten weekends. This is not the burden it seems, because my patients are rational about calling me at home. When the phone does ring at night, I don't have to deal with a patient I have never seen before. The patient is not confronted by a vaguely resentful doctor. I talk to someone whom I have examined before, whose history I know. I have an idea of how this particular person reacts to pain, whether he's stoic or panicky. Something they never teach in medical school is that the really tough decisions of today's medicine—hospital? house call? aspirin until morning?—are made over the phone, and then that pushcart industry doesn't look like such a bad idea after all. Real economies are achieved by reliable medical transactions over the phone day and night.

I am not saying that group practice and prepaid groups are bad medically or philosophically. I am pointing out that these arrangements have their inherent disadvantages as well as advantages, and that these disadvantages have been glossed over by many proponents. There is no doubt that fee-for-service tempts the greedy physician to provide unneeded services. On the other hand, salaried practice tempts the lazy physician to prolonged coffee breaks and extra reasons for not operating on a weekend. Institutions *can* provide ancillary services that the individual doctor cannot. However, it is axiomatic that the physician working for an institution, paid by the institution, must at times divide his loyalty between the patient and the institution.

Bigness, it should be added, is no guarantee of inefficiency. The Federal Government is hardly rational in its own allocation of physician-manpower (one could service several states with the doctors tucked away in various programs) and our great hospitals sometimes act like suburban housewives trying to impress one another with expensive acquisitions.

So I continue to practice by myself. I am not "isolated," as my critics would have it, for like almost all other physicians I must adhere to the standards of my local medical society, my colleagues, my specialty group, and the hospitals which have granted me admitting privileges. Working in a great city, I have access to dozens of other specialists, social workers and therapists. Some of us practice in the same medical building, but our finances are not intertwined. I treat all kinds of patients and I enjoy my work. I don't mind piecework payment—most professionals are paid this way and so is Renata Tebaldi. My practice is flexible and I don't have to worry about what my supervisor will say or whether O.E.O. is going to be funded this year. I don't have to worry about hurting my partner's feelings when I leave the cap off the lubricating jelly, because I don't have a partner. When I do indulge in political activism, I don't have to brood about damaging my employer's reputation or involing his subtle retaliation.

My friend, Nelson Goodman, practices in a prepaid group and he can't understand why I won't join up. He loves the lack of concern about billing patients, the freedom from business details. America's "nonsystem" of care provides multiple options within medicine for both doctors and patients. Nelson works best in his group, I work best in my un-group. His patients prefer a group, mine prefer a private practitioner (some of my patients used to belong to his group—and vice versa, I suppose).

The argument that private practice is a luxury which exists merely for the benefit of physicians not only ignores the points previously made, but skips the harsh fact that physician contentment is basic to any kind of practice scheme. Emigration of British physicians continues to bedevil the country's National Health Plan, discontent arising not only from heavy patient loads and bureaucratic restrictions, but also from a rigidly structured system of hospital specialists. A study of recent graduates of Aberdeen University showed that more than a quarter had emigrated. Doctors, like other humans, can vote with their feet.

Some economists, like Milton Roemer of U.C.L.A., feel that group practice is particularly desirable because it will enable consumer groups to bargain effectively with the providers of medical services. In this way fees, insurance and premiums could be held down. The trouble with this theory is that it assumes the providers of services won't organize as well. Despite the idea that doctors' fees are set by some kind of guild fiat, they are instead a matter of local custom. When fees go up, they do so almost by osmosis—one doctor raises his charges, tells his friends, they look at their books and decide to follow suit. If consumers and insurance companies start to bargain forcefully about fees, there is no doubt that physicians will do the same. Relative costs will not change very much.

Physicians will continue to be rather affluent people. Of all the complaints about doctors, this is the one which moves me the least. Concern about other people's income, whether they are pop singers, football players, neighbors, or fellow professionals, has always seemed a pawky way to dissipate one's energies. It bothers me most when one physician talks about another specialty—for example, an internist complaining about surgeons: "We get up in the middle of the night, spend an hour with the patient at home, make the diagnosis, call in the surgeon, and he operates for 45 minutes. We get $25 and he gets $250. Is that fair?"

My answer is basically, "Yes." I knew in medical school that internists earned less than surgeons, but no amount of money in the world would have made me want to be a surgeon. So far as I'm concerned, surgeons earn what they get. If internists don't earn enough, they ought to organize to change this without worrying about other specialists. Just for the record, I would add that I would have no objection to getting rich through practicing internal medicine, but to the best of my knowlesge it can't be done. My colleagues and I live solidly comfortable lives, just like most of our friends who went on from graduate school to business, *academia* or other professions.

Rather than brood about physicians' income, reformers should, as economist Fuchs has suggested, work to make medical insurance universal. The A.M.A. itself has accepted the principle of such insurance, but wants it provided through private carriers. Fuchs is for group-insurance plans that would include both the nonpoor and the poor, the latter to have their premiums subsidized by the Government. "Luxury options" would be allowed for those who value medical care above competing services, but basic care would be provided for all. I feel fairly sure that in 10 years a plan like Fuchs's or the A.M.A.'s will be in force.

In the next decade there will be significant evolutionary changes in American medicine, which will, I hope, become more humane and more patient-centered. Research will lose more of its primacy. Practicing physicians will start to pay more attention to the deeper needs of the poor—medical schools and teaching hospitals will start to pay some. A variety of occupations will

Another thing that happened to dear ole doc is that he joined a group........in an emergency, a patient served by a medical group is likely to be treated not by doc but by one of doc's partners.

grow up to supplant doctors in some procedures and assist them in others. Group practice, including prepaid, will continue to grow slowly but steadily. The hospitals will have an increasingly important role in regulating how doctors practice. All Americans will be covered by some kind of medical insurance, either by private companies or, if they are poor or old, through Government re-insurance. Instead of today's compulsory military service, which makes medicine unique among the professions, future doctors may have the option of serving in poverty programs. These reforms will relieve some of the more hurtful inequities of today's medicince, but I doubt if the medical profession will be any safer from criticism than it is today. For built into all of us is a profound ambivalence about the healer. We respect the physician and when we are ill we are genuinely grateful for his knowledge and compassion. Yet, when we have recovered, a bit of resentment often creeps in. For, despite what the World Health Organization feels, "health" for most of us is not a positive sensation, but an absence of negative ones. We do not routinely wake up and say, "How good to breathe easily, step lightly, and feel no pain in my head or chest."

We take these things for granted, and if we get sick, the physician who restores us to normal—or who helps while nature is restoring—has, in the long run, given us only what we had always taken for granted, and, usually, will soon start taking for granted again. Thus, when illness is over we resent the very dependence on the physician which sustained us while sick. He now becomes a reminder of our weakness and of the nasty fact that we are not eternal.

Neither the mature patient nor the mature physician expects their relationship to be one of unquestioned love and admiration. The link between doctor and patient, like that between parent and child, is too important to be tranquil. Conflict and resentment are inevitable, but these do not preclude mutual respect. The physician will continue to be the one we call when a bad pain awakens us at night. There is no one else who both cares and can do something about it.

For Further Reading

Breslow, Lester, and Paul Cornely, *Health Crisis in America.* New York, American Public Health Association, 1970.

Cleaver, Eldridge, *Soul on Ice.* New York, Dell, 1968.

Coser, Lewis, "The Sociology of Poverty," *Social Problems,* 13 (Fall, 1965), 140–148.

Duff, Raymond, and August B. Hollingshead, *Sickness and Society.* New York, Wiley, 1968.

Ehrenreich, Barbara and John, "The Medical-Industrial Complex," *The New York Review of Books,* 15 (December 17, 1970), 14–20.

Ellis, J. M., "Socio-Economic Differentials in Mortality from Chronic Diseases," *Social Problems,* 5 (July, 1957) 30–37.

Feingold, Eugene, *Medicare: Policy and Politics.* San Francisco, Chandler, 1966; esp. I, "Medical Care for the General Population," pp. 1–23; and II, "The Special Problem of the Aged," pp. 24–84. Positions both for and against medicare are given, and expensive bibliography is provided.

Graham, Saxon, "Socio-economic Status, Illness and the Use of Medical Services," in E. Gartley Jaco, ed., *Patients, Physicians and Illness,* Glencoe, Ill., The Free Press, 1958, pp. 129–134.

Greene, Charles R., "Medical Care for Underprivileged Populations," *New Eng. Jrl. of Med.,* 282 (May 21, 1970) 1187–1193.

Handler, Joel, *Reforming the Poor: Welfare Policy, Federalism and Morality.* New York, Basic Books, 1971.

Harrington, Michael, *The Other America.* New York, Macmillan, 1962.

Hollingshead, August B., and Frederick C. Redlich, *Social Class and Mental Illness.* New York, Wiley, 1958.

Muller, Charlotte, "Income and the Receipt of Medical Care," *Am. Jrl. of Pub. Health,* 55 (April, 1965) 510–521.

"Health Care and Poverty: What are the Dimensions of the Problem?" with articles by George Reader, Myron Wegman, Lisbeth Bamberger and S. M. Miller, in *New Directions in Public Policy for Health Care, Bulletin of the New York Academy of Medicine,* 42 (December 1966), 1126–1156.

Sanders, Marion K., ed., *The Crisis in American Medicine.* New York, Harper and Bros., 1961.

Scott, Robert B., "Health Care Priority and Sickle Cell Anemia," Y.A.M.A. 214 (1970) 731–734.

Sheps, Cecil G., and Dean A. Clark, "Medical Care: Its Social and Organizational Aspects—Expenditures for Health and Medical Care in the United States," *New Eng. Jrl. of Med.* 269 (Dec. 26, 1963), 1411–1417.

Sommers, Herman M. and Anne R., *Doctors, Patients and Health Insurance: The Organization and Financing of Medical Care.* Washington D.C., The Brookings Institution, 1961.

Stockwell, Edward G., "Socioeconomic Status and Mortality in the United States," *Public Health Reports,* 76 (Dec., 1961), 1081–1086.

Strauss, Anselm, "Medical Organization, Medical Care, and Lower Income Groups," *Social Science and Medicine,* 3 (1969), 143–177.

Suchman, Edward A., "Social Factors in Medical Organization," *American Journal of Public Health,* 55 (November 1965), 1725–1733.

U.S. Public Health Service, "Medical Care, Health Status and Family Income: National Health Survey Data." Series 10, No. 9, 1964.

Walsh, James Leo, and Ray H. Elling, "Professionalism and the Poor—Structural Effects and Professional Behavior," *Journal of Health and Social Behavior,* 9 (March, 1968), 16–28.

Yerby, Alonzo S., and William Agress, "Medical Care for the Indigent," *Public Health Reports,* 81 (January, 1966), 7–11.

Zola, Irving, "Illness Behavior of the Working Class," in A. Shostak and W. Gomberg, eds., *Blue Collar World: Studies of the American Worker.* Englewood Cliffs, N.J., Prentice-Hall, 1964.

Kosa, John, Aaron Antonovsky and Irving K. Zola, eds., *Poverty and Health, A Sociological Analysis.* Cambridge, Harvard University Press, 1969.

Norman, John, ed., *Ghetto Medicine.* New York, Appleton-Century-Crofts, 1969; esp. Chap. by L. S. Holloman.

III Proposals for Change—Payment and Financing

It is clear to most observers that money alone will not solve our health care problems. Additional money suddenly added in the form of universal health insurance, without increases in health manpower or change in medical care organization, would only generate more inflation and general chaos. Yet it is just as clear that the manner in which health workers are paid and services financed are essential matters closely intertwined with professional and patient motivation and other aspects of medical care organization.

Physicians and dentists in the United States have primarily organized their practices as small businesses. Thus they have been paid on a piece-work or fee-for-service basis—so much per office call, house call, or special procedure. Other groups of health workers—nurses, technicians, assistants, medical secretaries and librarians, etc.—have either worked on salary for physicians and dentists in their offices or for hospitals or other health organizations. Thus the dispute as to methods of pay has largely revolved

111

around physicians and dentists, for they have been the only ones on a fee-for-service basis, while the trend of the times was toward salaried arrangements. Physicians have a larger slice of the health care pie; thus it is primarily around their payment that the controversy revolves.

Sigerist found the worry that physicians would neglect their duties if they were on a salary "an insult to the medical profession." "And it is very queer," he wrote, "that this objection is frequently made by medical organizations. The Code of Ethics of the American Medical Association explicitly states that "a profession has for its prime object the service it can render to humanity; reward or financial gain should be a subordinate consideration."

Halberstam points to "the harsh fact that physician contentment is basic to any kind of practice scheme. . . . A study of recent graduates of Aberdeen University showed that more than a quarter had emigrated. Doctors, like other humans, can vote with their feet." Adequate income is one way to support physician contentment. "Physicians will continue to be rather affluent people."

Surprising or not surprising, depending on your point of view, there is little disagreement on this score. Halberstam cites Dr. Martin Cherkasky's recommendation that "private practice should be scrapped in favor of a salaried service at $80,000 a year." Halberstam admits that he would not mind earning this much. Glaser found that physicians earn high incomes relative to other people in countries with national health care programs.

The apparent difference comes with respect to the method of payment, not the amount. To proponents of a government-run national health service, salaried arrangements not only imply efficiences (some of which Halberstam recognizes—less surgery and hospitalization) but greater motivation on the physician's part to undertake preventive and rehabilitative measures as well as greater convenience and quality support from group organization. In the article that follows, Roemer develops this position in full. He cites evidence and offers some rationale why the organizational supervision that usually goes along with a salaried arrangement should lead to greater physician responsibility and higher quality of care. One might say that the extreme of this position was represented in the story (probably apocryphal) about the ancient Chinese system in which the physician was supposed to have received his regular stipend from a family only as long as its members were well.

But it is precisely the broader organizational implications of a salaried arrangement to which Halberstam objects. "The reason is that medicine still often amounts to one man asking another for help. In many (but not all) fields of medicine, effectiveness depends on a deep and continuing personal relationship between healer and patient. By introducing additional physicians and personnel, 'efficiency' may actually be counterproductive, just as mass-scale education and housing projects have been."*

One careful empirical study bears on this issue. It compared the effects on patients' utilization of services and physician satisfaction in an indigent medical care program in Baltimore when the method of payment was shifted from a capitation system (so much per patient per year regardless of how often the patient is seen) to a fee-for-service arrangement (so much per patient visit). Generally, patients were seen more often under the fee-for-service system with some increase in overall cost and some increase in fees paid to physicians per patient visit (from $2.59 in 1962 to $2.74 in 1964). Physicians with a large patient list under the capitation system saw the patients less often than did those with a small list. This evened out under the fee-for-service arrangements, with those having a large clientele receiving a slightly lower fee per patient visit than they had under the capitation arrangement.

> This study has found that the utilization of physician services and of prescriptions by MCI clients has increased. There has been no change in the utilization of clinic services or of inpatient care. There has been an increase in the total costs of the program, with most of it due to the increase in the MCI population. The proportion of administrative to total cost in the MCI program did not increase; in fact, it declined. Physicians with a large MCI clientele averaged a higher fee per visit during capitation than under fee-for-service. More physicians are in the program now

* This keystone of the conservative argument also has implications for new manpower and group practice arrangements as we will see in the next section.

than before. Clients make fewer complaints, apparently due to the continuing freedom of choice conferred by fee-for-service.

Such findings as the above imply that notwithstanding the "paperwork" and even the lower average fee collected by most physicians with a large MCI clientele, the fee-for-service method of payment is preferred by all physicians. The clients' satisfaction is also enhanced. Further, fee-for-service method insures the rendition of the service by the physician, whereas such a mechanism is absent under the capitation method.[1]

This was not strictly a salaried versus fee-for-service comparison and a health department clinic set-up was involved, not a group or solo practice. Also the level of payment was low under both the capitation and fee-for-service arrangements of this program. "The findings of the Baltimore experience need not necessarily apply to a change in the method of payment under conditions of adequate, or higher, payment."[2] Even with these several qualifications, this generally favorable experience with fee-for-service makes one entertain Halberstam's arguments much more seriously, and it calls the limits of Roemer's arguments into question.

Beyond the matter of method of payment to the physician, there is the all important question of overall financing. There have been "compulsory" health care programs in the U.S. for many years, if one considers special populations such as the military. But it was not until the passage of Medicare in 1965 that broad segments of our population were automatically covered by a reasonably comprehensive health insurance.

It is the persons 65 and over who suffer from the bulk of chronic disease in the society whose hospital and other institutionalized care bills are automatically paid for by this legislation (under part A). Often, long term hospitalizations, care in nursing homes or rehabilitation centers, or organized home care programs are required for the appropriate treatment of chronically ill patients. Before Medicare, these expensive cases ("bad risks") could not be covered by private, profit-oriented insurance companies of the private, nonprofit Blue Cross Plans if they were to come out in the black. Thus resistance from these quarters to a public program for the elderly began to melt.

But organized medicine still worried about government control of the business and practice of medicine. For the legislation to be passed at all, it had to be offered primarily as a money payment system with very little attention given to quality control mechanisms or to planning for manpower and reorganization of services to assure that the key health problems of older citizens would be attacked in the most appropriate way.

There are problems with the program in addition to its lack of quality assurances and planning. It requires a voluntary subscription on the pateint's part to qualify for coverage of physician's services (Part B). There are deductibles that the patient must pay, keeping some from appropriate use of services. Of course, other age groups (both the helpless younger age group and the productive middle age group) are still left to fend for themselves. The fundamental weakness is that "this is sickness insurance in the main. . .not health insurance, and it is not primarily geared to provide or support health service programs."[3]

As indicated in the introduction to this volume, several major plans have been introduced before the Congress. Their differences revolve primarily around the extent of Federal financing and administration versus private financing and administration. Falk is in a good position to lead us into these complex issues. He directed the research staff of the original Committee on the Costs of Medical Care. He served as principal technical advisor and member of the Committee of 100 for National Health Insurance headed by Walter Reuther until the latter's death in the summer of 1970. This group's bill for a national "Health Security Program" was just formally introduced in the Senate by Senator Edward M. Kennedy with the backing of 14 other senators.[4] It is one of a number of other proposals now before the Congress which have been usefully compared in a recent Social Security Administration publication.[5]

The new bill, as formally introduced, includes more detail on financing than do the others. A Health Security Trust Fund would be set up and funded by a 3.5 per cent tax on employers' payrolls. The part paid by employers and employees is left open. In addition, a 2.1 per cent tax would be assessed on individual income up to $15,000 a year.

Benefits would start in mid-1973 for anyone residing in the

United States and cover all services, including preventive examinations for the early detection of disease. (This was one of the serious gaps in Medicare as Falk notes in the following article.) Excluded would be custodial, psychiatric, and dental care and some drugs and appliances. "The four exceptions are dictated by inadequacies in existing resources or in management potentials," according to Senator Kennedy's introduction.

Users (patients) would not be charged any fee. Providers (doctors, hospitals, and others) would be paid directly by the program, but the system would allow fee-for-service, per-capita, or salaried arrangements.

"The program would set national standards of performance for professionals and institutions. It would supplement existing health manpower training programs. It would create a Health Security Board under the Secretary of Health, Education and Welfare—which would set national health policy." At the same time, "Mr. Kennedy emphasized that the bill would not set up a national health service of Government-owned facilities and federally employed doctors, as is the rule in Europe. He said the bill sought a 'working partnership' between the public and private sectors of the economy."[6]

There is little political likelihood of this bill or any other passing in the present or next session of Congress. But national health care is sure to be a major issue in the 1972 Presidential election. Falk's article provides some of the background thinking which can help us understand these developments, particularly the financial and administrative alternatives.

NOTES

1. C. A. Alexander, "The Effects of Change in Method of Paying Physicians: The Baltimore Experience," *American Journal of Public Health,* 57 (August, 1967), 1278–1289.
2. *Ibid.,* p. 1288.
3. I. S. Falk, "Response," in *Medical Care: The Current Scene and Prospects for the Future,* Proceedings of a symposium in Honor of I. S. Falk, Part II, *American Journal of Public Health,* 59 (January, 1969), p. 50. By contrast, recall Halberstam's argument that broad medical programs to achieve "health" may not be possible.

4. "National Health Insurance Proposed by 15 Senators," *New York Times* 119 (August 28, 1970), 1 and 13.
5. Saul Waldman and Evelyn Peel, "National Health Insurance: A Comparison of Five Proposals," Research and Statistics Note, Nov. 12, 1970, Social Security Administration, July 23, 1970. See the introduction to this volume for a brief summary of this comparison.
6. New York Times *cited above*.

6

On Paying the Doctor and the Implications of Different Methods

MILTON I. ROEMER*

Few questions in the organization of medical care
have provoked such heated controversy over the years as the
method of paying physicians for their services. With one method
or another there is associated a whole series of values involving
freedom, quality, costs, attitudes, and other important attributes
of professional service.

The method of paying doctors must be distinguished from the
method by which funds are raised for meeting the costs of medical care. Moneys for health purposes may be derived from private pockets, from insurance (to which, of course, individuals
have contributed premiums), from industry, from philanthropy,
or from governmental tax funds. Regardless of which of these
systems is used, the doctor may be paid in a variety of ways, and

Reprinted by permission of the author and the American Sociological Association from *Journal of Health and Human Behavior*, 3 (Spring, 1962), 4–14.

* M.D., M.P.H., Professor of Public Health, School of Public Health,
University of California, Los Angeles.

it is the latter mechanisms that are here discussed. The issue of medical remuneration, however, becomes more pressing under organized schemes of financing, like those of insurance or government, than under purely private economic arrangements. For in organized programs, a central disbursing agency tends to affect large numbers of doctors and, in various degrees, influences their modes of medical practice. And it is in this context that the polemics have long been waged about good or evil consequences of differing payment systems.

Often as the issue has been raised, a full-scale objective evaluation of the consequences of different medical payment systems has not been made. Yet the United States and the other countries abound with natural "field laboratories" where different payment methods are in operation. Here is a problem in medical sociology, therefore, where much analysis is possible from careful review of current experience, even before critical experiments may be conducted to answer the questions conclusively.

Basic Payment Methods

The principal ways that physicians may be paid for their services are usually described as (a) fee-for-service, (b) capitation, and (c) salary. Under each of these a number of formulations is possible. The fee-for-service system is like piece-work in industry, and in it the physician is paid a fee for each unit of service —an office call, a hospital visit, a surgical operation, an x-ray, and so on. There is a price for each such item, which may be separately determined by the doctor in each instance, varying with the difficulty of the particular case or the doctor's judgment of the affluence of the patient. (The latter is known as the "sliding scale of fees" and is justified as a method by which physicians can afford to serve the poor for low charges, at the expense of the well-to-do). Or the price may be stipulated in a fee-schedule, in which all possible types of service are categorized. Or, even without a fee-schedule, the price may be heavily influenced by custom in the community or by tradition in the doctor's own practice. Sometimes the fee-for-service system is applied to a "case of illness," like pneumonia or an obstetrical delivery, without exact regard to the number of medical acts performed.

The capitation system stipulates the person served, rather than the medical act, as the unit of remuneration. Thus, a physician in effect agrees to take care of a person—sick or well—for a certain length of time, for which he receives a given amount. A pediatrician may contract with a family to take care of a baby for the first year of its life for a fixed sum, regardless of the infant's medical needs. Usually the system involves a large group or panel of persons, on each of whose behalf an agency pays so much per month for all needed attention. The capitation or per capita amount may vary on a sort of "wholesale" basis, so that the first 1,000 members of a panel, for example, yield higher earnings for the doctor than the second 1,000. (This is designed to discourage the doctor from taking responsibility for an excessively large panel of persons whom he could not serve adequately.)

The salary method is essentially payment of the doctor for his time, regardless of the number of units of service provided or the number of persons whose health is supervised. Salaries may be full-time or part-time, and the latter may be defined in terms of a specific number of hours or days of work, or they may involve a "medical session" of elastic length. The amount of the salary is usually varied in accordance with the doctor's professional qualifications: his training, experience, special skills, level of responsibility, or other factors. Logically, the salary method could be used under any arrangement for raising medical care funds, but in practice it is nearly always associated with practice in an organized framework rather than in an individual office.

Historically, all three methods of medical remuneration have been used under diverse circumstances. Whether payment was in money or in kind, fees were paid in ancient times, and so were salaries. The Greek city-states paid salaries to designated physicians for taking care of indigent freemen (slaves being the responsibility of their masters). Physicians attached to feudal manors were paid salaries to serve the needs of the lord's family, as well as to look after the serfs. Medieval guilds and later fraternal orders of workingmen paid physicians by a capitation system—

so much per year for each member of the order, who would then be attended if he became sick. These precedents are worth recording, since there has been some tendency to assume that only the fee-for-service system has a long and honorable history in back of it.[1]

After the industrial revolution and the rise of the cities, physicians broke their attachments with feudal manors or occupational guilds and set up shops as private entrepreneurs. They offered their professional wares to anyone who sought help, and for each service they charged a fee. The fee-for-service system thus became firmly rooted in western society, at least for the treatment of patients at home or in the doctor's office. Hospitals were different; they were places of charity and in them physicians would be expected to serve without payment or receive only a small honorarium for care of the poor and destitute. Later in Europe hospital physicians were paid salaries. In America, the doctor's relations to the hospitals evolved somewhat differently. They became more typically places for private patients, for whose care the doctor charged fees. Even when insurance programs developed for raising the money, the fee-for-service system was so firmly established that it was retained as the principal method of disbursing insurance funds for both ambulatory and hospital care. Small wonder that this method of paying doctors should become dominant in the United States, and associated with a whole range of traditional values.[2]

Yet how can one evaluate the consequences—the relative advantages and disadvantages to doctor, patient, and community —of the different payment systems? This is an important and practical policy question that must be faced every day by organizations concerned with medical care, whether under governmental or voluntary auspices. Criteria for judgment may be of many sorts. The most important are probably the effects of the payment method on: (a) the quantity of medical care provided, (b) the quality of care, (c) the costs, (d) the administrative process in an organized program, and (e) the larger "politics" of the medical care field. Let us examine the three principal payment methods according to each of these criteria, drawing on field observations when they are available and otherwise speculating as best we can.

122 : MILTON I. ROEMER

THE FEE-FOR-SERVICE METHOD

The fee-for-service method of paying for medical care is associated with great freedom for the doctor, since—after the first contact made by the patient—the precise services to be given are essentially his decision, and each such service commands a fee. While the amount of the fee is influenced by supply and demand, restricted by custom, and may even be stipulated in a published fee-schedule, the final determination is in the hands of the physician; even with a fee schedule, the doctor has in effect agreed to follow that schedule. The importance of this pattern to the American physician is reflected in his great preference for health insurance plans that pay on an indemnity basis, leaving the physician free to charge his patient a higher fee than has been indemnified by the plan. This freedom also offers the physician a direct monetary incentive to work hard.

What are some of the consequences of the fee-for-service system for patients? As for its effect on the quantity of care, there is no question that it encourages provision of a great deal of service; the more units of service the doctor gives, the higher will be his earnings. This has been demonstrated in public welfare medical care programs that shifted from a salaried to a fee-for-service system, with a prompt rise in the volume of service rendered. In Saskatchewan, where fee-for-service and capitation plans for general practitioner medical service operate side-by-side in rural municipalities, the volume of hospital admissions is appreciably higher among the fee-doctors. In New York City a study was made of hospital admissions, and particularly surgical operations, by physicians on salary from group practice clinics, in comparison with doctors in private fee-for-service practice. While both series of doctors were remunerated by insurance plans, the volume of high-cost surgical and hospital services was much higher among the doctors getting fees.[3]

Unfortunately the fee incentive to a high volume of medical service may have negative influences on the quality of service. The amount of care may be excessive. Programs of organized medical care, like workmen's compensation or public assistance, have faced this problem for a long time, and various review procedures must be established to police this type of abuse. An excessive number of office or home calls may do no harm to the patient although it wastes money. An unnecessary surgical operation, on the other hand, may do positive harm. That this is a common problem associated with the fee system is reflected by the policy of most general hospitals to have "tissue committees" in their medical staff structure. These committees examine the pathologist's report on tissues removed during surgery, so as to permit discipline of physicians discovered to be removing more "normal tissue" than could be reasonably expected from diagnostic error. Such committees are almost unknown in European hospitals, where surgeons are paid by salary. In my own direct experience, a medical care program for prisoners was showing an inordinately high rate of appendectomies and elective orthopedic surgery, like excision of the cartilage in the knee joint. When the payment system was changed from fee-for-service to part-time salary (it was called a "monthly retainer"), the rate of surgical operations among the prisoners abruptly fell.

The fee system also has important qualitative bearings in the complex world of medical and surgical specialization. The best modern medicine calls for referral of many patients from general practitioners to specialists, or from one specialist to another. Outside of a group-practice clinic where income is shared, however, the referral of a patient ordinarily means the loss of a fee. Most physicians may not be deterred by this from doing what is best for the patient, but there can be no question that some are, and all physicians in fee-practice are subjected to this dysfunctional economic pressure. Witness only the fact that about half of the major surgery in American hospitals is performed by, what the American College of Surgeons calls, "non-qualified surgeons"—in other words, by general practitioners who do not wish to refer their patients to certified specialists in surgery. The same negative influence of the fee system tends to impede the operation of the much-discussed concept of hospital regionalization; that is, many rural patients are not sent from a rural to a central facility for diagnosis or treatment, because this would mean loss of a professional fee.

There are interpersonal aspects of medical care quality which must also be evaluated. Physicians devoted to the fee-system claim that it fosters a good personal relationship between the doctor and the patient. The cash-transaction is said to enhance the patient's appreciation of what the doctor is doing for him, and to heighten the doctor's solicitude for his patient. This line of reasoning was, indeed, used for years against the development of any form of health insurance, governmental or voluntary. Now that voluntary health insurance has become widespread, the argument is still used to buttress payment of the doctor by fees rather than by other methods. One may be surprised that physicians should so often claim these interpersonal advantages for the fee-system, as if to imply that attitudes toward patients would be less considerate if they were not enforced by an earmarked fee. But perhaps there is some truth to the claims.

As for the criterion of costs, there is little doubt that the fee-for-service system tends to result in greater costs to the community and higher incomes for the doctor than provision of the same amount of service by the other payment methods. This has been shown in the medical care program of the United Mine Workers Welfare and Retirement Fund, where generous salaries ($20,000 to $30,000 per year net) were paid to surgeons and internists in hospitals; if the work done by these men had been compensated at the customary fees in those areas, it was found that the costs would have been considerably higher. Small wonder that the fee system is usually preferred by doctors. Of course, there may be great differences among the earnings of particular physicians under the fee system, with some—especially the younger practitioners who have not yet built up a reputation and a clientele—earning relatively little, while others—especially experienced specialists—earn enormous incomes. The over-all cost to the community, however, is undoubtedly higher under the fee system.

It is possible, in a medical care program, to use the fee-for-service system and yet hold the over-all cost to the same level as that yielded from the capitation or salary systems. This is done through the device of "prorating" doctor's bills each month in accordance with the total funds available. Thus, if bills amounting to $1,000 are submitted one month and the funds available are only $900, then each bill is paid at a rate of 90 per cent; in another month, when funds are ample, bills are paid 100 per cent, with the balance carried over to the end of the year. At this time, any balances are distributed among the doctors toward their unpaid accounts, but even if debts remain, they are written off. This system has been used in many voluntary health insurance programs, including that among some 600,000 Farm Security Administration borrowers in the 1935–50 period.[4] It reduces the high-cost problem of the fee-for-service method, but does not alter its other effects, since all the doctors in a community are still competing for variously sized pieces of the budgetary pie. A slight modification of this scheme, popular in recent years, is the "unit system," by which each service on a fee-schedule is assigned a certain number of value units (an office call = 1 unit, a chest x-ray = 3 units, an appendectomy = 20 units, *et cetera*). The exact dollar and cents value of each unit is calculated, in relation to the premium income derived from various population groups covered; each doctor is then paid for the accumulated units of service provided to the members of a group.

With all these accounting procedures, medical reviews, applications of fee-schedules, and so on, it is easy to appreciate why the fee system is very cumbersome administratively. The bureaucratic expenses of operating it are far higher than for the other medical payment systems. The overhead of administering the fee-for-service Blue Shield medical care plans in the United States averages about 8 per cent, which is much higher than the expenses of administering salaried programs like that of the Veterans Administration. Moreover, the paper-work for the doctor is most elaborate with the fee-system, since he must make a payment claim for each unit of service. These written claims, one must recognize, do have another value—to permit studies of the distribution of disease and the receipt of medical care. They also permit accurate determinations of physicians' incomes, a fact which has not been ignored by internal revenue agents.

Finally there is the "practical politics" of the fee-for-service system to consider. There is no doubt of its popularity among private physicians in America. As a result, most community leaders concerned with the extension of health insurance, as a way to soften the economic blows of sickness, are quite prepared to accept the defects of the fee system in order to win the cooperation of the medical profession. Thus the most extensive forms of health insurance as well as many of the governmental medical care programs in the United States make use of the fee system. The hazards of the system, in terms of over-treatment, padding of bills, withholding of referrals, and so on are dealt with by various medical and administrative review procedures. Many students of medical care organization argue that only by compromise with the fee system can extensive health insurance be achieved in the United States. In time, they claim, the qualitative, financial, and administrative handicaps of the system may force it to be changed.

THE CAPITATION METHOD

The consequences of the capitation method of paying physicians, in theory and in practice, are very different. As for quantity of services, there is certainly no inducement to a maximum volume of care. The physician is paid the same amount per month or per year, for each person "on his list," regardless of the number of units of service rendered.

In practice, capitation has only been applied as a method of remunerating general practitioners or family physicians, and the most extensive experience with it has been in Great Britain. Since the first national health insurance legislation of 1911, as well as in the current British National Health Service, general practitioners have been paid on a capitation basis.

Criticisms of the operation of the general practitioner service in Britain have come from many sources. Observers from within Britain and from the United States agree that much of the care given is hasty and perfunctory.[5] The physician has the economic inducement of wanting to keep a maximum number of persons on his list, and dissatisfaction of patients can reduce this number if they leave to register with another physician. While patients are free to do this at any time, one can question the effectiveness of this protection, when the patient is not very sophisticated about medical affairs (probably in the majority of instances), or when an alternative practitioner is either inconveniently located or unable to enlarge further an already long patient-panel.

The other side of these common quantitative consequences of the capitation system is the qualitative aspect. While the fee-for-service doctor may hesitate to refer his patients for specialist consultations, the capitation doctor may make excessive referrals. Many professional observers get the impression that the British general practitioner is often little more than a traffic policeman, referring to the hospital out-patient department patients having diagnostic or treatment problems of the slightest complexity. It is sometimes claimed, however, that the capitation method induces a preventive viewpoint in the physician, since he earns no more if illness occurs and he has to treat it. Unfortunately there is no evidence for this contention in practice. The lack of such evidence may be due not to the operation of the capitation system as such, but rather to the associated pattern of solo medical practice in small private offices or "surgeries." There is also probably an inadequate supply of physicians, in relation to the population, in Britain as elsewhere; a general practitioner serving about 2,300 persons (the current average ratio) is usually too busy meeting day-to-day demands to give attention to periodic health examinations and other key measures of preventive medicine. The effects of the capitation system on doctor-patient attitudes are perhaps more democratic than with fee-for-service payment, since the awards are the same for the care of all patients.

The incomes of physicians and the costs to the community of capitation payment depend, of course, on the size of the capitation amounts. In practice, costs tend to be lower than with the fee system, since they can be accurately calculated in advance and they leave less room for bargaining by the doctor. But they need not be, if physicians present a strong case for increase of the capitation amounts, as has often been done in England.

Administrative procedures are undoubtedly simpler with the capitation payment system. The physician need only report at intervals, such as monthly, the number of persons registering with him for care. The laborious task of recording precise diagnoses and services rendered is eliminated, as is the enormous clerical duty of assessing bills in a central office and making payments. Some check is necessary to take proper account of the shifts of patients between doctors, of deaths, births, migrations, and so on, but the bureaucratic functions for both physician and administrative agency are much simpler than under the fee-for-service system. On the other hand, the very sparsity of reporting under capitation has its defects, since it makes difficult any evaluation of the content of services provided or any research on the epidemiology of disease and the effectiveness of various methods of care. The larger "politics" of the capitation system, has interesting implications for both physicians and public. Among physicians, it serves as a kind of buffer against sharp competition. Thus the financial pie in a community under the fee-for-service system would be divided in proportion to the number of services rendered for each physician. After the initial visit, most medical services are dependent on the doctor's rather than the patient's decision, and the aggressive doctor can, by rendering a high volume of services (whether justified medically or not), take an inordinately large piece of this pie. Under the capitation system, the volume of services rendered is immaterial, and the doctor's income is dependent on the proportion of patients that choose to be on his panel. Thus it is the public rather than the doctor that ultimately determines professional incomes.

With this dynamics, it is understandable why physicians in many communities have come to prefer the capitation method. In the prepayment medical care program of the U.S. Farm Security Administration, which flourished in the 1930's and 1940's, about 15 per cent of the plans in some 1,000 counties used the capitation system, the others using fee-for-service. Capitation would tend to be chosen by the profession in a locality where two or three doctors gave an especially high volume of service and the other practitioners resented the competition. It is not widely known that the British National Health Insurance Act of 1911 provided that the physicians in each local community could elect their own choice of method of payment (although the over-all funds allotted to the community were determined by an objective formula). At the outset many localities chose the fee-system, but in time the capitation system was found to be so much less troublesome that it came to be chosen by the British medical profession as the nationwide scheme.[6] It also came to be the prevailing pattern in Denmark.

Spokesmen for consumers often like the capitation method of paying doctors because it permits a more accurate control over costs which the people must pay. In 1945 in California, for example, with the end of the Second World War in sight, various health insurance bills were introduced into the legislature; the bill backed by the State Congress of Industrial Organizations (C.I.O.) required capitation payment.[7] The method of paying the doctor became such a contentious issue that the forces favoring health insurance were seriously divided. In sum, it is argued that capitation protects the patient not only against excessive costs but also against unnecessary services.

In practice, the capitation system has only been applied to the services of general practitioners under health insurance plans. The services of specialists for any single person or even for a thousand persons are too unpredictable to permit its application; much larger population bases are required to achieve such predictability, and even then the range of possible services by a particular specialist for a particular ailment may be extremely wide. For this reason, specialists are remunerated either by fees or by salaries. A team of physicians in a group-practice clinic may be paid by a kind of capitation system for the over-all services of the clinic, as is done in the Health Insurance Plan of Greater New York with its constellation of 35 medical groups. The physicians within each clinic, however, are paid by various forms of salary. The real *modus operandi* of capitation payment, therefore, assumes general practitioners working more or less independently in separate offices.

THE SALARY METHOD

In many respects the salary method of paying doctors is like the capitation method, in that the physician is awarded a relatively fixed sum for a period of time, regardless of the precise number of units of service he renders. Yet it differs in one substantial respect—that it is invariably associated with some form of organized framework of medical practice. This usually means medical care in a clinic or hospital, where a team of physicians work together. The organization may apply, however, to solo practitioners spread through a large geographic region, such as the salaried district physicians of Norway or Sweden; even the latter arrangement affords a system of professional surveillance over the actions of the individual doctor. It is this group-discipline implicit in the salary system that fundamentally distinguishes it from the other methods, and probably accounts in large part for either the ardour or the grimness with which it is viewed by different professional observers.

As for the quantity of medical services likely to follow from salary payment, there is obviously no built-in inducement to a high volume, as with fee-for-service. As among other salaried occupations in an industrial society, however, the inducement to optimal performance is lodged in the organized framework surrounding the doctor, rather than the financial mechanism per se.

There is much data to show that under the salary system of paying doctors, the volume of services tends to be lower than under the fee-system. The United Mine Workers of America program of medical care has been able to compare the volume of insured services rendered to similar socioeconomic populations served by doctors paid in different manners. Among those served by salaried physicians (in group practice clinics), hospital admissions were 32.5 per cent lower than for those served by fee-for-service doctors; surgical operations were 36.8 per cent fewer, and for appendectomies the differential was 59.4 per cent. Similar comparisons emerged from a study of services provided for steel workers; hospital admissions were at a rate of 135 per 1,000 persons per year for beneficiaries served by solo practitioners paid by fee-for-service, compared with 90 admissions per 1,000 for those workers served by salaried doctors in group clinics. The ratio of surgical operations was two-to-one—69 per 1,000 for the fee-for-service group and 33 per 1,000 for the salaried group.[8] We know, of course, that the vast majority of surgical operations, and for that matter hospital admissions generally, are elective matters depending mainly on the doctor's judgment.

One should not jump to the conclusion that the higher volume of service under the fee system always means unnecessary care and inferior quality or vice versa. Conceivably some patients served by salaried physicians are given superficial attention and inadequate care just because a financial incentive toward maximum service is lacking. The evidence in terms of end-results, however, favors the former rather than the latter interpretation. It is very difficult to establish comparable populations and examine end-results, but in the Health Insurance Plan of Greater New York (in which doctors are salaried), this was done; the experiences of H.I.P. members were compared with those of some 13,000 New Yorkers who were also insured but served by private fee-doctors. Taking peri-natal mortality as the measure, the H.I.P. population had a rate of 21.3 per 1,000 births, in contrast to 38.1 for the control population.[9] Moreover, it is generally conceded that the best quality of medical care in the United States is found in the medical schools and the great teaching medical centers, where physicians are conventionally on salary. The same high regard is held for non-university centers like the Mayo Clinic where physicians are on salary. Even in governmental installations, despite their social handicaps in attracting good personnel, the quality of medical care from salaried physicians is generally high; a survey of the Veterans Administration medical care program by the American Medical Association drew this conclusion.[10]

The salaried physician is provided no financial incentive for either a large or a small volume of service, but in an organized professional framework he has other forms of incentive toward optimal performance. He wishes to win the respect of his colleagues and his superiors, both for economic advancement and professional prestige. It is the judgment of other doctors, more than of patients, that counts. Nearly all salary systems base the level of remuneration on such factors as training, experience, and demonstrated skills, with increments being awarded for seniority and scope of responsibility. These qualifications are judged by other physicians or, at least, experts in personnel affairs and are theoretically based on rational criteria. Of course, there may be errors in judgment or even prejudices interfering with the reasonable operation of the system, and it is such factors that make many physicians apprehensive about salaries and in favor of taking their chances with the buy-and-sell market of fee-for-service practice.[11]

In a salaried medical organization with reasonable teamwork, the physician has every reason to consult with colleagues in other specialties on the handling of a case. Such a pattern also permits the physician to undertake post-graduate studies periodically, as well as to enjoy a rest or vacation, without loss of income. When a young physician starts work in a salaried framework, he can apply himself to full capacity at the outset, without many half-idle months or years waiting to "build up a practice" in a private office. At the same time, his work can be supervised by more experienced colleagues and can be adjusted to the level of his capacities. All these factors undoubtedly contribute to advancing the quality of medical care.

In one respect, the quality of medical care under salaried arrangements is believed by many to suffer. This is in the level of sensitivity of the physician to the personal feelings of his patient. Undoubtedly, many physicians of apathetic personality and weak ambition enter salaried employment, because they cannot thrive in the competitive medical market or they crave a secure job and an eight-hour day. Such physicians may well be insensitive to patients, as they probably would also be in private fee-practice. But there is no objective evidence that in the over-all American scene salaried physicians are less sensitive to patient-needs than physicians paid by the other methods. There are certainly enough complaints about callous or unsympathetic doctors in ordinary private practice.[12] In Europe, where salaried physicians are responsible for nearly all hospital-based medical care, the connotations of salaries are just as humane as of other forms of medical remuneration. Even in the Soviet Union, where all physicians are on government salary, American observers report professional attitudes to patients to be warm and considerate.[13]

Turning to the cost criterion of the salary system, there is no doubt that it generally tends to be less expensive for the consumer than any other method. Everything depends, of course, on the amount of the salary. The bargaining power of an organization hiring medical talent, however, tends to be greater than that of the individual doctor, so that his net earnings are bound to be lower than they would be if he levied a patient-fee for each service rendered. Despite this, as health services have become increasingly organized, the proportion of American physicians in full-time salaried employment has risen steadily. In 1959, the proportion came to 35 per cent of the total, including interns and residents; even without the latter young doctors in training, it was 23 per cent of the total.[14]

As the demand for salaried physicians in hospitals, public agencies, medical schools, and other organizations has increased, medical salaries have risen. The average income of physicians in research or public health work is still below that of private practitioners, but the salaries of physicians in most clinical specialties have come to exceed, on the average, earnings from independent practice. This can be seen in the relatively high earnings of salaried physicians in group practice clinics, compared with income from solo practice. Remarkably high salaries are paid also to specialists employed in community general hospitals (mental hospital medical salaries are still relatively low), particularly radiologists and pathologists. A survey in 1960 found the average net earnings of radiologists from hospital work to be $30,680 and of pathologists $28,000.[15]

Yet it has been shown that a given volume of services remunerated on a fee-basis would cost the consumers of medical care even more. The fact is that the extension of salaried medicine has gone hand-in-hand with a rise in the per capita volume of medical services received by the United States population. One can say, therefore, that the salary system has enabled the average American patient to receive an expanding volume of services at a somewhat lower cost than he would pay (directly or indirectly through taxes, philanthropy and so on) if fee-for-service were the exclusive method of medical remuneration. Consumer pressure for economy has, indeed, been a factor in the growth of the salary pattern, as reflected in the widening impact of the Group Health Association of America or the extension of new public programs like "Medicare" for military dependents.

As for its administrative implications, the salary system is manifestly simpler than any other. The paper-work for both physician and paying agency is much less. Neither units of service nor units of patient have to be accounted for, but only units of time like months or years. There are, of course, other phases of administration involved in a salary system, but they are incident to the process of organization, supervision, and coordination of the medical service, rather than the mechanism of paying the doctor.

Finally, the political implications of the salary system must be considered, and there is no question that this pattern is more beset with controversy than any other. This is by no means true of all countries, for in Europe salaried positions in hospitals are more prestigeful than any other. In England, competition for such posts is keen and it is the disappointed applicants who sometimes depart and make derogatory speeches about the National Health Service in other countries. In the United States, however, the great majority of physicians are strongly opposed to salaries as an exclusive scheme of payment. The reasons are complex, but they doubtless combine economic and professional factors. Economically, physicians oppose salaries because they believe, from observations in the past, that they mean lower income. Moreover, the opportunity for exceptionally high incomes —possible in private fee-practice—is virtually eliminated. Professionally, doctors oppose salaries because the organization of services associated with them means a restriction of their independence. An ellipsis between method of payment and method of medical care organization is readily made, and the physician —usually a staunch individualist—bridles at the thought of working under someone else's supervision. While he has, of course, done this throughout his years of training, the doctor embarking on clinical practice expects to be free and unfettered.

The bitterness with which many physicians feel about salaried employment has led to endless controversies about "socialized medicine" over the last 40 or 50 years. Even health insurance plans paying physicians on a fee basis have been opposed or viewed suspiciously, for fear that they might ultimately lead to salaried arrangements.[16] The most recent battles have been pitched in hospitals, where radiologists and pathologists have launched campaigns, and even law suits, to compel remuneration on a fee basis rather than by salary.[17] Accordingly, many specialists working whole-time in general hospitals are paid a percentage of the hospital's income from the services of their departments (especially radiology), rather than by a flat monthly amount. All sorts of circumlocutions, like "retainers" or "time-fees," are used to smooth the way for salary contracts, so strong are the feelings about them.

In view of these attitudes, and in spite of the steady growth of salaried arrangements in American medicine, the salary method of payment is least often included in various legislative proposals for health insurance in the United States. Most of the prepayment for physician's service that has grown extensively, like Blue Shield or commercial insurance, and the largest governmental programs, like welfare services for the indigent or workmen's compensation, are based on the fee-for-service system.[18]

CONCLUSION

This discussion of the three principal methods of paying doctors and their usual consequences has assumed the "pure" operation of each system. Actually various combinations are possible and are frequently undertaken. Many physicians work predominantly on a fee-basis, but engage in part-time employment for a salary also. Other physicians may work mainly on a salary, but are free to earn fees for special services rendered on the side. In the medical care systems of some countries, like Sweden, many physicians receive a governmental salary beyond which they may charge fees for services rendered to health insurance beneficiaries. In sparsely populated sections of Scotland, a basic salary is received as an underpinning for capitation payments. These combinations of payment methods often overcome the objections to one pattern or the other.

This review of the attitude of physicians toward different payment systems, and their varying consequences, has been based largely on the American scene. This is a setting in which the fee-system predominates and the other methods are associated with minority movements implying serious medical-social change. Yet, it must be realized that in a setting where the salary or the capitation system has come to predominate, the consequences of each pattern can be very different. The whole culture of medicine differs in a system like the British or the Soviet, where salaries and capitation payments are the general rule. Consequences of those patterns that are negative—when they are minority affairs, as in America—cease to operate. The financial incentive toward maximum performance, for example, identified in the United States with the fee system, becomes replaced by incentives for job advancement and reward built into nation-wide and highly structured systems of salaried medical care. Undoubtedly all methods of payment, in all cultures, must in some way satisfy the physician's need for both reward and recognition, and this can be achieved by many different formulas. It is the consequences of the payment system for meeting the needs of patients that make the difference.

The long-term trend in the United States is certainly toward an increased use of medical salaries. Even when fees are paid, the trend is toward standardization of their amounts under contracts with third-party paying agencies. The negative influences on the quality of service and their costs to the community, associated with the fee-for-service system, are becoming more widely recognized, and apprehensions about salaries are declining. On a world scale these trends are seen more strikingly. They are associated with more basic economic trends in the collective financing of medical care in the first place, as well as in the technical organization of services into more coordinated systems. It is all a part of the larger organization of social services in ways that can meet human needs most effectively.[19] Just as the industrial evolution from small artisans to large factories was beset with controversy and conflict, this evolution of medical care organization has its trials and tribulations. The issues surrounding the method of paying doctors are an eddy in this larger stream, and their eventual outcome will be determined by the course of the larger social movements. Objective studies of the full consequences of different systems of paying the doctor may help to guide this evolution toward more desirable goals.

NOTES

1. Henry E. Sigerist, "The Physician's Profession Through the Ages," *Bulletin of New York Academy of Medicine* (Second series), 9 (1933), 661–676.

2. Franz Goldmann, "Methods of Payment for Physicians' Services in Medical Care Programs," *American Journal of Public Health,* 42 (1952), No. 2.
3. Paul Densen, Eve Balamuth and Sam Shapiro, *Prepaid Medical Care and Hospital Utilization.* (Chicago, American Hospital Association, Monograph No. 3, 1958.
4. F. D. Mott and M. I. Roemer, *Rural Health and Medical Care* (New York, McGraw-Hill, 1948), pp. 392–431.
5. J. S. Collings, "General Practice in England Today," *The Lancet,* 1 (1950), 555–585.
6. I. S. Falk, *Security Against Sickness* (New York, Doubleday, Doran, and Co., 1936), p. 156.
7. California A.B. 449, January 22, 1945.
8. Caldwell B. Esselstyn, "The Next Ten Years in Medicine," *Proceedings of the Rip Van Winkle Clinic* (Hudson, New York), Spring, 1961, pp. 20–34.
9. Committee for the Special Research Project in the Health Insurance Plan of Greater New York, *Health and Medical Care in New York City* (Cambridge: Harvard University Press, 1957).
10. Roy R. Kracke, "The Medical Care of the Veteran," *Journal of the American Medical Association,* 143 (1950), 1321–1331.
11. William Glaser, "Doctors and Politics," *American Journal of Sociology,* 66 (November 1960), 230–245.
12. Selig Greenberg, "The Decline of the Healing Art," *Harper's Magazine* (October 1960), pp. 132–137.
13. U.S. Public Health Service, *Report of the United States Public Health Mission to the Union of Soviet Socialist Republics* (Washington, Government Printing Office, 1959).
14. Anon., "What 228,295 Doctors of Medicine Do," *Medical Economics,* 11 (1959), p. 136.
15. Anon., "Specialist Arrangements Not Changing," *Modern Hospital* (March, 1960), 67–71.
16. Richard Carter, *The Doctor Business* (New York, Doubleday and Co., 1958).
17. Alanson W. Willcox, *Hospitals and the Corporate Practice of Medicine* (Chicago, American Hospital Association, Monograph No. 1, 1957).
18. Herman M. Somers and Anne R. Somers, *Doctors, Patients, and Health Insurance* (Washington, The Brookings Institution, 1961).
19. Gunnar Myrdal, *Beyond the Welfare State* (New Haven, Yale University Press, 1960).

7 *Beyond Medicare*

ISIDORE S. FALK*

IS MEDICARE ENOUGH?

Medicare marked the beginning of national financing for personal health services on a social insurance basis in the U.S.A. Its enactment reflected national conviction that, without the intervention of government, the aged could not have ready access to needed health services.

Despite almost incredible complexities in its design, the Medicare program for the aged has been brought into operation. This is a tribute to the skill and imagination of those who have been charged with its administration. More specifically:

The administrative agencies, public and private, have developed functioning procedures.

Reprinted by permission of the author and publisher from *American Journal of Public Health,* 59 (April, 1969) pp. 608–619.

* Ph.D., Professor Emeritus of Public Health (Medical Care) Yale University School of Medicine.

The institutional and individual providers of service have adapted their practices to the requirements of the program, and they are being paid for their services to the aged.

The service loads of the system are proving to be close to what was anticipated.

A beginning has been made toward the establishment and observance of operational standards.

And twenty million persons who are 65 and older have an improved accessibility to health services.

Despite dire forebodings and forecasts, there are signs of increasing conviction, even among some who were most fearful, that Medicare has strengthened—not weakened—our society. Today, we are confronted by questions about the adequacy of the current Medicare and its course for the future.

Is Medicare enough for the aged? Is our social need satisfied with Medicare only for the aged, or is an equivalent program still needed for other social insurance beneficiaries—for the disabled as well as the widow, orphan and dependent-parent survivors of those who died during their working lifetime? To go still further, is such a program also needed for those who, though actively employed and embraced by the social insurance system, have no health protections under that system? Or, to pose the latter questions more generally, is an equivalent of Medicare needed for the non-aged who have only limited sickness insurance or none at all, and who may find themselves burdened or medically indigent when confronted by the costs of needed personal health services?

I submit that the current Medicare is necessary but not sufficient for the aged; and that an equivalent of an improved Medicare is necessary for the population as a whole.

INADEQUACIES IN MEDICARE FOR THE AGED

The *necessity* of Medicare for the aged was documented by a library of literature and testimony preceding its enactment in July, 1965. Its *insufficiency* is now equally well known but deserves recapitulation.

My criterion for an evaluation is the increasing national commitment to the social policy that comprehensive health care should be readily available throughout the country. A corollary is the elementary principle that the financial and administrative arrangements should effect such availability.

By these criteria, the current Medicare for the aged is insufficient on many grounds. Comprehensive health care is not readily available for the population as a whole, and even less for the aged. Medicare's financing does not extend to many services and commodities needed for comprehensive preventive, diagnostic, therapeutic or rehabilitative services. It deliberately interposes deductibles and prior hospitalization requirements as barriers, and co-insurances as disincentives to service. It requires termination of benefits even while care is still needed, precipitating financial burdens precisely when the costs are heaviest on the sick and their families. It not only accepts the traditional separateness of hospital and medical practitioner; it requires the separate payment of hospital and physician, and even excludes from the hospital payment the cost of the physician employed by the hospital. This contradicts the congressional declaration of policy not to interfere in the practice of medicine, or in the manner in which medical service is provided, or in the compensation of any employee, or in the operation of an institution. More serious, this interposes restraints on the development of organizational patterns that could contribute to efficient utilization of manpower and dollars, to better organization for the delivery of care, and to the containment of rising costs. Medicare provides little actual authority or incentive for effective review of utilization, and even less for encouragement or assurance of quality standards outside the accredited hospital. Finally, its financing covers about 35 per cent of personal health care costs for the aged, which is a great boon for many; but it does not even approach the 80 or 90 per cent coverage of costs which is essential for effective insurance protection.

The reasons for these elements of insufficiency are well known. The legislation was framed to make only a manageable beginning and to stay within boundaries of cost, mainly because of political considerations. Its *insurance* design was dictated largely by its *insurance opponents,* not by its proponents; and the apparent objective was to conform as far as possible—especially for the noninstitutional services—to insurance through cash indemnity rather than through service benefits. Its *medical service* design was dictated largely by its *professional opponents;* and the apparent objective was to conform as far as possible to solo medical practice supported by fee-for-service. These may have been unavoidable compromises, the prices that had to be paid to achieve enactment of the legislation in 1965. I suggest that these compromises should not have further longevity in Medicare for the aged, and that they should be avoided in the design of any extension to other population groups.

EXTENSIONS TO THE NON-AGED

We should recall that when the proposal was first advanced, in 1951, to provide health service benefits for the aged through the national social insurance system, the program intended that the benefits be made available not only to the aged, but also to the others receiving, or eligible to receive, social insurance benefits. Today, the case is just as clear that Medicare should be extended to the disability and survivor beneficiaries. Both categories have less-than-average means and resources for meeting the costs of health services; both have the same kind of need as the aged for paid-up insurance through the social insurance system; and both can be served as readily by the system's financial and administrative mechanisms. Thus, need and feasibility dictate that an improved Medicare be extended to all the OASDI beneficiary groups.

The need for an extension *beyond* the beneficiaries of the social security system—to the people who are not social insurance beneficiaries—is now evident from the clamor, day in and day out, for a mechanism that will really bring modern medical care within the financial reach of the population. The need for insurance to distribute the costs of personal health services arises, as we all know, from the very nature of medical care costs. The incidence of these costs is uneven, individually unforeseeable and unbudgetable for most people who are able to foresee, budget and meet their other essential costs of living.

In view of the increasing valuation placed on medical care since the 1920's, we have thought that the public would readily agree to pay for good medical care through an appropriate mechanism which would distribute the costs among groups of people and over periods of time.

Private insurance argued, persuasively to many, that it would effect the sale and distribution of adequate health insurance protection—if given time and the opportunity. Over the past 30 years it has successfully implemented a massive program of sales, so that nearly all who are in need of health insurance have some coverage today. For a while, the scope of the insurance, and its effectiveness in providing insurance protection, grew year after year; but that chapter has apparently come to an end. Now, when the proportion of people having some insurance is substantially maximal, the effectiveness of the insurance protection barely manages to keep pace with rising prices and costs, despite enormous effort and considerable success in persuading people to pay higher and higher insurance premiums.

The demand for health insurance protection, and the willingness to pay for it, are evidenced by the extension of private insurance to about 150 million persons under age 65, mainly through group insurance and the medium of the employment relation. The insufficiency of the prevailing private insurance is evidenced by its inability to extend protection against more than an average of about 40 per cent of the private costs for those who have insurance, and about 33 per cent of the private costs incurred by all in the population.

The massive growth of insurance enrollment is the great achievement of private insurance; and the nation is indebted to the industry for education of the public concerning the fact that medical care costs are insurable, and for the actual performance of the insurance contracts in reducing the burdens of sickness costs for millions of persons. The inability, however, of private insurance to achieve an adequate level of insurance protection for the population is its failure. This was always inherent in the very nature of private insurance, stemming from the limitations which its self-financing mechanisms could not avoid or escape. By and large, health service needs and the consequent costs are larger for the poor than for the rich; and most of the population cannot budget and self-finance their full health needs through available mechanisms for group and individual payment. Private insurance lacks the authority and the means to transfer the impacts of the costs from one economic level or sector to another.

Neither the insurance industry nor organized labor have been able to persuade employers that they could afford to effect the transfer adequately through the provision of fringe benefits to employment. And employees have been showing increasing resistance to the assignment of larger and larger shares of their wage and salary gains to pay for health insurance which provides only limited and substantially nonexpanding insurance protection.

Now, that which has been good should not be the enemy of the better. Private insurance should no longer stand in the way of insurance that can be designed to meet the public need, not only in the extensiveness of the population it reaches, but also in the effectiveness of the protection it provides.

A new health insurance for the general population should be designed to accord with the social policy of making comprehensive health care available to everybody; and not merely to give some partial protection against some of the costs to some, or even to many. It should also provide new stimuli for the attainment of both quality and economy goals. Toward these ends, a national system of health insurance has the right to rely upon the resources of the nation that can be applied to furthering the national interest in national health. Viewed in these perspectives, the extension of an improved Medicare to the general population would have the potential of achieving what the nation needs, and what has been demonstrably beyond the capacity of private insurance.

PERSPECTIVES FOR THE NEW HEALTH INSURANCE

Our goal should be the implementation of clear national objectives:

Comprehensive personal health care should be available for all the population throughout the country, with equal opportunity for access to the services by all persons, and without avoidable limitations dictated by geographical boundaries or by variations in state and local resources.

The services should be available under arrangements that are acceptable to the people to be served as well as to those who provide the services, without financial barriers when the care is needed and without financial burdens after it is received.

And the services should be available under arrangements which ensure—as far as is practical—high quality and effectiveness, efficiency in the utilization of personnel and facilities, economy in costs, and full accounting of operational experiences.

The design of a program to meet this goal should, I believe, be based on four policies which the Congress adopted when enacting hospital insurance for the aged:

1. The availability of the health service should be supported through governmental financing.
2. The services made available should be as comprehensive as is practical.
3. These health services should be provided by private practitioners and institutions.
4. Government should assume responsibility to encourage and institute procedures, private and public, for safeguarding and guaranteing the quality of the services for which it pays.

Toward this goal and on the basis of these policies, I suggest that the Social Security Act be amended to provide health insurance benefits for the nation's population. Such a new system of benefits should absorb both the present national system of Medicare for the aged, and the current Medicaid for needy and the medically needy persons under the federal-state assistance programs.

SOME BASIC SPECIFICATIONS FOR NATIONAL HEALTH INSURANCE

In order to explore the general outlines of a national system of health insurance benefits and to consider some of the main problems involved in its design, I submit for discussion the form which some of the basic specifications might take.

The Population Eligible for the Benefits

The primary objective is the availability of comprehensive personal health care fore everybody. Accordingly, the benefits of the system should extend to all persons resident in the country, without a means test, without requirement of an insurance contribution history, and with freedom to choose from whom to receive health care among the qualified service resources available in the community. Here I am pursuing the pattern already accepted by the federal government and by the nation for hospital insurance of the aged under Title XVIII, Part A, of Medicare. As will be evident later, substantially all who are gainfully employed would be required to pay contributions, but this should not be used as an explicit test of eligibility for the benefits.

The Health Service Benefits

In keeping with the objective for comprehensive personal health care, the system should undertake to provide its benefits in the form of services, not partial reimbursement dollars. Furthermore, the benefits should extend, as far as may be practical, to all kinds of services which can be usefully provided for the maintenance of personal health and the prevention of illness and disability; for care and treatment in illness and for medical rehabilitation. The benefits should extend to the services of physicians, dentists, nurses and other categories of professional, technical and supporting personnel; to the services of hospitals and other medical care institutions for both ambulatory and inpatient care; to the services of organized specialty and comprehensive group practice; and to prescribed medicines and appliances. There should be no arbitrary limitations on the place where a needed benefit service is provided. The guiding rule should be the provision of care where best done in the patient's interest, with regard for effectiveness of the service and economy in its provision. In such a broad spectrum of health services, as is proposed here, there is no place for deductibles, co-insurance, or arbitrary limits of number or time on the availability of services needed for reasons of health. Such protections as may prove to be needed—against excessive demands or other abuses of utilization—should be primarily administrative and professional; and not in the form of rationing in accordance with ability to pay.

Apart from emergency situations, access to specialty and in-bed care should flow through primary care, except possibly in the few specialties in which self-diagnosis of need may be justifiable.

The division between hospital and medical services—as in the demarcations between Parts A and B of the present Title XVIII —should be eradicated. Instead, the content and design of the service benefits, and the payment for them, should give every practical encouragement to their evolutionary integration. Such encouragement should have special regard for the provision of the services through the group practice team to bring about more efficient utilization of skilled and supporting manpower, increased availability of comprehensive and continuous care, maximal justified reliance on ambulatory service with concurrent reduction in the use of expensive inpatient hospital facilities, and extension of quality controls and evaluations throughout the spectrum of services.

Where boundaries or limits have to be specified—because of current inadequacies in particular categories of personnel, facilities or supplies—these should be held to the unavoidable minimum; they should be regarded as temporary compromises with comprehensiveness; and they should be removable by administrative decision as soon as the needed services and supplies can become available.

Administration

The system of health benefits should be built as an integral part of the national social insurance (OASDHI), with the primary administrative responsibilities lodged in the Department of Health, Education, and Welfare. The system should involve the Social Security Administration for the contractual arrangements to ensure the availability and financing of the benefits; and the Health Services and Mental Health Administration for those medical aspects concerned with medical care criteria, standards, professional relations, and priorities. In effecting arrangements for the availability of services, the national administration should be free to utilize—as national or regional agents—state and private agencies qualified for negotiations concerned with service benefits; and providers should be equally free to be represented by agents of their own choosing. With respect to the establishment and observance of national standards for the qualifications of practitioners, medical care groups and institutions, the administration may utilize state agencies and professional organizations as agents of the federal authority. The administrative structure should be broadly regional, compatible with regional organization of the institutional and service arrangements. Administrative policies should be formulated, and service performances should be evaluated, with the aid of consumer and provider advisory councils.

Payment for Services

The health insurance system should expect to pay for services, at fair and adequate rates, through methods that are acceptable to the providers and feasible for the administrative processes. Since there are no methods or rates of payment that are acceptable universally for each of the several categories of service, both the methods and the rates would have to be subject to explorations and negotiations. It may therefore be sufficient to suggest some of the possibilities.

Physicians and other practitioners, with whom there are agreements for service, may be compensated by fee-for-service (with or without fee or relative-value schedule), capitation, salary (full or part time), or combinations of these; and the choice of method may be left to their election in each major administrative area. The *rate* of payment should be negotiated periodically. It should have equivalent application and should yield equivalent results in average levels of compensation whatever the *method* of compensation, whether with or without *pro rata* adjustments as may be necessary. The total costs for a category of service should be substantially the same whichever method is selected.

Hospitals and related institutions should be compensated on a cost-reimbursement pattern, bounded by maxima which—while meeting criteria of reasonable adequacy in the community—discourage avoidable escalation of cost. The major details of the pattern will, no doubt, take form from national operations and studies now in progress.

For prescribed medicines, laboratory and radiological services, appliances, and so on, diverse methods of payment would have to be used—whether on cost-reimbursement, negotiated fee-schedules and prices, or combinations.

For group practice plans which involve various combinations of service categories (practitioner, hospital, laboratory, and so forth), negotiated all-inclusive rates, composited from the rates applicable to the several categories, would seem to be best indicated, since this pattern of payment can meet criteria of fairness and adequacy, and can at the same time encourage the organized provision of multiple or comprehensive services.

Standards

The health insurance system should undertake to preserve a balance between the objectives of: (a) free choice by the population in obtaining care from all qualified service providers in the community; and (b) guarantee of the worth of the services for which government pays. The administration would therefore have to establish and encourage the maximal observance of standards and operational requirements which serve the objective of worth, while effecting only minimal curtailment in the objective of free choice. To these ends, the system could draw upon the considerable achievements of Medicare in prescribing standards applicable to those who qualify for its payments, i.e., physicians and other practitioners, hospitals and related institutons, laboratories, group clinics and health centers, and so on. Obviously, such standards, existing and new, should continue to be developed by and with the statutory licensing and chartering agencies, and the professional organizations; and as far as may be feasible, they should be acceptable to and implementable by most of the providers.

In addition, the goals of the system should be served by the appropriateness of the methods of payment and the adequacy of the rates, and by systematic and continuing reviews of performances outside as well as inside hospitals and related institutions. Fortunately, many useful beginnings in these directions have already been made under Medicare. Also, new efforts are under way in that program and in Medicaid; in the special programs for children and regional medical programs; as well as in neighborhood health centers, medical schools and universities. We are hopefully optimistic that, if required by statute, increasingly useful standards of qualitative as well as quantitative adequacy will become operational. We should be encouraged by the growing interest in the improvement of organization for the delivery of care which encourages ready access first to continuing primary care, and then, and only then, to professionally competent referral to secondary specialty care, particularly through well-organized comprehensive group practice.

Finances

In the main, the costs of the health insurance benefits would not be new expenditures for personal health care, but a rerouting through the health insurance system of expenditures already being made through private and public channels. It may be useful to outline some of the potential patterns for the financing of the system.

As a benchmark, I would point out that in fiscal year 1968—when all expenditures for health and medical care were $53.1 billion and amounted to 6.5 per cent of gross national product —the total expenditures for *personal health care services* pertinent to our interest at this point were about $41.9 billion ($206 per capita).* Of this total 24 per cent ($10.0 billion or $49 per capita) were expenditures under federal, state and local governmental programs; and 76 per cent ($31.9 billion or $157 per capita) were private expenditures through personal expenditure channels and through private insurance. It is therefore sound and justifiable to suggest that the financing of the proposed system should rest primarily upon contributory social insurance. Inter-

* Of total expenditures for personal health care in fiscal year 1968, amounting to $47.8 billion (including the expenses for private prepayment, and the administrative expenses for Medicare and for veterans' hospital and medical care), I have excluded $5.889 billion—the expenditures of the Veterans' Administration ($1.382 bil), of the Department of Defense ($1.591 bil), of the federal and state workmen's compensation systems ($0.770 bil), and of state and local governments for psychiatric and tuberculosis hospitals, school health, and related programs (circa $2.146 bil). (Based on the preliminary estimates for FY 1968 of the Office of Research and Statistics, U.S. Social Security Administration. See: Research and Statistics Note No. 22, by Barbara S. Cooper (Nov. 11), 1968; and Social Security Bull. (Oct.), 1968, 31:10 and following, Tables M6 and M7. See also: Social Welfare Expenditures 1967–1968, by Ida C. Merriam; Alfred M. Skolnik; and Sophie R. Dales. Ibid. 31:12, p. 11.)

locked with the nationally accepted system of paying for OAS-
DHI, the contributions would be graduated in direct or adjusted
proportion to earnings, although the benefits would be uniform
for all eligible persons. This reflects the objective of comprehensive care for everybody and, in considerable measure, current
private expenditure patterns among families of different income
levels.

The health benefits system proposed would take over a large
share of expenditures for personal health care which are customarily and currently incurred through tax-financed federal, state
and local public programs. We have precedents for such a transfer in Medicare and in the Veterans' Administration, Defense
Department, Children's Bureau, and OEO programs. And since
the system would also surely be contributing to the national welfare in general, it is sound and justifiable that federal general
revenues should contribute substantially to the financing.

The allocation of the costs among persons to be served by the
benefits, employers, and the federal government, is endlessly arguable. For first consideration, I would suggest as a basic pattern
of sharing that two-thirds of the needed income should derive
from contributions—divided in one of various possible patterns
among employees, employers, and the self-employed, and even
allowing for negotiated divisions between employers and employees; and that one-third should be provided from federal general
revenues. The contributions should be interlocked with those for
OASDI, and should be collected jointly with other contributions
under the Federal Insurance Contributions Act (FICA),
whether or not with the same "ceiling" on taxable earnings as for
other social insurance benefits. The general revenue appropriations should be open-ended in order to meet all residual costs.

The *total* personal health care expenditures—private and public—with which we are concerned here, aggregated about 5.1 per
cent of *gross national product* (GNP) in fiscal year 1968. If the
costs to be incurred by the proposed system will need to increase
in the early years of operation, possibly by 5 or 10 per cent progressively with the development of the system, they may require
a somewhat larger share of the GNP of future years—perhaps
5.4 to 5.6 per cent, and moving up toward 6.0 or 6.5 per cent.
Such a progression would reflect that, even if the national prod-

uct increases in the years ahead, medical care costs may continue
to climb faster than the economy as a whole for some time to
come. These are easily manageable shares of the GNP if, as a
nation, we choose to allocate them to the support of the health
services.

The potential impacts of the allocated shares of the costs are
equally manageable. The *private* expenditures with which we are
dealing were about 5.6 per cent of *disposable personal income* in
fiscal year 1968. If two-thirds of the growing total expenditures
for a national system of health benefits are to be met by contributions, they would probably amount initially to about 5.2 per
cent of disposable personal income and could be expected to
move up toward about 6.0 per cent as the program proceeds.
The contribution rate under FICA would of course depend on
the arbitrary ceiling imposed on taxable earnings; but here there
is much room for flexibility. Obviously, the higher that ceiling,
the lower the contribution rate required, and the greater the
fiscal progressivity in the financing of the health care benefits.
These social insurance contributions, through fixed periodic payments from earnings, would be primarily a substitution for current partially regular and mainly irregular private expenditures.
The impact of the contributions on individuals and families can
therefore be readily acceptable because, in the main, the
amounts would be equivalent to what people are already spending for medical care. This would still hold true if contributions
had to provide more than two-thirds of the costs of the system,
or even all of the costs exclusive of those customarily met from
federal, state or local tax funds.

The federal share of expenditures to support the system would
represent a considerable increase in the expenditures for national
health purposes from federal general revenue. Such expenditures
for the personal health care services of the kinds with which we
are concerned now amount to about $3.4 billion a year.[2] If the
federal general revenue share were one-third of the total cost of
the system, it would have to increase progressively toward some-

2. Expenditures from federal general revenues for: Medicare benefits
   and administration; public assistance (vendor medical payments);
   general hospital and medical care; medical vocational rehabilitation;
   and OEO health and medical care.

thing like 2 percent of GNP, or about five times the current federal expenditures from general revenue for civilian personal health care. Should this be an unacceptably large federal sharing, it could be reduced to one-half as much (about 1 per cent of GNP) if individual social insurance contributions had to support as much as five-sixths of the total costs, leaving one-sixth (instead of one-third) as a charge on federal general revenue. In such a schedule, about one-fourth of the federal financing would result from relieving state and local governments of expenditures they have been making for personal health care. Though very large, all such increases in the federal role are within the means of our affluent society if, as a nation, we choose to undertake such an allocation out of our national means.

The success of the proposed system would depend in no small measure on the continuing development of manpower, facilities and organization needed for good personal health care. I therefore suggest that at least a substantial share of the federal support for these activities should become an integral part of the system's financing. If amounts equal to a small portion of the annual operating costs—perhaps 3 or 4 per cent of the total—were earmarked for these supporting purposes, these essential programs would be relieved of the annual agonies of fiscal uncertainty; and they could, I believe, go forward with renewed vigor, promise, and productivity.

The finances of the health benefits system should, of course, be managed through the trust fund procedures which have become well-established for our social insurance system since they were first included in the Social Security Act of 1935. Under this pattern, the income for the system is deposited in the trust fund; the amounts intended to pay for benefits are permanently appropriated and available as needed; and Congress controls the annual amounts which may be expended from the trust fund for administrative and related purposes. And since we are dealing with a system of social insurance which needs to be only on a current cost basis, the intricate problems of reserve financing associated with long-term risks are avoided, with only a contingency reserve in the trust fund as a stabilizer against annual or short-term fluctuations in income or expenditure.

Freedom and Responsibility

Many additional specifications are of course required for the complete design of a national system of health benefits. A few deserve mention here.

It is already clear, I trust, that all individual, group and institutional providers of service should have the privilege of deciding whether or not to participate in the system. It should be equally clear, however, that we have a right to expect their individual decisions to have regard for their obligations to the public need under our system of privileged licensure and charter. Participation by practitioners should of course be surrounded by the protections inherent in strict observance of professional independence and confidentiality in the doctor-patient professional relation, subject to professional review of professional performance. The group practice, the hospital, and the related institution, should be equally free from interference in the internal affairs of staffing and management—with the fullest possible latitudes in their patterns of organization, subject to over-riding national standards concerned with good quality of service and reasonable economy of cost.

The freedom of the patient to choose his doctor or his system of providers, and the freedom of the doctor or system to accept or reject, and the freedom of the doctor to practice by his best judgment and competence, must however have regard for the national interest in observing the value of what the national economy finances. Government must reserve the right to refuse to pay for what is not worthy of a draft on the public purse.

Finally, the administrative authority must be charged with clear and unambiguous responsibility for a full public accounting of performance under the system. This must, of course, extend to the counting of services and the flow of dollars. It should, however, go much further: to the relations of services and expenditures to recognized and true need; to the health values of performances; to experiments and studies of organizational patterns and performances; to unmet national needs for personnel and facilities and to the requirements for meeting those needs; and to methods of containing costs while adhering to standards of quality and the goals of health progress.

NATIONAL HEALTH INSURANCE FOR THE NATION

We are in quest of an adequate program for the personal health services. First, we strive for the acceleration of *health progress* for the whole population. Accordingly, if the program is to be adequate in this respect, it must be designed with awareness of what is already possible, and with alertness for what will become feasible through continuing progress in science and technology along with the growing support of national social policy for health care. Second, we strive for the strengthening of *health security* for the whole population. And if the program is to be adequate in this respect, it must be designed to ensure effective protection against the financial impacts and burdens that sickness brings in its wake. Third, we strive for enhancement of the general public welfare through all that *both health progress and health security* can contribute or make possible for the broader foundations of well-being in our society.

Toward these objectives, I have submitted the outline for a system of personal health care with the hope that it is sufficient in detail to serve as the basis for constructive discussion. It does not propose a national health service; but rather it proposes an extension of our national social insurance to support and finance our private resources for personal health service. In this pattern, it proceeds along the course on which we began with the Social Security Act of 1935, building on the framework which has been evolving over a third of a century. It is a pattern which has demonstrated its feasibility, and has won national acceptance and confidence.

Since the proposal is only concerned with the personal health services, it is obviously self-limited; for it does not extend to those preventive and other services which must be provided as community programs. The boundaries between personal and community areas are not always sharp or clear, and each must be adapted to the other. Therefore, as we fix the specifications for the personal services, we must be alert to the implications for the complementary community services, and for their coordination with the personal health services. I suggest, however, that the more we strengthen the personal health services, and the more secure we make their national financing, the more we increase the opportunities to improve the community health and related services. These opportunities will be augmented, especially if state and local governmental agencies are relieved of their present large expenditures for personal health services that would, under the proposal, be financed through the national system of health benefits.

The precipitating occasion for national action now, with respect to personal health care, is the increasing national recognition that the delivery of the care is inadequate, and that the inadequacy is approaching near-crisis intensity in urban areas. The timeliness of national action now results from the successful implementation of Medicare. What has been achieved for the aged can now be done—and, I believe, better—for the whole population. Extension from Medicare for 20 million aged to national health insurance for 200 million of all ages means a tenfold expansion of persons to be served; but, of course, it means only a relatively minor expansion among the providers of health services to be involved—because Medicare has already achieved the negotiated participation of most medical care practitioners and of nearly all the hospitals and related institutions of the country. The system I have submitted for discussion does involve extensions among the providers, however, because it intends application to a broader scope of services, leading to comprehensive health care benefits. I believe that such extension is manageable.

Should expansion from Medicare for the aged to national health insurance for all be undertaken in one stage or through multiple stages? The answer is arguable; but no one should think lightly that all the advantages or all the disadvantages are with one answer or another.

Nor should expansion be quantitative alone. Important changes are also needed—in the administrative organization of the health benefits system, in the methods of paying for services, in the organization for delivery of care, in the provision of resources for care, and for the utilization of these resources. Both the strengths in our present system of medical care, and the weaknesses in our "nonsystem," are too well and extensively known to need documentation here. The discussions and debates on this subject are a rising cacophony in the public domain and in the professions, made more intense in recent years by steeply rising costs which are already threatening little short of disaster to the health services. This is all the more embarrassing to us as a nation because it grows in intensity at a time when public demand for good health, the potential for good health care, and national affluence to support all essential services, are at unprecedented heights.

This is a proposal for a national system of personal health care services through our national system of social insurance, with all in the population equally eligible for the benefits. There would be no means tests—public assistance would have no role in such a system—and there would no longer be any medically needy citizens. The system would operate through organizational and financial arrangements which, I believe, would be found adaptable to our social and economic patterns; and which would meet the needs of those to be served while providing supports and protections for those to whom our society looks for the services.

It is almost gratuitous to record the expectation that my proposal as a whole, and its every major specification, will meet with differences of opinion. I hope, however, that the discussion can be of a kind and at a level worthy of the importance we in the public health professions attach to personal health care, and to the opportunities for improving its availability and delivery.

On another occasion I expressed the opinion that there is no turning back from the basic goals and policies incorporated in recently enacted public programs for health care; and that extension of those programs to more of the population is socially inevitable, whatever political winds blow most strongly on the domestic scene.

I suggest that these views are still sound and pertinent—because the public need will continue to press for satisfaction; and no partial and ineffectual compromises will long withstand the pressures of public need, demand, and expectation.

For Further Reading

PAYMENT OF PHYSICIANS

Alexander, C. A., "The Effects of Change in Method of Paying Physicians: The Baltimore Experience," *Amer. Jrl. of Pub. Health* 57 (August, 1967), 1278–1289.

Carter, Richard, *The Doctor Business*. New York, Doubleday, 1961.

Glaser, William A., "Doctors and Politics," *Am. Jrl. Soc.,* 66 (November, 1960), 230–245.

————, *Paying the Doctor: Systems of Remuneration and their Effects.* Baltimore, Johns Hopkins Press, 1970.

Goldman, Franz, "Methods of Payment for Physicians' Services in Medical Care Programs," *American Journal of Public Health,* 42 (February, 1952), 134–141.

Hogarth, J., *The Payment of the Physician.* New York, Pergamon Press, 1963.

Klarman, Herbert, "Approaches to Moderating the Increases in Medical Care Costs," *Medical Care,* 7 (May, June, 1961), 175–190.

Lees, D. S., and M. H. Cooper, "Payment per Item-of-Service, The Manchester and Salford Experience," *Medical Care,* 2 (July–September), 1969, 151–156.

Mencher, Samuel, *British Private Medical Practice and the National Health Service.* Pittsburgh, University of Pittsburgh Press, 1968.

158   :   *For Further Reading*

Report of the National Conference on Medical Costs. Washington, D.C., U.S. Department of Health, Education, and Welfare, 1967.

Royal Commission on Doctors' and Dentists' Remuneration, *Report*, 1957–1960, Cmnd. 939. London, HMSO, 1960.

Somers, Herman M. and Anne R., *Doctors, Patients, and Health Insurance.* Washington, D.C., The Brookings Institution, 1961.

Willcox, Alanson W., *Hospitals and the Corporate Practice of Medicine.* Chicago, American Hospital Association, 1957.

NATIONAL HEALTH INSURANCE

Andersen, Ronald, and Odin W. Anderson, *A Decade of Health Services: Social Survey Trends in Use and Expenditures,* Chicago: University of Chicago Press, 1967.

Andersen, Ronald, *A Behavioral Model of Families' Use of Health Services.* Chicago, Center for Health Administration Studies, Research Series, No. 25, 1968.

Burnes, Eveline M., "Health Services for All: Is Health Insurance the Answer," pp. 9–18; and "Commentaries" by Nelson H. Cruishank (pp. 18–22); and Steven Janos (pp. 23–24); and "Response" by I. S. Falk, pp. 27–33, in *Medical Care: The Current Scene and Prospects for the Future,* Proceedings of a Symposium in Honor of I. S. Falk, Part II, *Am. Jrl. Pub. Health,* 59 (January, 1969).

Cohen, Wilbur J., "Current Problems in Health Care," *New Eng. Jrl. Med.,* 281 (July 24, 1969), 193–197.

———, "National Health Insurance—Problems and Prospects," The 1970 Michael M. Davis Lecture. University of Chicago, Center for Health Administration Studies.

Eilers, Robert D., "National Health Insurance: What Kind and How Much (First of Two Parts)," *New Eng. Jrl. Medicine,* 284 (April 22, 1971) 881–886.

Fein, Rashi, "The Case for National Health Insurance," *Saturday Review* (August 22, 1970), 27–29, ff.

Paxton, Harry T., "The A.M.A. lobbies *for* national health insurance," *Hospital Physician* (March, 1969), 39 ff.

Rohrlich, George F., "Implications of the New Social Insurance Mechanisms for Other Population Groups," pp. 1109–1125, in *New Directions in Public for Health Care, Bulletin of the New York Academy of Medicine,* 42 (December, 1966).

Somers, Herman M., and Anne R. *Medicare and the Hospitals: Issues and Prospects.* Washington, D.C., The Brookings Institution, 1967.

Waldman, Saul, and Evelyn Peel, "National Health Insurance: A Comparison of Five Proposals," Research and Statistics Note, Nov. 12, 1970, Social Security Administration, July 23, 1970.

Holloman, John L. S., Jr., "Toward a National Health Program," Editorial, *Amer. Jrl. Pub. Health,* 60 (Sept., 1970), 1680–1682.

IV Manpower and Organization

The manpower problem is far from a simple matter of calculating demand, numbers now available, and additional numbers remaining to be attracted and prepared.

The availability of sufficient numbers of adequately prepared health workers to provide care under whatever system of payment a society has, is, in part, a function of that system of payment (since it creates demand and choices). Availability of health manpower is a function of a number of other factors:

—the growth or decline of demands from other fields of endeavor such as industry, education, and agriculture;

—personal and family influences on career choices;

—attractive or discouraging aspects of the health field and each of its many work groups;

—specialization within the field and the organization of the full spectrum of health work;

—restrictive covenants such as professional secrecy, entrance requirements to schools, licensure laws, accreditation standards;

—technological developments and other factors.

Once sufficient, well trained personnel are engaged in each of the more than 200 occupational groups in the health field, the application of their abilities in a concerted, effective fashion to solve the health problems of our people is complicated by inter-occupational-group struggles.[1] In this connection, it is important to realize that an individual's place in the prestige-reward hierarchy of a society is largely determined by the place of his occupational group in that hierarchy. Thus we find the manpower picture importantly influenced by occupational groups vying with one another over tasks, work schedules, other work conditions, titles, and control of certain monetarily (and otherwise) rewarding relationships—e.g. the doctor–patient relationship. In short, there are many artificial shortages with especially prestigeful, rewarding, yet simple tasks reserved for dominant groups when less dominant groups could perform these tasks perfectly well.[2]

Kissick provides a broad, yet fairly detailed, factual overview of the health manpower problem. He reaches the general conclusion that we do indeed face serious shortages, given present rates of training and present forms of health services organization.

The provision of new money through a universal, compulsory health insurance system (which we can anticipate in the next few years) will do little more than raise demand and health care costs, unless significant new departures in preparing and organizing health personnel are undertaken now. In general, we might suggest an important principal: persons with the *least* formal preparation adequate to a given task should be the ones to perform it.[3] The patient, in this view, should be educated to take over a significant number of the most general health care tasks, including many preventive and continuing care efforts now guarded as "professional" secrets.

But we must recall Halberstam's position here. It bears on the crucial area of primary care and is based on the relative inflexibility of the public's wish, as he sees it, to consult a doctor when they are sick and not some other health worker.

This matter of deep, continuing contact with a physician also serves as Halberstam's principle objection to group practice. Weinerman's article in this section points up other inadequacies of groups as they have operated in the past, and he identifies some needed experimentation and change, including new types of health personnel and greater consumer involvement in health policy and decision-making. With such changes, he defends group practice as the most promising form of medical care organization at the primary care level.

In its most developed form, group practice includes salaried physicians and other health workers representing a range of specialties to meet the demands for personal health services made by members of some defined population whose care is prepaid on a time period, capitation basis. This prepayment may be in the form of annual premiums paid by the individual or his employer for himself and family or be assured by public taxes. Some form of group practice, generally tax supported, is an important component of most national health systems—be it the Soviet polyclinic; the health center in Yugoslavia where the physician in charge is also the health officer in charge of preventive, public health measures; or, somewhat differently, the hospital-based group of specialists in Britain. Group practice has developed in the United States too, but not as rapidly as its proponents believe it should have. No doubt this is explained in part by some of the culturally rooted themes which Halberstam sounds—individual freedom from bureaucracy; deep, continuous, personal contact with patients; enterprise and initiative.[4]

N O T E S

1. R. Elling, "Occupational Group Striving and Administration in Public Health," in M. Arnold, L. V. Blankenship and J. Hess, eds., *Administering Health Systems* (New York, Atherton Press, 1971).
2. Eliot Freidson, *Professional Dominance, the Social Structure of Medical Care,* (New York, Atherton, 1970).
3. "The Joint Committee Report" by H. Fry in collaboration with W. P. Shepard and R. H. Elling, *Education and Manpower for Community Health.* (Pittsburgh, University of Pittsburgh Press, 1967), p. 95.
4. Rosen examines pertinent historical trends, and cultural and sociological forces that help us understand how important organizational innovations in medical care such as group practice meet opposition in some settings from some quarters and receive support in other times and situations. George Rosen, "Provision of Medical Care; History, Sociology, Innovation," *Public Health Reports,* 74 (March, 1959), 199–209.

8 Health Manpower in Transition

WILLIAM L. KISSICK *

Doctor Michael M. Davis, one of the pioneers in the study of medical care and health policy in the United States, identified the basic elements of medical services as 1. people, 2. professionals, 3. facilities, 4. organization and 5. finances.[1] In his opinion, finances represented the foundation that supported professionals, facilities and organizations, which functioned as a ". . . complex aggregate of human beings and material facilities. . ." to deliver health services to people.

The frame of reference for this discussion of health manpower differs slightly. Manpower will be considered as one of three *basic* health and medical resources—1. health manpower (professional, technical and supportive); 2. facilities, including

Reprinted by permission of the author and publisher from *The Milbank Memorial Fund Quarterly,* 46 (January, 1968), Part 2, 53–90.

* M.D., Ph.D., Professor and Chairman, Department of Community Medicine, School of Medicine, University of Pennsylvania.

equipment and supplies; and 3. biomedical knowledge, or "state of the art." In this context, organization and financing are the intangible resources or mechanisms that serve to translate the three basic resources into health services for the consumer. An adequate analysis of health manpower at a minimum requires its consideration in this, or an alternative context that attempts to relate these variables, which together make up a highly complex, interdependent system.

In general, health manpower has not received the attention accorded to the other two basic resources. Although not impressive when contrasted with expenditures for defense or space exploration, society's investments in the resources of biomedical knowledge and facilities over the last two decades are substantial. Expenditures for medical and health related research have totaled almost $14 billion since the end of World War II. More than two-thirds of the two billion dollars spent in the pursuit of new biomedical knowledge during 1966 was derived from public sources, and expenditures for this type of research will be even higher in 1967. For the construction of hospitals, nursing homes, health departments and other facilities for the delivery of health services, the Hill-Burton Program has been appropriated more than $2.7 billion since 1948, and these funds have been matched through the appropriation of public monies at the state and local level, through private philanthropy, loans and other means of financing, to achieve a total investment of $8.5 billion.

Until 1963, on the other hand, investments in the development of health manpower were relatively neglected, especially as a responsibility of the federal government. Although a substantial portion of the educational costs of health manpower have been publicly financed, largely from appropriations by state legislatures,* federal support of manpower development has been

---

* The nation's 87 medical schools reported total expenditures of $695,684,904 (regular operating programs $286,157,698; sponsored programs $409,528,206) for the 1964–1965 academic year. Major sources of funds included: federal research grants and contracts, $252,284,161; federal training grants and contracts, $80,506, 064; state appropriations, $75,554, 188; overhead on federal grants and contracts, $40,201,471. *Source;* Medical Education in the United States, 1964–1965, *"Journal of the American Medical Association,* 194, 760 (November 15, 1965).

limited to grants for research training, except for some specialized efforts on a small scale; e.g., support of graduate preparation of nurses for careers as teachers, supervisors and administrators; support of preparation at the graduate level of public health personnel; and a relatively few fellowships and training grants in maternal and child health, rehabilitation and related disciplines. One major exception to the rule has been the program of the National Institute of Mental Health, which from 1948 through 1965 supported 35,000 trainees in psychiatry, psychology, social work, psychiatric nursing and related fields; the trainees were in service, as distinct from research positions.

A federal concern for the preparation of adequate numbers of health manpower was established, however, with the passage of the Health Professions Educational Assistance Act of 1963. Passage of this act represented the culmination of a legislative effort lasting 15 years. In 1965, the legislation was amended to add formula and project grant support of basic educational costs and scholarships to the original program of construction grants and student loans, in an effort directed toward increasing the nation's supply of physicians, dentists, pharmacists, optometrists and podiatrists. The Nurse Training Act, enacted in 1964, has comparable provisions, and the Vocational Education Act of 1963 emphasizes the support of programs geared to those areas in the nation's economy which have ". . .actual or anticipated opportunities for gainful employment." These Congressional actions signify the beginning of what will undoubtedly become sustained and increasing support by the federal government of the education and training of health manpower. But at this juncture, thorough review and analysis of the forces influencing both the preparation and the utilization of health manpower deserves the highest priority. Careful assessment of the relevant issues is needed as a prerequisite to the formulation of a rational manpower policy to guide the investment of vast sums of public monies during the years ahead. Lacking such a policy, billions of dollars could be expended without significantly increasing the availability and accessibility of health services to meet the population's rising expectations.

CURRENT STATUS OF HEALTH MANPOWER

Definitions

An even more basic prerequisite to policy formulation is definition of terms. In its usual connotation, the term *health manpower* does not extend beyond the categories of physician, dentist and nurse. Such a definition is both restrictive and deceptive, as well as unrealistic in view of the diversity and array of personnel necessary to sustain a complex social enterprise that now represents expenditures in excess of $45 billion annually. Health manpower should rather be considered as comprising individuals ranging from the highly sophisticated, extensively educated biomedical scientist, who requires many years of postgraduate education and training, to the aide or attendant working in a hospital after only limited on-the-job training.

Two major classifications of health manpower are currently in use, frequently cited in the literature, sometimes interchangeably. The first of these classifications is used by the Bureau of the Census, which divides the civilian labor force into 71 separate industries. The "health services industry" at the time of the 1960 census ranked third among these industries, employing 2,578,214 persons. Between the 1950 and 1960 census, the "health services industry" gained almost a million workers, for a growth rate of 54 per cent. Only seven of the 71 industries experienced a higher growth rate.[2]

Approximately one-third of the individuals employed in the "health services industry," however, are clerical workers, craftsmen, laborers and others who assist the provision of health services by functioning in a supportive role, but whose skills and work are not unique to health services. The importance of the approximately one million clerical, technical and kindred workers in health services is not to be ignored, but their recruitment, education and utilization constitute problems that are generic to most enterprises in an industrialized, specialized society.[3]

The second classification of health manpower—"health occupations"—is more appropriate to this discussion since it focuses on those individuals possessing knowledge and skill unique to the health establishment. Also, this classification includes health manpower counted in industries other than "health services" by the Bureau of the Census; e.g., only three per cent of veterinarians and seven per cent of pharmacists are counted in the "health services industry." The "health occupations" are the categories of manpower that come to mind when one hears the often repeated statements of "shortage," "gaps" and "limited supply."

The National Center for Health Statistics has been collecting manpower data for these health occupations categorized into 35 fields, and it has been estimated that the health manpower in these fields totaled nearly three million in 1965 (Table 1). When these categories are subdivided into more discrete units, the range and diversity of health careers can be more readily appreciated. The *Health Careers Guidebook,** published recently by the United States Department of Labor, identifies approximately 200 health career opportunities, subdividing each of the 35 general categories—"health careers briefings" as they are called in the book, several of which cover more than ten individual careers—into the distinct and separate careers each comprises. Thus each medical specialty is presented as a separate career.

Trends

The changes in the types and characteristics of health manpower are perhaps the most striking to be found in the health establishment—an area where striking changes are the order of the day. It is estimated that the health professions requiring college education or professional preparation accounted for approximately 200,000 persons in 1900. In 1920, the number of individuals in these categories increased to 409,000; in 1940 to

* United States Department of Labor, *Health Careers Guidebook*, 1965. The 31 "Health Career Briefings" listed in the book and the 34 fields for which the National Center for Health Statistics is collecting data differ in several instances. The *Guidebook* does not list chiropractics as a health career. The National Center combines medical and osteopathic as one category and has separate categories for "automatic data processing" and "medical secretarial" as well as "miscellaneous."

692,000; and in 1960 to 1,140,000.* Whereas, at the turn of the century, three out of five health professionals were physicians, by 1960, rapid growth in other disciplines reduced the proportion of physicians to one out of five professional health workers; a continued decline is to be anticipated as other disciplines experience more rapid rates of growth and new categories of personnel emerge. Also at the turn of the century, individuals in the health occupations accounted for 1.2 per cent of the experienced civilian labor force. This proportion increased to 2.1 per cent by 1940; 2.4 per cent by 1950; and 3.0 per cent by 1960.⁴ A projection of this trend forecasts a total of between four and five per cent of the civilian labor force employed in health occupations by 1975.

During the decade ending 1960 alone, the number of workers in health occupations increased at a rate twice that of population growth—from 1,531,000 in 1950, to 2,176,700 by 1960, an increase of 42 per cent in contrast to a population growth of 19 per cent. The rate of increase among occupational categories differed, being greatest among those with the shortest periods of training (e.g., practical nurses, x-ray technicians and hospital attendants) and among the occupational categories that have arrived relatively recently (e.g., medical technology, medical record librarians, physical therapy, occupational therapy and speech and hearing therapy).

The trend toward new careers is yet to be fully appreciated. Among the 200 plus careers listed by title in the *Health Careers Guidebook,* the majority represented but a small segment of total health manpower prior to World War II. Many careers, including inhalation therapist, nuclear medical technologist, radiologic health technician, cytotechnologist and medical engineering technician, did not exist. Admittedly, the three basic careers—medicine, dentistry and nursing—still constitute approximately 40 per

* *Manpower in the 1960's, op. cit.* Includes physicians, dentists, nurses, pharmacists and other persons who are college educated or professionally trained among those employed as biological scientists, biostatisticians, chiropractors, clinical psychologists, dental hygienists, dietitians, health educators, medical laboratory technologists, medical record librarians, optometrists, podiatrists, rehabilitation counselors, sanitary engineers, social workers—medical and psychiatric—veterinarians and therapists—occupational, physical, speech and hearing.

TABLE 1: *Health Manpower—1965*

Health Field	Estimated Persons Employed[1]
All fields	2,778,900 to 2,898,700
Administration of health services[2]	31,500 to 37,000
Anthropology and sociology	600 to 800
Automatic data processing	300[3]
Basic sciences in the health field	44,200
Biomedical engineering	7,500
Chiropractic and naturopathy	25,000
Clinical laboratory services	85,000 to 95,000
Dentistry and allied services	230,900[4]
Dietetic and nutritional services	30,000[5]
Economic research in the health field	500
Environmental health	32,500 to 35,000[6]
Food and drug protective services	16,500
Health and vital statistics	1,400 to 2,400[7]
Health education	16,700
Health information and communication	5,000
Library services in the health field	8,000[8]
Medical records	37,000
Medicine and osteopathy	305,100[4]
Midwifery	5,000
Nursing and related services	1,409,000[9]
Occupational therapy	6,000[6]
Orthopedic and prosthetic appliance making	3,300
Pharmacy	118,000[6]
Physical therapy	12,000[6]
Podiatry	7,600
Psychology	9,000
Radiologic technology	70,000
Secretarial and offices	150,000 to 250,000
Social work	17,500[6]
Specialized rehabilitation services	5,300 to 5,900
Speech pathology and audiology	14,000
Veterinary medicine	23,700[4]
Visual services and eye care	40,400

Vocational rehabilitation
counseling   4,200
Miscellaneous hospital services   6,200[10]

[1] Each occupation is counted only once. For example, all physicians are counted in "Medicine and osteopathy" even though certain specialists perform in other health fields.
[2] Excludes business, clerical and maintenance workers.
[3] Estimates not available for programmers, operators and electronic technicians.
[4] Includes total personnel (active and inactive) for dentists, physicians and veterinarians.
[5] Estimates not available for food service supervisors, clerical workers and other workers.
[6] Estimates not available for aides and technicians.
[7] Estimates not available for statistical clerks.
[8] Includes technical and clerical workers in medical libraries. Estimates not available for paitents' librarians.
[9] Estimates not available for ward clerks.
[10] Estimates not available for electrocardigraph technicians and hospital aides—obstetrical, pediatric, surgical and so forth.
Source: Health Resources Statistics: Health Manpower, 1965. United States Department of Health, Education and Welfare, Public Health Service Publication No. 1509, Washington, D.C., 1966, p. 177.

cent (1.0 to 2.7 million) of persons in health occupations; however, specialization within these fields and the emergence of new disciplines are major factors to analyze in any discussion of health manpower. Although the data are limited, it can be anticipated that specialization and diversification will continue as the two foremost characteristics of health manpower in future decades.

The institutionalization of health services, and the effects of this institutionalization on health manpower, is an issue yet to be faced. The anachronistic features of the "one doctor-to-one patient mythology," the changing technology, and the emergence of new skills and professions are well illustrated by a recent account of the diagnosis and treatment of a 28-month-old girl with phenylketonuria (PKU). The patient's physician was backed up by a team of 14, including medical specialists, microchemists, psychologists, speech pathologists and social workers, not to mention nurses, aides and other hospital personnel. In situations such as these, organization is essential. Health services has moved from the era of the "cottage industry" to that of space exploration, and as more and more medical care is provided within an institutional structure—118,000,000 visits were made to the hospital outpatient departments, emergency rooms and specialty clinics in 1963[5]—mechanisms for effective utilization must be sought. The goal is one of maximum efficiency in delivery of services without composing the quality of those services.

The growth of institutionalization and specialization is an effort to cope effectively with the requirements for depth and thoroughness in a wide range of tasks. These are essential to adequate provision of many new services. The exponential growth of scientific knowledge has contributed to both this inexorable trend and to a vast potential for improved health care. A physician could provide a wide range of services in the early part of this century, but now these services are provided more effectively, with greater skill and competence and in greater depth by several individuals with professional and technical skills, no one of whom represents the diversity of service that was once found in a single practitioner.

Specialization in medical practice, a post-World War II occurrence, and concentration of health manpower in hospitals, or institutionalization, have reached major proportions. As recently as 1940, 80 per cent of physicians had not specialized. In 1941, a total of 5,256 residency positions were offered and 78 per cent of them were filled. At the present time, the situation is rapidly approaching in which almost nine out of every ten graduates of the nation's medical schools enter specialty training. In 1964, 1,317 hospitals had sponsoerd 5,440 approved residency programs offering a total of 38,373 residencies; 80 per cent of these were filled. For the young physician seeking specialty training in July, 1966, more than 40,000 positions were offered.[6] This represents almost a ten-fold increase during the past 25 years and a doubling of the residencies offered since 1951. It is stimated that now seven of every ten physicians in private practice are full-time specialists.[7]

In 1941, hospitals had approximately one professional nurse for every 15 beds and one practical nurse, aide, attendant or auxiliary person for every ten beds. Personnel increased over the next ten years so that by 1952 the figures were one to seven and one to five. By 1962 the continued proportionate increase of nursing personnel resulted in one professional nurse for every five beds and a practical nurse or auxiliary person for every three beds.[8] This increasing concentration of nursing personnel per hospital bed may come as a surprise to many who are familiar with the complaints of lack of personal service and attention being voiced by many of the millions of Americans hospitalized in a general hospital during a single year. These comments beg the question, "What are the services provided and tasks performed by these categories of manpower?" This of course bears on the whole question of utilization of health manpower. In addition to nursing personnel, hospitals are increasing the numbers of personnel in other occupational categories, e.g., occupational and physical therapists, dieticians, medical record librarians, medical technologists, x-ray technicians, pharmacists and social workers, at a rate that exceeds both the expansion in hospital beds and the climb in the total annual admissions to short-term general hospitals.

In summary, one finds divergence in the types of health manpower and a convergence of the settings in which services are delivered. Organization becomes the ranking imperative, but it is hardly the full solution to the problem.

REQUIREMENTS AND RESOURCES

This, then, is health manpower. The next step is to establish what the boundaries of *needs* are to be, for any statement of need for health manpower, as for health services, is to a certain degree arbitrary. Few would disagree that a person suffering from acute appendicitis is in need of specific health services—particularly those of a surgeon. Likewise, a patient with diabetic acidosis is in need of an array of health services to save his life. But in many areas need is determined by a highly judgmental process. How many times does a patient with well-controlled diabetes need to see a physician? How many times does a patient with hypertension need to see a physician? How many times ought an infant to see a pediatrician during his first year of life? If one definitive answer could be cited to each of these questions, a definite need would exist for a specific amount of health manpower.

However, economists and manpower specialists agree that manpower forecasts based even on a finite need for future health services are unrealistic. Instead they suggest approaching manpower forecasting in terms of demand for health services in the classic economic sense of supply and demand. For the most part, demand is the economic expression of need, but some suggest demand may go beyond actual need. Illustrative of this point of view is the affluent hypochondriac who may be expressing a demand for health services that is in excess of actual need. Others feel that anxiety expressed by a patient for a physician's services is a valid need and not an inappropriate demand.

Both need and demand for health services are greatly affected by biomedical advances. Using Phenylketonuria as an illustration shows dramatic needs and demands for health services, neither of which existed prior to the discovery of the technique for detecting, diagnosing and treating inborn errors of metabolism and congenital malformations. It might be argued that preventing mental retardation and correcting heart lesions achieves a net saving in the utilization of health services. In the absence of data to support such a contention, these advances have increased rather than decreased the requirements for health services. The same applies to the developments in renal dialysis, exfoliative cytology, rehabilitation and the like, not to mention an advance such as the discovery of insulin, which has transformed a once-fatal disease to an abnormal varient of the metabolic process with late sequelae that require extensive and, frequently, intensive health services.

In any case, demand for health services has and will continue to increase. Anne Somers identified the "significant long-run social and economic trends over the past century that have already greatly enlarged the demand for medical services and altered the character of that demand." The trends listed were: 1. overall increase in population, 2. the increase in the over-65 population, 3. the rising proportion of nonwhites in the population, accompanied by their improved socioeconomic status, 4. increasing portion of women in the population, 5. steady increase in urbanization and industrialization, 6. steady increase in educational levels, 7. steady rise in income levels, and 8. rise in national income.[9]

The purchasing power of the aged for health services has increased with the establishment of the Medicare program, which, it is estimated, will cost well over three billion dollars in 1967. How much of this sum represents displacement of funds that were expended for health services and how much represents added expenditures is not known. Many take the position that this increased purchasing power, whatever the amount, will allow the aged to translate needs into demand, while others state that this will allow the aged to generate demand for health services in excess of actual need.

Instead, this issue will be set aside and health manpower requirements will be considered, recognizing that the term *requirements* blurs the difference between need and demand. It may mean primarily need or mainly demand; or it may mean a mix of need and demand. As one reviews the literature of projection of manpower requirements, the distinction between need and demand is frequently unclear.

In many respects the requirement for health services can be virtually insatiable, depending on a society's level of expectation and the resources it wishes to allocate. This was suggested by participants in the first seminar when they alluded to "a visit to the dentist every six months," "a complete medical check-up each year" and Nelson's aspiration, "an analyst for every adult." At any rate, it would appear that any characterization of the dimensions, quantitative and qualitative, of requirements for health services is arbitrarily defined, at least within the limits of the present scientific ignorance.

Determination of Manpower Requirements

Whatever the definitions employed, predicting or forecasting the requirements for health manpower is a hazardous enterprise. As Hechinger commented in the *New York Times,*

> Why, then, make projections? The answer appears to be that modern society's dependence on highly skilled talent has made obsolete the theory that if everybody just pursues his interests, everything will come out all right.[10]

Forecasting has become essential.

To date efforts to forecast health manpower requirements have used various methods, each with its own deficiencies, each risky:

1. *Population Ratios:* The application of existing health-manpower-to-population ratios to the projected population base is the most frequently used and accepted method for predicting fu-

ture manpower requirements, but this technique is seldom used without qualification and recognition of its limitations. Admittedly, it is a crude indicator that ignores changes in patterns of utilization and increases in productivity. Furthermore, it does not take into account anticipated changes in economic conditions, awareness of health problems, sophistication in seeking health services, general level of educational attainment and availability of resources, each of which can result in an increased demand for health manpower.

This method was used by the Surgeon General's Consultant Group on Medical Education (the Bane Committee)[11] in 1959, to project physician requirements by 1975. The maintenance of the ratio of 141 physicians per 100,000 population existing in 1959 was accepted as a minimum goal for 1975. The committee recognized and discussed the implications of the various factors that would probably serve to increase the need and demand for medical services (chronic disease, aging population, specialization, regional disparities and changing patterns of practice) and concluded that the existing physician to population ratio was a "minimum essential to protect the health of the people of the United States."

2. *Economic Projections:* A second method employed in attempts to forecast manpower requirements uses a formula in which projected expenditures are the numerator and expenditures per worker are the denominator. This is an effort to translate effective demand into manpower requirements.

Using this formula and assuming a national biomedical expenditure of three billion dollars and a cost of $39,000 per professional research worker in 1970, the National Institutes of Health has forecast a medical research manpower requirement of 77,000. Allowing for attrition from among the 39,700 research workers in 1960, a net additional requirement (1961–1970) of 45,000 was calculated.[12]

The Center for Priority Analysis of the National Planning Association has been using this technique to estimate the manpower requirements in health for 1975. Two premises have been used for the calculations: 1. continued expansion of total expenditures for health and medical care at the existing rate—a maintenance of effort level—and 2. expansion of effort to pursue realistically the health goal of narrowing ". . .the gap between the potentialities of the modern health technologies and the availability of medical care for most Americans," recommended in 1960 by the Presidential Commission on National Goals. The Center estimates that the attainment of this goal would result in an increase in ". . .public and private spending for health and medical care rising. . .to 8.7 percent of GNP in 1975"[13] or between $85 and $90 billion. Using these alternative premises, the projected manpower requirements for 1975 are: physicians (M.D.) 310,000 to 400,000; dentists, 118,000 to 140,000; registered nurses 840,000 to 1,091,000; licensed practical nurses 442,000 to 575,000; hospital attendants 930,000 to 1,229,000; and medical and dental technicians 279,000 to 352,000.*

3. *Professional Judgment:* The Lee-Jones' study, completed in 1930, for the Committee on Costs of Medical Care, remains the major effort to calculate manpower requirements on the basis of professional judgment, or expert opinions as to medical needs. Roger I. Lee and Lewis W. Jones examined the nation's morbidity experience and computed the manpower required for preventive, diagnostic and curative health services. The authors estimated the requirements at 135 physicians per 100,000 population, 220 nurses per 100,000 populations, and between 99 (with use of dental hygienists and assistants) and 179 (if dentists do all the work themselves) dentists per 100,000 population. Although all of these requirements fell below existing ratios, the authors doubted that the country during the Depression had the economic capacity to respond to this need.[14]

The Surgeon General's Consultant Group on Nursing[15] based its calculations of nurse requirements, totaling 850,000 by 1970, on the opinion that adequate services were provided by registered nurses, 30 per cent by licensed practical nurses and 20 per cent by aides or attendants. Qualitative judgments were also made as to the requirements for public health, occupational health, nursing education and so forth. The need was considered unobtainable, fully 25 per cent in excess of a feasible goal of 680,000 professional nurses by 1970, 920,000 in 1975.

* Estimates from study nearing completion by the Center for Priority Analysis, National Planning Association, undertaken for the United States Department of Labor.

More recently, professional judgment was used to estimate the requirements of some ten million disabled Americans for rehabilitation services, including the services of certain allied health specialists. Assuming a 2,000-hour work-year for professional personnel, the author concluded that present service requirements called for seven times the existing number of physical therapists, eight times the number of occupational therapists and five times the number of medical social workers.[16]

The State of Health Manpower—1966

In 1966, using both the tools of economics and professional judgment, the American Hospital Association, in cooperation with the Public Health Service, undertook a survey of hospital staff and staffing requirements. The study was made to determine the number of personnel employed, current vacancies and estimates of personnel needs, and thus to provide a more adequate picture of the present health manpower situation. Data from the first 4,600 hospitals that reported, have been used to estimate totals for all 7,100 hospitals in the United States registered by the American Hospital Association. These reports indicate that the total number of professional, technical and auxiliary personnel employed in hospitals is about 1.4 million. About 275,000 additional professional and technical personnel would be needed to provide optimum patient care, an increase of about 20 per cent over present staffing. Over 80,000 more professional nurses and more than 40,000 practical nurses are needed. Some 50,000 aides are needed in general hospitals; another 30,000 in psychiatric institutions. Over 9,000 more medical technologists, almost 70,00 social workers, and about 4,000 more physical therapists, 4,000 x-ray technologists and 4,000 surgical technicians are required.

Resources

The main pool of manpower resources from which the health occupations can draw to fill these requirements is that of the nation's youth. Viewing the situation in terms of numbers, the nation has a virtually unlimited pool of manpower from which to draw, each year bringing a bumper crop of 18-year-olds—more than 3.5 million in 1966—all of them seeking careers and making choices, many of them potential recruits to the health occupations. This figure will increase gradually over the next 15 years to reach 4.2 million in 1980.

Two other dimensions of this manpower resource warrant consideration. During the 1963–1964 academic year, three-fourths of those 17 years old graduated from high school, and during recent years the percentage of young people completing high school has steadily increased. Further increase in this percentage is projected, reaching almost 85 per cent by 1975. Furthermore, approximately one-half of all high school graduates in 1962 went to college (44 per cent of 18- to 21-year-olds were enrolled in institutions of higher education during 1964). Five hundred thousand bachelor degrees were awarded in 1965, and this number will increase to almost 750,000, a 50 per cent increase, by 1975.[17] The size of this manpower resource is impressive.

The growing proportion of women in the labor force will also be of benefit since, by and large, the health occupations are a woman's field. The proportion of women in the labor force has been increasing steadily during the past several decades, from 24 per cent in 1940, to 27 per cent in 1950, to 32 per cent in 1960. Also, the working wife or working mother is an increasing phenomenon in society. In 1940, one-third of the women who worked were married; in contrast, by 1965, almost two-thirds of women who worked were married.[18] In 1960, 70 per cent of workers in the health services and 75 per cent of individuals working in hospitals were females.[19] Within the health occupations, of course, the proportion of women varies—ranging from 90 per cent in fields such as nursing and dietetics to less than ten per cent in dentistry, medicine, optometry and pharmacy.

If other nations can be taken as a guide, more women will choose the health professions in the future. Dentistry, for example, is a woman's field in other societies. More than 50 per cent of all medical students in the Soviet Union are women, as are about 25 percent of those in the United Kingdom. In the United States, women have never accounted for more than 12 per cent of all M.D. degrees awarded in any year. In 1965, only 7.3 per cent of these degrees went to women.

Looking at the resources for health manpower in the context

of the total economy, the signs are encouraging. The decline in agriculture as a source of employment—a 38 per cent decrease in manpower between the 1950 and 1960 census—automation in industry and the development of a productive capacity that exceeds consumption of goods, would suggest a greater availability of manpower for the service aspects of the economy. As has been noted earlier, health and educational services represent the two most rapidly growing segments of the service economy. As the society pursues the policy of full employment, health services will be viewed increasingly as a source of employment.

Attempting to develop health manpower from these basic resources is when problems arise. In the fall of 1960, one first-year medical student was admitted for every 45 baccalaureate degrees awarded the previous June. One first-year dental student was admitted for every 100 baccalaureate degrees. Projecting these ratios ahead ten years, one can anticipate for the fall of 1975 a potential for 16,500 first-year medical students and 7,400 first-year dental students. Can the medical and dental schools accommodate them? Not on the basis of current estimates; these figures exceed the probable school capacity in 1975 by at least 50 per cent.

Federal Manpower Programs to Develop Resources

Action has already been taken by the federal government to avert the full effects of health manpower shortages by promoting efforts to increase the nation's training capacity in the health field, as well as by encouraging health personnel and institutions to accompany this expansion by the most productive use of existing health resources.

Within the past few years, several significant legislative measures have been enacted whose impact upon the nation's supply of health personnel can already be measured. Under the Health Professions Educational Assistance Act of 1963, the federal government has provided grants to certain professional schools—medical, dental and others—to expand and modernize their teaching facilities and to support student loan programs. In 1965, the Act was amended to continue these programs and to add two new categories of assistance: grants to support basic educational costs and student scholarships. Awards made in the first 18 months for which funds were available are adding 2,442 first year places in schools of medicine, dentistry, public health, nursing, pharmacy and optometry. Eight new schools of medicine, one new school of dentistry, and one new school of public health are being established under health professions assistance.

The Nurse Training Act of 1964 has comparable provisions. These include: grants to enable collegiate, associate degree and diploma schools of nursing to strengthen and expand their teaching programs; a loan program for students of all types of professional nursing schools; and grants for the construction of new schools and the expansion or modernization of existing teaching facilities.

Significant progress has been made also in training allied health personnel. The Vocational Educational Act of 1963 emphasizes support of programs geared to those areas in the nation's economy which have "actual or anticipated opportunities for gainful employment." This Act, which authorized greatly increased federal aid for vocational and technical education at less-than-baccalaureate level, is already stimulating the growth of educational opportunities in high schools, technical schools and community and junior colleges for existing and new categories of technical and supportive health manpower. The Vocational Rehabilitation Amendments of 1965 authorized increased project grants for traineeships, and fellowships to assist with the training of physical therapists, occupational therapists, rehabilitation counselors and other categories of rehabilitation personnel.

The most recent legislation in this area, and perhaps the most responsive to many of the problems produced by current changes within the health occupations, is the Allied Health Professions Personnel Training Act of 1966, passed by Congress on November 3, 1966. The goal of this Act is to fill a critical health manpower gap: meeting a growing need for supervisors of subprofessional workers, for teachers in the allied health professions, for highly skilled technical specialists and for new types of allied health professionals.

The qualitative aspects of this program are important in view of the limited number of people to be trained in relation to the total demand. The legislation encourages the creation of broad, multidisciplinary training programs and the expansion of many high-quality existing programs. Improvement grants will be awarded to selected schools with three or more interrelated allied health professions curricula. Some universities with medical centers have developed comprehensive groupings of health curricula, including medical technology, physical therapy, occupational therapy, x-ray technology. In such coordinated programs, individuals who will later work together in providing health care are trained together.

Traineeships will help prepare teachers, administrators, supervisors and specialists in the various allied health professions. They will permit people with basic preparation or work experience in their field to return to school for limited periods to obtain the further training needed to fit them for teaching or supervisory duties.

Finally, project grants for developing, demonstrating or evaluating new curricula to train new types of health technologists yet unknown will allow educators flexibility and room for experimentation. This is perhaps the most important aspect of the program since the organization and technology of health care will continue to change. New kinds of technologists will both use and develop radically new diagnostic and therapeutic equipment, which in turn will require changes in allied health professions personnel training.

FACTORS INFLUENCING FULL REALIZATION OF MANPOWER POTENTIALS

The improvement in the capacity for training, which the above legislative measures are designed to insure, is a first and vital step, but the full realization of manpower potentials for health services requires consideration of the effectiveness of both the preparation and utilization of professional, technical and supportive health workers. It also requires consideration of the obstacles that will be encountered in improving effectiveness and fully realizing potentials.

Income and Salaries

One of the foremost obstacles encountered is presented by the economics of health manpower. As the opportunity to fulfill humanistic drives has been diffused throughout a variety of social institutions, health services can no longer rely principally on this value for attracting manpower. Consequently, the multiplicity of elements that together constitute working conditions must be considered. For physicians, the opportunity still exists for the satisfaction of both altruistic drives and economic needs. A recent study by the United States Department of Labor reported that physicians enjoyed the highest median annual earnings ($14,561) of male workers in 321 selected occupations,[20] and a survey conducted by *Medical Economics*[21] found that the average physician in private practice netted in excess of $28,400 during 1964, up from $25,000 in 1963, and ranging from $26,000 in the East to $31,000 in the Midwest. Admittedly, the work week is closer to 60 hours than 40; however, this intensity of work is probably not greater than that undertaken by most professionals. For physicians at least, participation in the healing of the sick does not require significant financial sacrifices.

The same cannot be said for the profession of nursing. A survey of the annual salaries received by school teachers, not a particularly high-paid occupational group, reveals that on the average women with comparable educational experiences can earn $1,000 per year more in teaching as contrasted to nursing. A 1962 study of 810 selected agencies revealed the median salary of a staff public health nurse to be $4,442 in a voluntary agency, $4,902 in an official health agency and $6,090 with the board of education.[22] This disparity has led to a particularly acute situation in which nurses have left nursing practice to take positions with boards of education or school systems, where their knowledge and skills are not fully utilized.

As noted recently,[23] this is not the only unfavorable comparison—"In New York City, a nurse starts at an annual salary some $400 lower than that of a beginner in the Sanitation Department." A 1963 survey of short-term general hospitals revealed average weekly earnings of $86.50 for general duty nurses, $98.50 for head nurses and $110.50 for nurse supervisors.[24] The recent demands for higher wages by nurses suggest that the issue of wages and working conditions must be faced realistically in the near future.

Other health occupations do not fare much better. Average weekly earnings in mid-1963 were: dietitian, $103.50; medical record librarian, $106.50; medical social worker, $116.50; medical technologist, $94.00; physical therapist, $106.50; and x-ray technician, $82.50.[25] Even though these salaries reflect the disparity in incomes of men and women in society, the figures are substantially below the earnings of individuals with comparable education and training in other fields.

The low earning potentials in health occupations take on added significance if one hopes to increase the attractiveness of the health occupations for men. It has been suggested that a definite association exists between the increasing portion of teachers who are men and the rising salary scales in elementary and secondary education; the $6,164 estimated average annual salary for a nine-month contract exceeds all of the salaries for the health occupations listed above.

Educational Inflexibility

Restricted opportunities for job enlargement through continuing expansion of the individual's horizons and opportunities present another obstacle. For the most part, a recruit to the health endeavor is expected to select his or her ultimate goal and then enter a highly structured—"locked step"—curriculum that presents first general and then specific information. Once graduated, the individual is supposedly prepared to perform certain functions for the ensuing decades. In general, any attempt to move from the discipline or profession originally selected—from practical nursing to professional nursing, pharmacy to medicine, social work to clinical psychology, or physical therapy to physiatrics—requires individuals to return to the beginning of the educational sequence. This is less true among the most extensively prepared members of the health professions; for example, it is not unusual to see interchange in career lines among M.D.s and

Ph.D.s in the biological sciences. But since both the individual and the society gain when each citizen achieves the fullest potential within the limits of his innate capacity, this would seem to be ample stimulus to establish a more flexible educational framework.

At the same time a point of entry to the educational continuum commensurate with the individual's general capacity should be considered. At present, it is not ludicrous that a recent college graduate and middle-age matron who has successfully raised a family of three through adolescence during the 20 years since she graduated from college, require, or for that matter necessarily benefit the most from the same two-year graduate experience? Such is the case in social work, and innumerable similar cases may be found in the health field.

Consumer Expectation

In attempting to modify or change the existing patterns and mechanisms for the preparation and utilization of health manpower or for the delivery of health services, the factors exerting influence on patient acceptance must be identified for consumer expectation will be one of the more formidable obstacles to many contemplated improvements. As noted by George Silver,[26] a patient may desire to consult with a physician and only a physician even when the difficulty could better be handled by another professional who has more suitable training—in this instance, a social worker for problems of social and psychological adjustment. Reluctance on the part of patients to settle for a dental hygienist as the most appropriate practitioner to administer dental prophylaxis is another illustration, and use of private-duty nurses by the affluent patient who wishes every whim catered to is characteristic of the inappropriate utilization of scarce manpower.

The prevailing philosophy of allocation and provision of services according to one's ability to pay is another obstacle to rationalization of the utilization of health services. Income and not medical need appears to determine whether one is treated by a psychiatrist or a social worker, an ophthalmologist or an optometrist, an orthopedist or a podiatrist.

The disparity between need and utilization of professional manpower in the case of maternity services was discussed in a recent lay publication.[27] The authors, in discussing infant mortality in the United States in contrast with other countries, note:

> No country on earth has enough obstetricians and pediatricians to supply . . . [the full scientific resources of medicine] to all mothers and all newborn babies. But it is relatively easy to supply top-quality care to the 25 to 35 percent of pregnant women who really need it and to their babies. It is in this selection of high-risk women for high-quality care that the United States lags far behind countries like Sweden and the Netherlands.

The authors inform the reader that Fellows of the American College of Obstetricians and Gynecologists or an obstetrician who is board-certified are qualified to handle "high risk" pregnancies. The logic of the presentation notwithstanding, it is doubtful that the middle-class reader of the magazine will settle for less than "top-quality care" no matter how normal her pregnancies. Thus do many obstreticians become the highest paid midwives in the world.

Professional Conservatism and Isolationism

Health professionals are likewise unwilling to accept modifications of traditional patterns. Most established professions are conservative in orientation—a desirable trait when viewed as an effort to safeguard standards and enhance quality. But professional conservatism produces a natural reluctance on the part of a profession to share functions or responsibilities previously recognized as its sole prerogative. This attitude frequently can create conflicts between the older and newer professions as each seeks the same end—patient well-being—by different means. The resultant "jurisdictional disputes" are comparable to those prevalent in other sectors of the economy. The defenses on the grounds of quality are frequently noteworthy for their lack of supporting evidence. Moreover, these conflicts can be socially devastating when the fight over prerogatives occurs in the midst of a need and demand for health services that surpass the present capacity of health manpower.

Some of the problems inherent in this subject are related to those posed by the educational framework. Frequently, the pressures for annexation of new responsibilities and expansion of the scope of interests results from individuals who have selected a discipline or profession that ultimately fails to place the greatest demand on their intellectual resources. These individuals are prevented from moving up into more prestigious and privileged groups that have greater responsibilities.

In anticipation of encroachment, some professions; e.g., physical therapy, have resisted the inauguration of training programs for assistants. Interdisciplinary relationships within health services are of critical importance. Herein both existing and emerging health disciplines must be considered. As new specialties take form in an effort to cope successfully with the potential offered by scientific and technological breakthroughs, one can anticipate additional careers. Since few, if any, new disciplines confine their activities to new techniques or problems, areas of overlap can be expected.

Resistance to the pressure for change can be even more difficult to overcome when the *status quo* is firmly imbedded in a multiplicity of statutes, accreditation procedures and criteria for certification. Even these can be minor obstacles, however, when compared to the economic vested interests that are supposedly a hallmark of guilds rather than professions. In such situations the forces of logic and rationality may be no match for tradition and vested interest.

The irrationality of many standards that become fixed in state statutes is evidenced by the differing privileges accorded dental hygienists in various states. Almost one-half of the states prohibit a dental hygienist from providing dental prophylaxis that requires scaling beneath the margin of the gum. "Why should a dental hygienist who can successfully scale and polish teeth below the margin of the gingivae in Michigan be forbidden to do so in New York?" asked the New York State Committee on Medical Education.[28]

The problems raised in accreditation have been forthrightly reviewed by William K. Selden, former Executive Director of the National Commission on Accrediating and an interested student of the problems associated with the accreditation of professional programs of study. Increasing the supply of health manpower, through both the expansion of existing programs and the creation of new curricula, often faces the dilemmas of quality versus quantity in the arena of accreditation. As noted by Selden:[29]

> Professional accrediting, most of which is supported indirectly by licensure laws in the various states is intimately related to the desires of individuals to attain a high vocational status. When individuals in a particular group discover that they are using a common body of knowledge . . . inevitably they band together . . . [and] develop an impelling motive to raise individual status by restricting admission to the profession—sometimes with more emphasis on the interests of the practitioners than on public welfare. The issue of control over admission is extremely important to any profession. This is especially true in the formative stages of a profession as it fights for recognition and struggles against the superior attitude of the established professions.

These comments can also apply to a host of "semiprofessional," "subprofessional" and technical areas in which the individuals in an occupational category share an identifiable common body of knowledge that is transmitted through educational programs.

The issues vary from the "delicate balance between the institutional and the public interest" that are of a general nature and ever present, to the more discrete conflicts in which each of the protagonists claims to represent the public interest, as in the present struggle between the National League of Nursing, advocating accreditation of professional programs, and the American Association of Junior Colleges, arguing for institutional accreditation. Some observers have suggested that inclusion of more generic concerns within the accreditation procedures of individual fields is required.

Since "quality" as a criterion for accreditation has been discussed up to now, a pause is in order to recognize that although the expression "quality of health services" is widely used, discussed and argued, it is imprecise and lacks an accepted definition. The expression usually connotes a value judgment as to whether or not the professional is performing his tasks to the best of his ability and in accordance with some generally accepted standards. Actually, as suggested by the Surgeon General, standards promulgated by a profession are but one part of a notion of quality of health care. The other basic dimensions to any determination of the quality of health services are the criteria established by the consumer and the society. Admittedly some overlapping occurs; nevertheless, each set of criteria has distinct features.

The criteria established by the professional are those of peer judgment and are concerned with diagnostic excellence, the scientific validity of one's decisions and the technical skill manifested in one's provision of service. These are some of the factors with which record audits and comparable approaches to measuring and evaluating standards are concerned. This is also the dimension that is most severely challenged by the growth in scientific knowledge that has resulted in shortening the performance half-life of the practitioner and created an awareness of the need for well-developed and utilized continuing education.

The second dimension of quality of health services is that advanced by the consumer. Although he recognizes the importance of the "science of medicine," he is also concerned with the "art of medicine." His assessment of quality of health services is subjective and emphasizes the patient's emotional needs. For the consumer, accessibility and compassion are very important elements in determining the quality of health services. That is not to suggest that he is willing to sacrifice scientific quality to have accessibility and compassion; but neither is he particularly desirous of sacrificing them to receive care of the highest caliber.

The third dimension of the quality of health services is that developed by society. In some respects this dimension is concerned with achieving a balance between the previous two. For a society, efficiency, reasonable costs and unit productivity are all extremely important variables. A fair statement would be that the societal dimension seeks the most effective utilization, the lowest cost and the greatest unit productivity without sacrificing the expectations of the professional or the consumer. It is here that conflicts are found as those concerned with the formulation of social policy take cognizance of individual and group expectations and seek to achieve satisfactory resolution of incompatibilities. This emphasizes the importance of seeking an arena in which the interests of both the provider and consumer of health services can bargain over the requirements for preparation and utilization of health manpower.

Organization and Utilization

On the more positive and slightly less problematic side, with the growth in the size and complexity of the institution of health, an increasing organization has been noted in an effort to achieve more effective utilization of skilled manpower. The institution of health has been slower than many of the other institutions in society to adopt the principles of organization and many of its benefits are therefore only now beginning to be reaped.

Also, slow but continuous changes have occurred in the utilization of manpower. Attempting to analyze these changes from 1940 to 1960, Weiss[30] grouped health occupations into three levels of job content—high, medium and low—using as measures, in the absence of more concrete data, relative earnings and estimates of educational and training requirements. Comparing employment at each level over this period, he found the largest percentage increases in the occupations with low job content and the smallest increases in the occupations with high job content. This inverse relationship was valid also when the data were analyzed by region and sex. Furthermore, his analysis showed that "if the 1950 job coefficients [earnings and educational requirements] for health manpower had been maintained [in 1960], an additional 100,000 health jobs with a high level of job content and 113,000 health jobs with a middle level of job content, would have been required to produce the 1960 output of health services. Instead, 117,000 with a low level of job content were substituted for these 113,000 jobs." In addition, analysis of specific groups of jobs indicated improved utilization of health manpower. For example, productivity of dentists has increased from 1950 to 1963, and the evidence suggests that this increase is partially due to additional dental auxiliary personnel. Similarly, the field of nursing has seen an increase in the productivity of nursing care and the proportion of low-level content jobs.

Therefore, although not actively pursued as a policy, in effect improvement has taken place in some fields in utilization and organization of health manpower. But this is only a beginning.

Problems of Under-Utilization

Traditionally qualified manpower has been under-utilized by "capital-poor institutions," such as universities and hospitals, in the service section of the economy. As Ginzberg has stated:[31]

> Partly because we have so many non-profit institutions which tend to be capital poor, productivity tends to be low. . . . The kinds of supporting personnel that even a broken-down business organization would have on the payroll to economize the use of the more expensive personnel are scarce in non-profit institutions. Being capital poor, these institutions squeeze their dollars and try to make them go as far as they can. From a productivity point of view, I think you have a substantial under-investment in capital, with corresponding under-utilization of personnel which on balance gives you a bad result.

Everyone can cite examples of the waste of talent and training in hospitals and other institutions as well as in private medical and dental offices. Hospitals, the major employers of health manpower, generally are unable to afford supportive clerical and administrative personnel in the numbers needed to free their professional and technical staffs from the routine and the repetitious. The result, as they recognize and as Ginzberg points out, is a less-than-desirable method of operation that requires specialized personnel—who must be employed—to function for a good portion of their time at less than their highest levels of capability.

A recent time-motion study of practicing pediatricians by Bergman, Dassel and Wedgwood[32] raises many questions concerning the appropriateness of training and utilization of pediatricians. Although the study included only four pediatricians, the data revealed that 48 per cent of the pediatrician's day was spent with patients, 12.5 per cent on the phone, and nine per cent on paper work. Fifty per cent of the time with patients was spent with well children and 22 per cent with children who had minor respiratory illness. Less than two per cent of the total work week of the pediatricians studied was spent on the types of illnesses that constituted the vast majority of pediatric residency training, namely on the inpatient care of nephrosis, meningitis, inborn errors of metabolism, leukemia, cardiac disease and severe infectious disease. As a result, the authors concluded, "intellectual understimulation seems to arise from spending the majority of time with children who did not require their special talents." One consequence has been a trend to subspecialization in a search for intellectual challenge. With rising demands for child health care and an increasing population, the pediatrician manpower gap will become larger and larger. If current manpower trends continue, it has been estimated that by 1980, 59,000 additional physicians would have to be trained to maintain the current physician-child ratio.[33] Obviously, that is not going to be possible. Different patterns of child health care will be necessary.

Ross, commenting on this study, has made some suggestions for new patterns:[34]

> Can we not set up teams comprising trained individuals to interpret normal growth and development, give advice on nutrition, and carry out planned immunization procedures, and reserve to the pediatrician a supervisory role, the performance of physical examination, and the care of illness? As the head of the team the individual pediatrician should be able to provide good care to a much larger number of children and satisfaction not only to his patients and their parents but also to his professional teammates themselves.

The issue—an issue relevant to every discipline—is how long even a wealthy society can rationalize the investment of years of education and training beyond high school in individuals who will subsequently devote significant portions of their time to routine duties that might be provided very effectively by people trained in half the number of years.

ESSENTIALS OF A MANPOWER POLICY

The number and variety of health occupations considered in juxtaposition to society's pool of manpower resources is a challenge to formulate a rational policy for health manpower. A continuum must be developed in which the preparation and utilization of different types of professional and technical workers are related in an optimum fashion. This will require consideration of health manpower at all levels of knowledge and skill.

The range of skill, aptitude and general interest required of health manpower is as great as that found in virtually any societal endeavor. Careers exist in the health disciplines for individuals with highly disparate backgrounds, diverse levels and duration of preparation and significantly divergent interests and capacities. Moreover, critical shortages exist of highly trained and specialized manpower. Efforts to create jobs that comprise only circumscribed tasks and a limited number of skills can contribute ancillary and supportive activities that aid highly competent manpower to achieve a greater output of health services. Individuals with innate capacities that will enable them ultimately to pursue higher levels of education need to be considered. So do individuals with lesser talents who can be expected to perform work that requires the mastery of only limited skills.

Education Programs

To clarify the various levels of preparation in health occupations is difficult since every group considers itself professional and use of the terms technician and technologist and vocational and technical is interchangeable. The confusion in nomenclature notwithstanding, education and training for the health occupations occurs essentially in six levels or clusters, namely:

1. *Advanced professional:* programs that admit students holding a baccalaureate degree to study at the graduate level; four years for an M.D., D.D.S. or Ph.D. in the behavioral or biological sciences and two-year curricula leading to masters degrees in social work, hospital administration, etc.

2. *Intermediate professional:* programs that require two years of college prior to a four-year curriculum leading to a Doctor of Optometry, Doctor of Pharmacy, Doctor of Podiatry or Doctor of Veterinary Medicine.

3. *Basic professional:* programs based in colleges or universities and leading to a baccalaureate degree. Included are physical therapy, occupational therapy, speech therapy, medical laboratory technology, medical record librarianship, dietetics and nursing. In some instances as much as a full year of clinical or practi-

cal work in a supervised setting is required for professional certification; in the four-year program, the practical or clinical work is frequently accomplished during summers and vacations. Programs for the preparation of cytotechnologists and dental hygienists represent a variation on this level of preparation since six months and one year of practical training respectively follow two years of general education in a college or junior college.

4. *Technical:* programs offered by community colleges, vocational institutions or hospitals, are usually of two-year duration, although less when little, if any, general education is included in the curriculum. Illustrations include programs for associate degree nurses, diploma nurses, x-ray technicians and dental laboratory technicians.

5. *Vocational:* training offered primarily by vocational high schools or hospitals, usually six to 12 months in duration and almost completely practical in orientation. Training programs for licensed practical nurses, inhalation therapists and certified laboratory assistants are illustrations.

6. *On-the-job training:* programs that have virtually no educational prerequisites and are limited to short orientation courses or in-service instruction in limited procedures.

The differences between the technical and vocational clusters are the least distinct. The terminology used is arbitrary and attempts to distinguish between training programs of one year's duration or less and those requiring two years of study beyond high school.

The relations between the two principal types of programs for the preparation of health manpower—educational institutions (universities, colleges, community colleges, vocational schools or departments of education) and service institutions (mainly hospitals)—needs resolution. The recent trend is toward increasing the portion of training sponsored by primarily educational institutions with hospital affiliations for the clinical or practical component of the program. Expansion of this trend will require a major shift of administrative responsibility for technical and vocational training service to educational institutions. This trend is being stimulated by the tremendous growth of two-year community colleges in the United States and a redirection of public, vocational education from industrial trades to those of service careers.

Two benefits of a merger of educational and service institutions with respect to the preparation of health manpower are to be anticipated. A majority of the programs for training health technicians have less than ten students. Many have as few as two. The question is being raised as to whether or not a program of this size has the necessary "critical mass" to justify the energies of a faculty, no matter how small its numbers or the portion of time devoted to that effort. The character of the training approximates apprenticeship far more than an organized curriculum. Another salutary effect of this merger would be the expanding influence of educational accreditation. Currently, regional accreditation, the main mechanism through which society assesses and acknowledges the adequacy of its programs of formal instruction, is not used for the technical areas.

In any event, an adequate health manpower program should be aimed at obtaining the most effective yield possible from the nation's educational resources, represented by almost 600 junior colleges, universities and other institutions offering four or more years of higher education, augmented for purposes of supervised practical experiences by the approximately 1,000 short-term general hospitals with 200 or more beds.

Theory-Skill Spectrum

Developing new educational programs and changing existing ones will constitute one of the most important avenues to the improvement of utilization. Kinsinger, who has been concerned with developing increasing numbers and kinds of health technicians, has proposed a "theory-skill spectrum in the health field."[35] Such an idea with the added dimension of "capacity for independent action," as proposed by Mase,[36] offers a context in which to deduce the interrelationships among specific disciplines with respect to both their preparation and utilization. Approaching health manpower as an interrelated whole rather than merely an agglomeration of disparate categories of personnel is essential.

The "theory-skill spectrum" suggests a hierarchical continuum in which generalizable academic and experience equivalents are common to several levels of functioning. The technical or professional health worker is faced with the necessity of mastering varying portions, in both range and depth, of biomedical knowledge and specific skills. Flexibility in both the development and use of health manpower requires that educational and experience equivalents must be identified and measured wherever they might exist. This, together with the development of adequate measures of capacity for independent action, is a prerequisite to accomplishing a downward transfer of functions from the higher-trained to the lesser-trained individuals (see below), as well as to developing "job enlargement," i.e., assuming increasing responsibility commensurate with one's skills.

It is suggested that the curricula found in the various clusters of health manpower described above (advanced professional, intermediate professional, basic professional, technical and vocational) could be examined both for the common elements within each cluster and the relationships among the hierarchy of clusters. A determination of the portion of each curriculum devoted to generalizable knowledge and to technical skill could assist and enable an individual completing a program in one cluster to receive advanced standing in a curriculum in another cluster located above it in the hierarchy. In addition, to facilitating and encouraging each individual to obtain the fullest margin of his capacity, the existence of such a continuum could open positions in the clusters of "basic" through "advanced" health professions to students making a lateral or diagonal transfer.

For example, the nation's medical and dental schools lose approximately ten per cent of their students between enrollment and the start of the third year. It would seem that the possibility of filling these 800 plus vacancies in the third year medical class and the 300 vacancies in the third year of dental school with "transfers" from other programs in the health professions through the vehicle of related curricula is worth exploration. The increasing portion of the medical curricula given over to electives (two of the four years in the new curriculum at the Duke Medical School) increases the options for developing overlaps with curricula in other professional schools. Advanced placement is now a widespread phenomenon in the movement of the student from high school to college. Honors study offered to students of nursing, pharmacy, optometry, physical therapy and so forth to qualify them for advanced placement in a medical curriculum should not be impossible to devise.

At the present time, high school graduates spending three years in a diploma school of nursing in a hospital receive no credit toward a college degree; the assumption is, therefore, that the program has zero academic equivalents. On the other hand, a girl spending two years in a community college qualifies for licensure as a registered nurse at the same time that she receives academic credit, suggesting that the program has fewer technical equivalents. The Bachelor of Science in Pharmacy degree, however, that required five years beyond high school, represented four years of academic equivalents for enrollment toward a Ph.D. in most universities.

Core Curricula

New curricula may well have to be devised and planning and inauguration of core curricula at various levels of health manpower must be pursued. With an increasing number of health professions, relationships among the various members of the health team who will be sharing responsibilities will become critical, and interaction among these health workers must be encouraged. At the same time, consideration must be given to making maximum use of limited educational resources through such mechanisms as the sharing of faculty, which the development of core curricula would facilitate.

Indications are that community colleges will attempt to develop core curricula as they consider initiating programs for a whole range of health technicians.* The similarity of the curri-

---

* Kinsinger, *op. cit.,* Appendix III, lists the following 21 Community College Career Programs in Allied Medical and Auxillary Dental Occupations:

Biomedical Electronics Technician	Director of Hospital Volunteer
Dental Assistant	Services
Dental Hygienist	Medical Laboratory Assistant
Dental Laboratory Technician	Nursing (ADN)

cula for many of these programs with respect to the biological sciences supports the logic of such an approach. One program in Minneapolis, Minnesota,[37] using core curricula, currently offers preparation in seven health occupations: 1. medical laboratory assistant, 2. medical record technician, 3. medical secretary, 4. nurse technician, 5. occupational therapy assistant, 6. radiologic technologist and 7. food service supervisor.

In addition, the use of core curricula is found in graduate schools and universities where the basic science faculty provides instruction for students in the biomedical sciences, medicine and dentistry. Some faculty also teach in several clusters by varying the scope and intensity of the subject matter covered—for example, in teaching clinical pathology and medical technology. Efforts to develop core curricula at the basic professional and intermediate professional levels, as well as increasing the effort at the other levels, would appear to warrant careful study and implementation.

Education as a Continuous Process

But the education of health manpower cannot be considered solely a preparatory experience, as it has tended to be to date. The increasing rate at which scientific and technological advances are being achieved indicates the foolhardiness of considering any preparation as terminal. It has been suggested, and advocated, that the intimate relationship between educational and service programs discussed above would enable education to become a truly continuous process. The individual health worker could learn new techniques relative to his or her discipline, and he might also have more chance to enlarge his theoretical knowledge. Opportunities for the latter—that is, increasing the level of one's mastery of theory and generalizable knowledge—are essential to upward movement on a career ladder.

X-ray Technician	Inhalation Therapy Technician
Occupational Therapy Assistant	Operating Room Technician
Medical Record Technician	Ophthalmic Dispenser
Medical Secretary	Radioisotope Technician
Medical Assistant	Prosthetist
Medical Emergency Technician	Environmental Health Technician
Food Service Supervisor	Ward Manager

Career Mobility

Any increase in opportunities for movement on a career ladder will be of paramount importance in achieving the most complete utilization of health manpower. At the present time, mobility is limited in either a lateral or vertical direction among health careers. As noted above, with the present system of education and training an individual has to select one of the many possible health careers prior to enrollment in a specific program. In effect, the student who chooses one health career bars himself from all others, unless he chooses to go back and begin at the beginning in a new course of study that may well repeat what his previous training and experience have already taught him. But, as noted by Ginzberg and his associates,[38]

A person's occupational choice is not a one-time decision but the cumulative result of many decisions over time. These decisions re-enforce each other until the occupational path open to an individual has been narrowly delineated.

A more flexible system fostering both lateral and vertical career mobility among health disciplines could serve to offset premature restriction or closure of occupational choice.

The absence of vertical mobility among the health disciplines and the restriction of occupational decisions to only one or at most a couple of "points of entry" virtually close the majority of the health careers to the socially and culturally disadvantaged in society. The odds against motivating an impending high school dropout to complete secondary schooling, four years of college, four years of medical school and four years of post-graduate work so that he might practice medicine are beyond his comprehension, his innate intelligence and aptitude notwithstanding. Providing him with a series of short-range goals encompassing a step-by-step elevation in responsibilities—all accompanied by general educational opportunities—might provide the individual with sufficient challenge and motivation to reassess his career aspirations in the light of recent achievements and newly perceived horizons.

Can several of the health disciplines be related in an education continuum to provide multiple points of exit to jobs and reentry for further study preparatory to a higher level of functioning? It seems that combinations of some parts of existing curricula reinforced by the current thinking about education as a continuous process could produce a plausible first step to truly exciting opportunities. One of the major policy recommendations of the Conservation of Human Resources Project[39] is that of work-study programs designed to stimulate the "awareness of occupational opportunity," an approach that warrants scrutiny.

A continuum of enlarging experiences through a work-study program could enable an individual to derive motivation from an "awareness of occupational opportunities." Although it is usually argued in educational circles that the general or broad education should precede training for specific activities, this sequence is not always possible and frequently is impractical. A widely recognized example of specific or technical training occurring before rather than after general education can be found in many case histories of "self-made" men. In these situations, so frequently idealized and venerated in folklore, circumstances necessitate the individual's entrance into the labor market through the performance of menial tasks. Energy combined with innate ability and good fortune enables the individual to progress to a point where he can acquire a broadened and general education through the vehicle of life experiences.

Similarly, the opportunity to work in health services, even at a very basic or rudimentary level, could represent the beginning of a broader horizon of basic education, adult education, self-study and similar experiences. It is important to recognize that efforts aimed at adapting jobs to individuals do not preclude consideration of the educational facets of these programs. On the contrary, these efforts ultimately can contribute to the educational enhancement of the individual. Thus, he can grow to fill larger, more complex and more demanding responsibilities in the future. The experience of the armed forces in preparing hospital corpsmen, laboratory technicians and personnel for other health occupations suggests that career ladders in health are feasible, and it should be noted that one-quarter of the medical students in the Soviet Union have had prior education and experience in one of the health occupations.[40]

The widely publicized two-year, post-high-school curriculum initiated recently at Duke University Medical Center to train physician assistants could be used as part of a foundation for construction of a career ladder. This program is aimed at increasing the productivity of medical practitioners by preparing a new category of paramedical manpower to perform a large array of procedures under supervision. The information available to date does not suggest that the graduates of this program will possess skills that vary significantly from those found in many nurses, but a great contribution of the program may be in establishing new opportunities in the health field for men as an alternative to nursing, characterized as predominantly a female profession. The most far-reaching impact could be achieved, however, if thought is given to devising future educational opportunities, in combination with work experiences, that would permit one of these or subsequent "physician assistants" to move up the occupational ladder to become a physician.

The subject of the "indigenous, nonprofessional" is stimulating the curiosity of many service professions. The idea of career development is included in the thinking on this subject, and the shortsightedness of concentrating on jobs, and therefore failing to look for careers, is recognized. As noted by Reiff and Riessman:[41]

> The concept of employing indigenous nonprofessionals calls for the possibility of promotion to various levels of subprofessional and professional positions. For this to occur, both public and private sector requirements will have to accept combinations of work experience plus education which can be acquired concomitantly with employment or intermittently with leaves of absence.

Downward Transfer of Functions

Complementary to establishment of career mobility as an approach to effective utilization is a downward transfer of functions. Giving each service the level of skill it needs, no more and no less, may be the principal challenge to health manpower. Meeting this challenge requires detailed study of health services and a subdivision of specific functions into the component tasks. Then individuals possessing only a limited range of skills and competencies can be drawn into the manpower pool to perform many of the tasks, freeing those more highly trained and skilled for the performance of duties requiring their more advanced level of competency.

Extensive research and analysis to determine the limits of safety is, of course, a necessary prerequisite to this approach. Then, attention must be focused on those services that can be provided by more than one discipline and on the fact that the greatest economy is realized when disciplines in shortage areas are devoting the greatest possible percentage of their time to those services that they, and they alone, are equipped to provide.

Success in programs of "downward transfer of functions" usually hinges on effective organization and supervision of the services performed, and, accordingly, the approach requires an institutional setting for effective implementation. That should not present a problem in the health enterprise, however, since health comprises a variety of institutions and agencies—hospitals, health departments, nursing homes, group practices and voluntary health agencies—located through the nation and extensive in both number and kind. Moreover, as was noted earlier, the trend toward institutionalization of health services, in a functional sense, suggests an increased opportunity for new approaches.

The increasing use by dentists of auxiliary personnel is one illustration of a downward transfer of functions. A recent survey of dental practice,[42] which assumed dentists' incomes reflected productivity, found that their income or productivity increased with each additional dental auxiliary that they employed. Furthermore, the addition of a second assistant increases income more than the addition of the first assistant, and the addition of a third assistant increases income more than the addition of a second. Since most dentists now employ one or two full-time assistants, the study implies the need for further improvements in utilization.

A downward transfer of functions has frequently resulted in the creation of new disciplines and some interesting innovations involving assistants to physicians now being tried may well create more. Of these, the following programs are illustrative:

1. Training of personnel as "medical emergency technicians" for emergency service, being conducted at Ohio State University.
2. Duke University's two-year program for training "physician assistants," comparable to the experienced medical corpsman of the armed forces.
3. The "pediatric public-health nurse practitioner" being trained at the University of Colorado to assume an expanded role in child health.
4. The "unit manager," developed at the University of Florida Health Center, who orders supplies, stocks, medications and linens, handles requests for and records results of laboratory and technical procedures, schedules orderly service and patient transportation and manages meal service, thus freeing nurses for patient care.

Application of Technology

Increased application of technology to provision of health services would also serve to improve utilization of health manpower. In contrast to other industry, "the health service industry" has substituted technology for manpower to only a limited degree. No doubt, a variety of reasons may be cited, ranging from an inherent distrust of the appropriateness of the extensive use of automation and instrumentation in what must be a personalized, service activity, to the lack of capital for investment in developmental activities and purchase of hardware. Nonetheless, when the health endeavor is viewed as a $45 billion labor-intensive industry, with labor costs approximating three-quarters of the total, the impetus to substitute technology for manpower becomes inevitable.

Several examples of "labor-saving" developments can be cited: disposable supplies (syringes, needles, transfusion sets and gloves), prepackaged formula and intravenous solutions, simplified laboratory tests (Clinitest for Benedict's solution) and so forth. The potential of automated laboratories, computer analysis of electrocardiograms and similar developments is suggested by the Kaiser Permanente multiphasic screening project[43] under development in Oakland, California, since 1962. Approximately 40,000 health-plan beneficiaries are screened annually with a battery of 20 automated and semi-automated tests, including a self-administered health history questionnaire. Only approximately two and one-half hours are required to complete the automated survey and it is conducted by nurses, technicians and other supportive health manpower. Conventional methods would require two days and between four and five times the $42 cost established in this program.

CONCLUSION

Careful exploration of each of these avenues to improved utilization and application of new ideas and practices encountered in this exploration can profoundly affect the capacity to insure that every individual receives the best in health care. For utilization is a critical variable. As such, it is considered in a new book by Rashi Fein of the Brookings Institution.[44] Working on the premise that manpower requirements are a function of requirements for services, now considered by some to be the only meaningful and realistic basis for forecasting, Fein asserts:

> The "need" for medical personnel depends on the demand for medical services and on the quantity of services a given amount of personnel can and is prepared to offer. Both the demand and the supply change over time. The former is affected as the health and socio-economic characteristics of the population alter, as research in medicine advances, and as government helps transform medical needs into demand by instituting new medical services or financing programs. The latter changes as new patterns of medical organization come into being, as new types of personnel are trained and new technology is developed, and as the productivity of personnel changes.

Not all of the variables involved are quantifiable, but estimating the effects of each to the extend possible and using existing patterns of utilization as his base, Fein projects an increase in demand of at least 22 to 26 per cent for 1975, and a 19 per cent increase in the number of physicians. For 1980, he predicts a 35 to 40 per cent increase in demand and a 29 per cent increase in physicians.

Obviously, utilization of health manpower in such a way that the benefits of modern medicine may be made available to all will require much in terms of creative energy and innovative approaches. The introduction to this paper expressed the belief that billions of dollars could be invested in the education and training of health manpower without making a significant impact on the availability of health services, and thereafter, attempted neither a thorough review nor analysis of all the relevant factors. Rather the attempt has been made to suggest issues and to provoke a discussion of health manpower policy.

Planning for the effective preparation and use of health manpower is the subject of the first two of the 23 recommendations of a task force that has spent considerable time in examining the subject of health manpower.[45] But, as always, the recommendation is easier than implementation. Nonetheless, "plan we must!" As planning proceeds, visualizing the problems and formulating solutions must precede and guide the computerization of the data.

N O T E S

1. M. M. Davis, *Medical Care for Tomorrow* (New York, Harper & Brothers, 1955), p. 7.
2. *Manpower in the 1960's,* Health Manpower Source Book No. 18. Washington, United States Department of Health, Education and Welfare, Public Health Service Publication No. 263, 1964, pp. 2–3.
3. *Ibid.,* pp. 7–10.
4. M. E. Altenderfer, "Trends in Health Manpower," Staff paper No. 1 for the Task Force on Health, Education and Welfare Manpower Requirements and Training Programs (November 30, 1965).
5. E. R. Weinerman, *Dilemma of the OPD: Epilogue or Epicenter,* Hartford Foundation Conference on Ambulatory Care and Rehabilitation (October 15, 1965, publication pending).
6. "Medical Education in the United States, 1964–1965," *op. cit.,* p. 771.
7. "Health Information Foundation, Where Physicians Work," *Progress in Health Services,* 13 (May–June, 1964).

8. *Trends in Health Manpower,* Table 8.
9. A. R. Somers, "Some Basic Determinants of Medical Care and Health Policy: An Overview of Trends and Issues," *The Milbank Memorial Fund Quarterly,* 46 (January, 1968).
10. "Expert Guessing," *New York Times* (July 12, 1964).
11. United States Department of Health, Education and Welfare, *Physicians for a Growing America.* Washington, United States Government Printing Office, 1959.
12. *Manpower for Medical Research: Requirements and Resources, 1965–1970,* United States Public Health Service Publication No. 1001, 1963.
13. L. A. Lecht, *The Dollar Cost of Our National Goals.* Washington, National Planning Association, May, 1965, p. 27.
14. R. I. Lee and L. W. Jones, *The Fundamentals of Good Medical Care.* (Chicago, University of Chicago Press, 1932), Tables 7 and 11, and pp. 115 and 123.
15. *Toward Quality in Nursing: Needs and Goals,* United States Department of Health, Education and Welfare, Public Health Service Publication No. 992, (February, 1963).
16. B. D. Daitz, "The Challenge of Disability," *American Journal of Public Health,* 55 (April, 1965), 528–534.
17. Office of Education, unpublished data.
18. *American Women,* Presidential Commission for the Status of Women, 1963.
19. *Manpower in the 1960's, op. cit.*
20. M. A. Rutzick, "A Ranking of U.S. Occupations by Earnings," *Monthly Labor Review,* 88 (March, 1965), 249–255.
21. "Physicians' Economic Health: Excellent," *Medical Economics,* 42 (December 13, 1965), 77 and 81.
22. V. Freeman and G. Levenson, "Salaries of Nurses in Selected Public Health Agencies: 1962," *Nursing Outlook,* 10 (December, 1962), 815.
23. Nationwide Crisis in Nursing, *Medical World News* (January 28, 1966), 77.
24. J. E. Elliott, *Facts about Nursing: A Statistical Summary* (New York, American Nurses' Association, 1965), p. 130.
25. *Ibid.,* p. 223.
26. G. A. Silver, *Family Medical Care,* (Cambridge, Harvard University Press, 1963).
27. R. Brecher and E. Brecher, "The Disgraceful Facts About Infant Deaths in the U.S.," *McCalls* (February, 1966), 82.
28. *Education for the Health Professions* (Albany, New York State Education Department, 1963), p. 25.
29. W. K. Selden, *Accreditation* (New York, Harper & Brothers, Publishers, 1960), p. 56.
30. J. H. Weiss, "The Changing Job Structure of Health Manpower, Cambridge," (Harvard University, unpublished doctoral dissertation, July, 1966), pp. 117–120, 156.
31. E. Ginzberg, "Manpower Aspects of the Service Sector of the Economy," Joint Economic Committee Hearings on Employment

Growth and Price Levels, 86th Congress, First Session, September–
October 2, 1959, Part 8, pp. 2661–2670.
32. A. B. Bergman, S. W. Dassel, and R. J. Wedgwood, "Time-Motion
Study of Practicing Pediatricians," *Pediatrics,* 38, (August, 1966),
Part I, 254–263.
33. *Ibid.,* p. 262.
34. R. A. Ross, "Commentary: Time, Motion and Pediatric Practice,"
Pediatrics, 38, 165–166, August, 1966, Part I.
35. R. E. Kinsinger, *Education for Health Technicians: An Overview,*
American Association of Junior Colleges, 1965.
36. D. Mase, "The Utilization of Mindpower," paper presented to the
American Public Health Association, Health Manpower Section,
November 2, 1966.
37. *Ibid.,* p. 17.
38. E. Ginzberg, J. K. Anderson, and J. L. Herma, *The Optomistic
Tradition of American Youth* (New York, Columbia University
Press, 1964).
39. *Ibid.,* pp. 145–158.
40. *Medical Education in the Soviet Union,* Report of the Delegation
on Medical Education, U.S.–U.S.S.R. Cultural Exchange Agreement,
1964.
41. R. Reiff and F. Riessman, "The Indigenous Nonprofessional: A
Strategy of Change in Community Action and Community Mental
Health Programs," *Community Mental Health Journal,* Monograph
No. 1 (November, 1965).
42. American Dental Association, Bureau of Economic Research and
Statistics, The 1962 Survey of Dental Practice, *The Journal of the
American Dental Association,* 66 (May, 1963), 722.
43. M. F. Collen, "Periodic Health Examinations Utilizing an Automated Multitest Laboratory," presented at a joint meeting of the
Section on Preventive Medicine and the Section on General Practice,
American Medical Association, June 23, 1965.
44. R. Fein, *The Doctor Shortage: An Economic Diagnosis* (Washington,
D.C., The Brookings Institution, 1967).
45. Task Force on Health Manpower, National Commission on Community Health Service, *Health Manpower: Action to Meet Community Needs* (Bethesda, 1966).

9 Problems and Perspectives of Group Practice

E. RICHARD WEINERMAN*

Through most of history the role of the healer has been a lonely one. As tribal shaman, priest, or medicine man his occult and magical power required the aura of mystery as the basis of effectiveness. As itinerant hawker of medicinal wares or robed dignitary of the Galenic school he shared neither his methods nor his records with his fellow-practitioners.[1] In more recent times the physician has been harnessed into teams more reluctantly than most of the rest of society. The dominant professional mode—at least in the United States—is still lonely, still ritualized, still basically solo.

Yet the current trends are all toward the grouping of medicine as specialization and technology have their day. Hospital staffs in western Europe, polyclinics in Eastern Europe, rural health

Reprinted by permission of the author and publisher from *Bulletin of the New York Academy of Medicine,* 44 (November 1968) pp. 1423–1434.

* M.D., late Professor of Medicine and Public Health, School of Medicine, Yale University.

centers in developing countries—all are group formats developed in response to the inevitable social adaptation of this essential public service. But the particular form of association which we call group practice is thoroughly and almost solely American—as American as jazz or baseball or political conventions. In my view neither the form of group practice nor the nature of its counterparts in American life are accidental.

The scientific and economic forces which compel such rational forms of social organization as division of labor and programmed production—when coupled with the peculiarly American brand of competitive individualism—must produce that mixture of teamwork and star performance which characterizes groups named for Mayo, Ochsner, or Leahy, just as it does those named for Goodman, Gillespie, or Brubeck.

The fabric of American group practice is, then, woven from the warp of individualism and the woof of productive organization. Its design, its utility, and its impact can be comprehended, I think, only in terms of such crossed threads and historically determined patterns.

All fabrics of social organization, while historically determined in the fundamental sense, are woven ultimately to fit the needs of those who own the loom and set the weaving pattern. The outpatient departments of teaching hospitals serve first the needs of staff and of students, then of patients. Industrial clinics, college dispensaries, military medical stations—each meets the special requirements of its managers in the name of service to workers or students or soldiers.

So is it with group medical practice. Those few groups which have been organized by and for consumer cooperatives or labor unions differ from the many units which are the products of organizational efforts made by physicians themselves.[2] Since most group practice in this country has been developed by doctors it should surprise no one that the resulting pattern is better for them than for their patients. Those who control the policy-making boards of future group centers will determine both form and content, not according to prevailing ideology about health service, but according to their own perceived needs.

Few aspects of American medical care have shown more promise or have been given more attention than has group practice. The idea has been prominent since the report of the Committee on the Costs of Medical Care in 1932,[3] and it has been reinforced by the policy declarations of the American Public Health Association in 1949[4] and endorsed—albeit guardedly— by the Larsen Report of the American Medical Association in 1955.[5] It has been echoed in every governmental document on medical care in recent years; the newest of these are the reports of the National Conference on Group Practice in October 1967[6] and that of the National Advisory Commission on Health Manpower in November 1967.[3]

But the glowing hopes of the medical care ideologists of the 1930's and 1940's and the statesmanlike pronouncements of public officials in the 1960's—often the same individuals—have been met with hesitant professional acceptance and with lackadaisical response, despite the seeming advantages to both groups. To what extent does the tradition of medical mysticism, which requires privacy for the practitioner, explain this? What is the effect of the star system so characteristic of the American team? Can consumers be consistently attracted by group programs designed by and for managers and physicians? Perhaps we have been looking for the right answers in the wrong places.

GROWTH OF GROUP PRACTICE

One can argue the growth rate of group practice according to one's own prejudice. It booms, say the protagonists, who cite a doubling of the number of physicians in it from 1959 to 1966. It falters, counter the critics, who use the same raw data to describe an advance during this period of only a few percentage points in the small production of all active clinicians who practice in formal groups. The total number of groups has more than doubled from 1959 to 1966, but a close look at the data reveals that only 221 general service groups had been added to the 1,154 counted in the earlier year; all the rest constitute that form of private medical partnership labeled "single specialty" groups. While the files of the American Association of Medical Clinics now contain data on 4,287 group practices of all kinds in the United States, almost half of these are composed of only three to five physicians

—again a form not very different from the popular pattern of less formal office partnership.[6, 8]

The story of prepaid group practice is even less reassuring. While the national population increased by about 25 million in the past decade, enrollment in group health plans grew by little more than 1 million, and much of this increase was due to expansion of the two coastal giants; the Health Insurance Plan of New York and the Kaiser Foundation Health Plan, Inc.[6,9] In total, only about 7 per cent of visits in the country are made by ambulatory patients to all group offices, and only 3 per cent to prepaid group practices.[10] Yet all prepaid groups have survived, if not prospered, once they have passed the formidable hazards of getting started. There has been neither clear-cut success nor abject failure in the 30 years since Michael Shadid's heroic effort in Elk City, Okla.[11] This ambivalence in public response is the essence of the difficulty we face today.

Along with so many of you, I have been trying for 20 years to learn the reasons for such modest results from such promising labors. My own work as clinician, administrator, consultant, and researcher in group practice has afforded me the opportunity to view this brand of medical care from all vantage points except the crucial one of the nonprofessional consumer.[12-14] Perhaps it is precisely this bias which prevents us all from seeing the forest of group *health service* instead of the trees of *medical practice*.[15] We can only be sobered by the reminder from Eveline Burns: "If a new policy or program is found to be good, even though initially limited in scope, pressure will be exerted to extend it to other groups or problem areas."[16]

PREMISES REVISITED

The need, then, is for a fresh look at the premises and the promises of group practice in the light of the experience of the past three decades. Many influential advocates of medical progress have called in recent times for review of our somewhat fixed ideas. Surgeon General William Stewart thus challenged the 1967 National Conference on Group Practice: "There is a need for imaginative experimentation in new forms and formats of group practice. We cannot afford to be frozen in a few tried and true patterns. We need to reach out for new incentives and new financial and organizational mechanisms."[6]

The National Advisory Commission on Health Manpower states the proposition directly: "It is only by exploiting the innovations and technologies of other sectors and by developing new techniques appropriate to its own problems that the health care system can adequately respond to social change and scientific advance."[7]

How, then, do we look again at group practice? Why has it not fully caught on, as have such contemporary innovations in the medical care system as intensive care units, group hospitalization insurance, or automated clinical laboratories? Why has this rational, wholly voluntary, and uniquely American idea lagged in its application? What have been its major premises?

Premise 1. Group practice is advantageous to the physician. For the physician, group practice has been a relatively good thing. This follows from the fact that it has been developed essentially by and for doctors and represents merely a portion of the spectrum of associative medical practice which now characterizes so much of private medical office arrangements. Modern medical technology and the economics of specialization require some form of association in office as well as hospital practice. While less structured medical partnerships satisfy many of these needs and attract a larger proportion of practitioners, the formal group can and does appeal to many of the younger and less entrepreneurial physicians.

Further, most studies indicate that the net incomes and income equivalents are as good or better for solo as for group practitioners.[17] Control of work hours and recompense for activities that do not produce income are also more feasible in the group setting.

In an age of specialization, of impersonal urban relations, of dependence upon mechanical and technical aids, the group medical center is as relevant to the expectations of the modern doctor as are the blood bank or the smoothly intermeshed open-heart surgical team.

Group practice does suit the physician, although the degree of its formalization is seemingly of less importance. The number of clinically active physicians in associated practice now bids to equal the number who remain purely solo, although those in formal multispecialty groups comprise less than 8 per cent of the total. Of the "true" group practices counted in 1966 more than 1,200 were owned and controlled by physicians and only about 200 by consumers.[6] He who writes the ticket, as we have seen, determines the destination.

Premise 2. Group practice is better for the patient. Here the evidence is equivocal, as measured by the response of consumers. The established larger clinics do expand, after a difficult period of initial capital financing and scepticism on the part of the community. But relatively few new consumer-sponsored groups appear: of the present total of about 200 group health plans, more than 125 were already in existence a decade ago.[9, 18] The significant amount of membership turnover, the use of "outside" services by plan members, and the choice of nongroup practice plans in dual choice elections also reflect this ambivalence on the part of the consumer.[15, 19]

Some advantages to the patient are clear-cut, even though the fact is not always understood by the public. Benefits per prepaid dollar are higher, use of hospitals lower, and certain end results of care—such a perinatal mortality—have been shown to be better in group than in individual practice.[20, 21] But the last word on comparative quality is not yet in.[22]

The judgment most clearly pronounced by the consumer—interestingly enough, also by those who have not yet personally experienced group medical care—is that the group clinics provide more competent care but with less personal interest in the patient than do independent practitioners.[19] I believe that competence and personal interest are equally important components of good medical care. The premise that group practice improves the lot of patients remains incompletely documented.

Premise 3. Group practice is good for the community. Here again, the proposition is by no means proved. Certainly, resources in the community are augmented by new group health centers; competent personnel are attracted; the array of services available to patients is extended and, it may be hoped, rationalized. A degree of sophistication about comparative forms of medical care is developed in the community; in some cases the standards of equality are pushed a notch or two upward for all the medical competitors.

Yet in balance the effect on the community is unclear. Over-all costs of care continue to rise, for patients of groups as well as of solo physicians. The group pattern, as we have seen, has not spread with the velocity of the supermarket. The bankers and other financing agencies have not been as impressed with the long-range potentials of group practice as with those of motels or gas stations. Only a minority of group centers is responsible to the community rather than to a special category of owner. Most important, the poor are usually excluded—except by the handful of neighborhood health centers and a few experiments with welfare patients in group practice clinics. Over-all the controversy about group practice, especially prepaid group practice, continues to rage—not the least dramatically in my own community of New Haven.

Problems in Group Practice

We must come to grips with the question of *why?* Promises and premises, it seems, have not fully withstood the test of time. We are urged to reappraise—and, presumably, to redesign. Where are the flaws in the model at hand?

The primary difficulty, as has already been suggested, is that American group practice reflects the needs of doctors rather than of patients. The services of group practice are oriented to acute and categorical sickness rather than to the maintenance of health; the customers tend to become those who can pay, or negotiate, their bills. Group practice seeks a hospital image rather than the role of a community center intended to provide a continuum of health services, from prevention through long-term care. Its preoccupations are with fees or premiums, with building plans, and with office hours rather than with new forms of service and effective methods of delivery. The most successful groups are big and thus more efficient financially, more supportive of the physicians but more impersonal and fragmented to the patient. Finally, the group clinics are themselves usually in independent or solo operation; only rarely, as in the Kaiser and

Ross-Loos plans, do they function under regionalized or echelon arrangements.

Most private clinics today (and, unhappily, much of the pre-paid variety that has maintained the standard group-practice format) can be characterized as either the "Noah's-ark" or the "inverted-pyramid" types. The former designation fits those which assemble one or two varieties of every known species of medical specialist under one roof, regardless of the distribution of needs in the community. A minor variant is the other type of group whose large complement of superspecialists depends for its support, like an inverted pyramid balanced on its apex, upon a few "intake" practitioners, who may indeed be nurses or clerks. Here is reflected most clearly the effect of doctor-dominance and episode-of-sickness orientation on the structure of the group itself.

The detailed structure of most groups carries out this conceptual orientation. Departments reflect the classification of physicians more than of patients. Nurses, technicians, and other therapists function as aides to the physician, not as interdependent members of a health care team. The work rules, appointment systems, office hours, and telephone arrangements are all calculated to make life more bearable for the doctors, while the time and comfort of patients and nonmedical staff receive secondary consideration.

Most important, the real potentials of cooperative medicine are only partially exploited. Physicians usually deal independently with patients; they are separated from colleagues in the routine of the day's work by rushed schedules, compartmentalized buildings, and the self-sufficient style of work of the solo practitioner. Group conferences, medical audits, and informal office consultations are, in my experience, more common in the descriptive literature than in daily practice.

The group clinic provides the opportunity—but not yet the reality—for new and more useful roles for public health nurses, health educators, social workers, and other potential members of the health care team. Although new mechanical and laboratory aides are rapidly adopted by medical groups, they rarely take full advantage of the nonmedical professionals.

Perhaps most disappointing has been the hesitation on the part of most medical groups to effect changes in the "way of life" of the medical team itself. This would involve acceptance by the group as a whole of collective responsibility for the health of its patients or members. This would mean actively reaching out into the community of the apparently healthy for screening and early detection. It would mean identification and special protection for those at specific risk of disease. It would imply particular concern for those patients who do not use the service, and for those who break appointments or fail to comply with prescribed regimens. It implies as much concern with *rapport* as with diagnostic labels, as much with education as with prescription.

New Models Needed

Such assumptions draw us, inevitably, to a consideration of methods in group medical care which are rather different from most of those now in operation. The pilot trials for such innovations have been presented, at least in part, by previous contributors to this conference. The major characteristics of the model I propose can be indicated briefly.

Policy Direction and Control

Any community-service program (and a group practice clinic, especially when prepaid, falls into this category) should be controlled directly by the community of consumers for whose benefit it exists. If it is true that the man who pays the piper can call the tune, this prerogative must be recognized as the necessary basis for a health-oriented program. It is as bitter a pill to swallow for physicians as is the self-expression of a black community for many philanthropic whites or as equality between the sexes is for chauvinistic males. But swallowed it must be, if improvement is to take place.

Internal Structure of the Group

A new format of organization is needed, with emphasis on the health care forward line as well as on the backfield of specialists. Experience with health-maintenance projects such as those at

Montefiore,[23] Yale,[24] and Cleveland[25] suggest that the most effective team for primary care includes either the "comprehensive-care physician" of the Millis report[26] or—less effectively —the presently popular combination of internist and pediatrician *plus* public health nurse and community health worker. Depending upon the size of the community served, a number of such teams form the forward line of the program. In isolated rural areas and sequestered urban districts, this combination can function as the peripheral component of a supporting "parent" group.

To the usual array of physician-specialists in the backfield must be added such essential experts as social workers, nutritionists, and health educators—these to serve as consultants rather than as primary practitioners. Only the more commonly needed specialists (i.e., obstetricians, psychiatrists, social workers) needed be located physically in the primary-group center. Some, whose services are used in predictable volume, as in ear, nose, and throat, radiology, nutrition, etc., can be scheduled regularly on assignment from a secondary level, each serving a number of primary units. The highly specialized and irregularly needed consultants (i.e., neurosurgeons and hematologists) and those dependent upon special equipment (as in ophthalmology and urology) can be used on an individual referral basis as indicated, and can be grouped in a central base facility.

The pyramid is thus inverted, to rest on its natural foundation of general health service, which supports the narrowing superstructure of specialist-assistants.

Group Practice Among Medical Groups

This format of primary health service units and secondary specialist support implies a regional system of cooperative echelons—in fact, group practice among medical groups. An isolated medical group, much like an isolated solo practitioner, can provide neither a well-balanced nor a complete service to a finite population. The number of physicians adequate for, let us say, a community of 30,000 persons must provide far more primary than secondary medical care and cannot include all the talents of the specialists which might occasionally be needed. As already suggested, the solution is to be found in the regional interconnection of multiple local health care units with a smaller number of secondary specialty stations (probably related to general hospitals) and with a central major medical resource (ideally a teaching medical center).

Maintenance of Health as the Focus

In such a setting, the work of the team in the local unit can be oriented primarily to the maintenance of health and the long-term control of chronic disorders—items which rank higher among the needs of people than among the interests of medical specialists. In this context the health nurse and the community aide are placed at the very interface of the medical group and the family members, often primary to the physician himself. Thus the "way of life" of the group would embrace the concept of active responsibility for the health of the community, rather than that of waiting passively for the appeals of the already afflicted.

Group Health Centers and the Continuum of Medical Care

The new model of group practice requires a further refinement. The ambulatory and acute hospital-care cases to which most medical groups are now restricted must be linked by coordinated function with the extended and home-care components of the local service area. Thus the group health system would achieve a full network of continuity for care of the acutely and chronically ill.

Role of the Medical Schools

Inherent in this concept of community-controlled and regionalized group practice within a continuum of health services is the opportunity for a wholly new role for the medical schools. Much of this potential has already been described in papers previously presented.

The role of the medical school at the hub of the regional

wheel can be described as fourfold: 1) cooperative planning with the rest of the community, 2) specialty support, 3) innovative experimentation, and 4) teaching and research activities at all levels of the system. A model unit of comprehensive care at the university center can serve both as a laboratory for testing new forms of delivery of medical care and as a supervised classroom for teaching family-health maintenance to students.[24]

Such an effort is now underway at Yale University in a concentric three-ring model. The inner core is the medical center itself, which offers a continuum of ambulatory, intensive, and extended care. Interaction takes place at every point with the surrounding second ring, the local area serviced, i.e., greater New Haven, in which three new group practice health units are now being developed by academic, labor, and communities of the core-city in close liaison with the medical teaching center. The network of associations with outlying small-town and rural hospitals and practitioners through the Connecticut Regional Medical Program constitutes the third ring; this completes the integration of school and community. The unit training and research of the service complex is the Family Health Care Project of the medical school, which serves as a pilot experimental station for the testing of new teaching and organizational methods. The advantages to both the local group practice health centers and the medical school are more than theoretical.

Financial Group Practice

In the final analysis, the problems of paying for group or solo medical care are similar. This is so even though prepaid group practice plans are able to provide substantially greater benefits per premium dollar and even though the rate of hospitalization in the group plans is very much lower. The voluntary prepayment method, even when coupled with the efficiencies of group practice or organization, cannot finance the complete spectrum of needed preventive, therapeutic, rehabilitative, and custodial services. Neither can it provide for services to the poor, to the irregularly employed, or to migrant workers.

The answers must be found in a public and universal financing arrangement that uses the methods of social insurance and tax support. Group health experience demonstrates the advantages of rational *organization* of services rather than the solution of the problem of *financing* the full costs of such care.[12, 13]

CONCLUSION

My thesis is that both the concept and the design of group practice require modification if protective health services are to attain greater relevance to the needs of contemporary society. The essential new elements of the proposed model are: 1) the primary health care team, 2) the local community health center, 3) the functional continuum of long-term care, 4) the regionalized system of affiliation between the health center, hospital, and teaching institution, 5) consumer involvement in the design of programs, and 6) relation to a universal system of financing which supports a single standard of care for all.

Quite obviously there is nothing really new in this formulation. The entire model (except for aspects of the financing mechanism) was proposed by the Committee on the Costs of Medical Care in 1932 and its main features have been reproposed by most of the study commissions appointed since then.[3-7] The reports presented at this conference have described key elements of the total pattern which are now in successful operation. Important lessons must be learned from experiences closely related to regionalized health centers in other countries.[27] The need now is for a functional synthesis of the best elements of these experiences.

Perhaps, then, group practice will fulfill the primary criterion for success in innovation: the new idea must be, in the first instance, relevant to the social needs of its time.

NOTES

1. H. E. Sigerist, *Medicine and Human Welfare* (New Haven, Yale Univ. 1941).
2. J. L. Schwartz, *Medical Plans and Health Care* (Springfield, Ill., Thomas, 1968).

3. Committee on the Costs of Medical Care. *Medical Care for the American People.* (Chicago, University of Chicago Press, 1932).
4. American Public Health Association; Subcommittee on Medical Care. The quality of medical care in a national health program, *Amer. J. Public Health 39* (1949) 898–924.
5. American Medical Association. Report of the commission on medical care plans, Larson Report, Part 1. *A.M.A. 94* (1955), 54–65.
6. Public Health Service, Division of Medical Care Administration. *Promoting the Group Practice of Medicine,* Report of the National Conference on Group Practice, U.S. Department of Health, Education and Welfare (Washington, D.C. Government Printing Office, 1967).
7. *Report of the National Advisory Commission on Health Manpower,* Volume I (Washington, D.C., Government Printing Office, 1967.
8. American Association of Medical Clinics, American Medical Association and Medical Group Management Association. *Group Practice: Guidelines to Forming or joining a Medical Group* (Alexandria, Va., American Association of Medical Colleges, 1967).
9. L. S. Reed, A. H. Anderson, and R. S. Hanft, *Independent Health Insurance Plans in the United States—1965 Survey,* Social Security Administration, Research Report No. 17 (Washington, D.C., Government Printing Office, 1966).
10. M. A. Morehead, *Geographic Distribution and Organization of Manpower and Facilities for High Quality Health Care.* 1968 National Health Forum, Los Angeles (New York, National Health Council, 1968).
11. A. Shadid, *A Doctor for the People* (New York, Vanguard, 1939).
12. E. R. Weinerman, "Essentials of a Successful Group Health Plan." *Information Letter,* Cooperative Health Association of America (October 1951).
13. ——— An appraisal of medical care in group health centers. *Am. J. Public Health, 46* (1956), 300–09.
14. ——— Medical care in prepaid group practice. *Arch. Environ. Health 6* (1961), 47–59.
15. ——— Patients' perceptions of group medical care. *Amer. J. Public Health 54* (1964) 880–89.
16. E. M. Burns, "Policy Decisions Facing the United States in Financing and Organizing Health Care." *Public Health Rep. 81:*675–83, 1966.
17. Medical Economics Continuing Survey. "Physicians' Economic Health: Excellent." *Med. Econ.* (December 13, 1965) 75–127.
18. D. G. Hay, "Independent health insurance plans, 1961 survey. *Social Security Bulletin 26* (1963), 3–11.
19. E. Freidson, *Patients' Views of Medical Practice* (New York, Russell Sage, 1961).
20. Committee for the Special Research Project in the Health Insurance Plan of Greater New York. *Health and Medical Care in New York City.* (Cambridge, Harvard University Press, 1957).
21. P. M. Densen, E. W. Jones, E. T. Balamuth, S. Shapiro, "Prepaid medical care and hospital utilization in a dual choice situation," *Amer. J. Public Health, 50* (1960), 1710–726.
22. E. R. Weinerman, Research into the organization of medical prac-

tice. "Health Services Research II, *Milbank Mem. Fund Quart.* 44: 1966, 104–45, Part 2.
23. A. Silver, *Family Medical Care* (Cambridge, Harvard University Press, 1963).
24. J. S. Beloff, and E. R. Weinerman, "Yale studies in family health care: I. Planning and pilot test of a new program. "*J.A.M.A. 199* (1967) 383–89.
25. J. H. Sloss, W. R. Young, and E. R. Weinerman, Health maintenance in prepaid group practice: I. Planning and early development of a project at the community health foundation in Cleveland." *Med. Care 6* (1968), 215–30.
26. Citizens Committee on Graduate Medical Education. *The Graduate Education of Physicians,* Millis Report (Chicago, A. M. A., 1966).
27. E. R. Weinerman, "Organization of Health Services in Eastern Europe." *Med Care 6* (1968).

For Further Reading

Health Manpower

Baker, Timothy D., and Mark Perlman, *Health Manpower in a Developing Economy: Taiwan, A Case Study in Planning* (Baltimore, The Johns Hopkins Press, 1967).

Cherkasky, Martin, "Medical Manpower Needs in Deprived Areas," *The Journal of Medical Education,* 44 (February, 1969), 126–131.

Darley, Ward, and Anne R. Somers, "Medicine, Money and Manpower—The Challenge to Professional Education;" I. "The Affluent New Health-Care Economy;" II. "Opportunity for New Excellence;" III. "Increasing Personnel," *New Eng. Jrl. of Medicine,* 276 (June 1, June 8, June 22, 1967), 1234–1238, 1291–1296, 1414–1422.

Elling, Ray H., "Occupational Group Striving and Administration in Public Health," in Mary Arnold, L. Vaughn Blankenship and John Hess, eds., *Administering Health Systems* (Chicago, Aldine • Atherton, 1971).

Fein, Rashi, *The Doctor Shortage, An Economic Diagnosis.* (Washington, D.C., The Brookings Institution, 1967).

Field, Mark G., "Health Personnel in the Soviet Union: Achievements and Problems," *Am. Jrl Pub. Health,* 56 (November, 1966), 1904–1920.

Freidson, Eliot, "Paramedical Personnel" in *International Encyclopedia of the Social Sciences* (New York, Macmillan and Free Press, 1968), V. 10, pp. 114–120.

221

———— *Professional Dominance, The Social Structure of Medical Care* New York, Atherton, 1970.

Friedman, Milton, *Capitalism and Freedom* (Chicago, University of Chicago Press, 1962).

Ginzberg, Eli, with Miriam Ostow, *Men, Money and Medicine* (New York, Columbia University Press, 1970).

Fry, Hilary G., in collaboration with William P. Shepard and Ray H. Elling, *Education and Manpower for Community Health* (Pittsburgh, University of Pittsburgh Press, 1967).

Garbarino, Joseph E., "Price Behavior and Productivity in the Medical Market," *Industrial and Labor Relations Review.* 13 (October, 1959), 3–15.

Godber, George E., "The Future Place of the Personal Physician," The 1969 Michael M. Davis Lecture. University of Chicago, Center for Health Administration Studies.

Hughes, Everett C., *Men and Their Work* (Glencoe, Ill., The Free Press, 1958).

Judek, Stanislaw, *Health Manpower in Canada* (Ottawa, Royal Commission on Health Services, 1964).

Levin, Lowell S., *Study of Manpower Needs in the Basic Health Sciences* (Washington, D.C., Federation of American Societies for Experimental Biology, 1963), 3 Vols.

Morris, J. N., "Tomorrow's Community Physician," *The Lancet* (October 18, 1969), 811–816.

Office of Health Economics, *Medical Manpower* (London, 1966), No. 20.

Silver, George A., "New Types of Personnel and Changing Roles of Health Professionals," in *New Directions in Public Policy for Health Care, Bulletin of the New York Academy of Medicine,* 42 (December, 1966), 1217–1225.

Standish, Seymour, "The Work-up of Olive Gray," *Medical Opinion and Review* (April, 1969), 58–64.

Strauss, Anselm, *et. al.* "The Negotiated Order," in E. Freidson, ed., *The Hospital in Modern Society* New York: Macmillan (Free Press), 1963), pp. 147–169.

Taylor, Carl E., Rahmi Dirican and Kurt Deuschle, *Health Manpower Planning in Turkey* (Baltimore, The Johns Hopkins Press, 1968).

Wise, Harold B., "The Family Health Worker," *American Journal of Public Health,* 58 (October, 1968), 1828–1838.

GROUP PRACTICE

Brindle, J. K., "Prospects for Prepaid Group Practice," pp. 37–45 and the following "Commentaries" by F. D. Mott, T. H. Tulchinsky, and G. K. MacLeod and "Response" by I. S. Falk in *Medical Care: The Current Scene and Prospects for the Future, Part II, American Journal of Public Health* 59 (January, 1969).

Falk, L. A., G. J. Mushrush and M. E. Skrivanek, *Administrative Aspects of Prepaid Group Practice,* an annotated bibliography. Pittsburgh: University of Pittsburgh Press, 1963.

Feldman, Louis L., *"Organization of a Medical Group Practice Pre-payment Program in New York City."* Health Insurance Plan of Greater New York (mimeo.).

Freidson, Eliot, "Medical Care and the Public: Case Study of a Medical Group," *Annals of the American Academy of Political and Social Science,* 346 (1963), 57–66.

Freidson, Eliot, and John N. Mann, "Organizational Dimensions of Large-Scale Group Medical Practice," *Am. Jrl. Pub. Health* 61 (April, 1971) 786–795.

Freidson, Eliot, and B. Rhea, "Processes of Control in a Company of Equals," *Social Problems,* 11 (1962), 119–131.

MacColl, W. A., *Group Practice and Pre-payment of Medical Care* (New York, Public Affairs Press, 1966).

Makover, Henry, "The Quality of Medical Care: Methodology of a Survey of Medical Groups Associated with the Health Insurance Plan of Greater New York," *Am. Jrl. Pub. Health,* 41 (July, 1961), 824–832.

The New York Academy of Medicine, *Group Practice: Problems and Perspectives, Bulletin of the Academy,* 44 (November, 1968).

Roemer, M. I., "Group Practice: A Medical Care Spectrum," *The Journal of Medical Education,* 40 (December, 1965), 1154–1158.

Rosen, George, "Provision of Medical Care; History, Sociology, Innovation," *Public Health Reports,* 74 (March, 1959), 199–209.

Rothenberg, R. E., Karl Richard, and Joel Rothenberg, *Group Practice and Health Insurance in Action* (New York, Crown, 1949).

Stern, Bernhard J., *Social Factors in Medical Progress* (New York, Columbia University Press, 1927).

Weinerman, E. Richard, "Patients' Perceptions of Group Medical Care," *American Journal of Public Health,* 54 (June, 1964) 880–889.

V Interorganizational Relations and Planning

A vast array of medical knowledge, personnel, and resources must often be applied to the health problems of patients, families, and larger social units. In the United States, these resources are presented through a myriad of agencies and programs. Two decades ago an investigation in a semi-urban county of West Virginia found several hundred health agencies of possible direct relevance to the care of members of a family.[1] If anything, the numbers of agencies have increased since then. These numerous organizations (hospitals, clinics, medical practices, nursing homes, social service agencies, specific-disease voluntary agencies, local health department) are subject to different control structures, receive their support from different sources, cover different areas, and are accepted and used in varying degrees by different members of the population. While all these health and related welfare organizations are subject to limits imposed by broad social approval, or legitimation, which is based largely

225

on uninformed public images of the extent to which they are rendering good care, these outside impressions leave great latitude for mixed quality, competition, even conflict, among agencies and programs.

But this is in the best tradition of this country. It is sometimes called "the American voluntary way." A social and political philosophy of free enterprise and competition lie behind this outlook. The market is seen as the most appropriate distribution mechanism and it should be left to operate without hindrance, even in the medical realm.[2] Halberstam would wish to continue practicing without direction from central or regional planning and control structures.

Since the relevant elements of care are expanding and the bulk of problems requiring care are shifting to the more complex ones of chronic disease, the often referred to "crisis in health care" can be attributed in significant part to the increasing lack of coordination of care. Several elements are involved: (1) The care of individuals is not meshed with preventive efforts directed to population units. (2) Care of individuals often lacks *comprehensiveness*—doing all that needs to be done to (a) avoid, mitigate, or erase disability; (b) prevent or cure specific disease; (c) relieve discomfort; (d) alleviate emotional distress; and (e) postpone premature death. (3) *Continuity* of care often suffers—the pursuit of all necessary efforts in a logical order. In part, the problems of coordination can be attributed to interoccupational group struggles and manpower shortages. But in significant degree they are due to interorganizational competition over support and general position in the health care complex.

Wysong and Eichhorn examine this problem sphere with special attention to organizational domains and breadth of agency interest in serving tuberculosis patients. They suggest the need for serious efforts to undertake and evaluate organizational innovations that might have a better chance of providing continuity and comprehensive care.

I see a complete reordering of the myriad of agencies and programs in our present highly fractionated health system as politically and practically impossible. The suggested approach is based on seeking new concerting forces to reshape the present system. The plan combines some elements of decentralized populism with centralized public control and advice of a professional, scientific sort. In addition to a compulsory national health insurance, the two main components to be added to regionalize the present system and make the best use of existing facilities and other resources are (1) consumer-controlled local-neighborhood-centers (the periphery of the regional system); and (2) consumer-controlled regional health services boards (the center).

Illich's provocative piece brings us up short. By examining the situation in "developing" countries, he reminds us that overall health planning goals are inextricably bound up with the general conditions and directions of a society.

In Peru there are approximately 5,500 physicians for a population of some 14 million. There are fewer nurses than physicians. With 60 per cent of all "scientifically trained" health workers located in Lima, it is clear that major portions of the largely rural population go without the benefits of modern medicine.

Similarly, in the United States, urban ghetto dwellers, rural residents, particularly migrant farm laborers, and others are without easy access to the services of well trained health workers —this in spite of the growing public demand for good health care as a basic human right.

Effective approaches to planning health services are required. And health services can not be planned in isolation from the rest of the social, economic, cultural, political, and physical environmental context. The provision of funds through a compulsory health insurance system is only one, perhaps minor, aspect of a socialized system of medicine designed to achieve high marks on the several dimensions of care that I identify in my chapter. The fundamental problem under which all others are subsumed is one of developing the appropriate human systems and relationships so that all men will benefit from available and developing medical knowledge, skills, and resources as these can be suitably applied in a given context. Illich underlines this understanding through his focus on "developing" countries. His article makes us think seriously of really significant alternatives. His piece should disabuse us of blind attempts simply to replicate the traditional.

NOTES

1. Milton I. Roemer and Ethel A. Wilson, *Organized Health Services in a County of the United States*. Washington, D.C.: U.S. Public Health Service Publication No. 197, 1952.
2. Milton Friedman, *Capitalism and Freedom*. Chicago: University of Chicago Press, 1962.

10

The Health Services Complex: Inter-Agency Relations in the Delivery of Health Services

JERE A. WYSONG*
ROBERT L. EICHHORN*

There are remarkable similarities between the ways in which Americans solve the problems of providing health services and their solutions to the problems of making war, making money, or governing the society. In the medical sector, as in the economic, political, and military sectors, problem solving is increasingly the province of the specialist and the computer. Specialization in medicine is obvious (33 distinct specialties are listed in the American Medical Directory), but the increasing division of labor is particularly striking in the increasing numbers of new kinds of paramedical personnel. More and more, the doc-

* Ph.D., Assistant Professor, Department of Sociology, The Ohio State University.
* Ph.D., Professor of Sociology, Purdue University and Immediate Past Deputy Associate Director for Program Development, National Center for Health Services Research and Development, Health Services and Mental Health Administration, Department of Health, Education, and Welfare.

tor's services are supplemented and extended by the laboratory technician, the social worker, the nursing aids, the medical record technician, the inhalation therapist, the engineer, and the medical librarian. In 1967, 3.4 million people were employed in the health occupations and services in the United States; yet only 200,000 of these were physicians actively involved in patient care.[1] Further, in the best hospitals and clinics, these specialists and technicians are aided by an impressive and varied assortment of machines and computers for data processing, record management, laboratory tests, patient monitoring systems, and other tasks. Within perhaps five or ten years, automated in-patient and out-patient medical care systems will be developed, and the doctor will be assisted in history-taking, diagnosis, treatment, and followup by a computer console in his own office.

Yet while medicine is like the economy or military in the importance of specialization and automation—indeed, many of the new computer techniques now being applied to the problems of medicine were first developed to further economic or military activities—the striking difference between them is the lack of centralization or consolidation of activities. In the economy, the trend is toward increasing consolidation of activities through conglomerate mergers; in the polity, through the growth and expansion of a massive federal bureaucracy; in the military, through reorganization and expansion of the Defense Department since World War II. In contrast, the health services complex in the United States is an elaborate and loosely-knit structure of thousands of autonomous units, and while these units are dependent on each other for goal achievement, no single organization or group of organizations has the power to direct or coordinate their activities.

These units range in size and complexity from county health departments with a part-time physician and full-time nurse to the Public Health Service with 25,000 employees. Included among the providers of health services are 146,470 doctors in solo practice and approximately 1,600 medical groups enrolling 14,850 physicians. They care for their patients in the 13,500 hospitals of the United States, refer them to the 19,000 nursing homes, and are reimbursed most often through the facilities of 1,045 insurance companies, the 75 Blue Cross-Blue Shield Plans, or the hundreds of state and local medical assistance plans. (All states include Medicare; some include Medicaid.) These private efforts are supplemented by public health organizations in 50 states, with 100 distinct state health districts, 1,600 city and country health departments, and thousands of school health departments and voluntary organizations. Even in the area of health planning, there is decentralization and autonomy. In the difficult task of health planning, the state organizations and Public Health Service are joined by more than 60 areawide health facility planning agencies.[2]

The major difficulty with the organization of health services is not, however, that it is elaborate and decentralized, but that it is cumbersome, unplanned, and uncoordinated. The results are duplication of facilities and services, higher costs, delays and difficulties in obtaining services for individual clients, gaps in service, and an inability to respond effectively and quickly to changing health needs.[3] In effect, neither skills, facilities nor records are fully integrated in the service of the community. As Herman and Anne Somers remark: "In medical care, as in other spheres of activity, the scientific and technological revolutions and their far-flung implications have not yet been organizationally assimilated."[4] Significantly, many of the most recent innovations in health care services, such as the Regional Medical Programs or Model City Projects, are attempts to rationalize the organization of health services.

Organization, then, is the "perilous imperative."[5] The most difficult task for health planners in the United States, however, is not simply to organize the health services complex, but to choose between alternate forms of organization. If reorganization of health services is to be meaningful and effective, it must be based on an adequate understanding of the factors that now govern the relationships between health units. The argument here is that the structure of these relationships at the community level is now largely determined by the existence of independent sources of support and general agreements on organizational domains and by variations among organizations in the scope of their interest in clients.

ORGANIZATIONAL DOMAINS

In the local community setting, relationships among health units are governed primarily by agreements or prescriptions on organizational domains. Among service organizations, in general, organizational goals are usually announcements of an intention to produce some change in clients; domains indicate what specific organizations or groups may legitimately do to or with clients to bring about these changes. As Levine and White suggest, in the health field domains specify the disease covered by an organization, the population served, and the services rendered.[6] The set of activities an organization may and may not engage in are often defined by law. In most states, for example, local health departments are given the power to hospitalize recalcitrant tuberculosis patients forcibly, but tuberculosis hospitals or physicians do not have this power. Domains are also limited by informal agreements among organizations and professional groups. Local medical societies encourage TB associations and school health departments to test school children for tuberculosis but usually prohibit them from prescribing prophylactic drugs for those who are found to be infected. Since most organizations are in effect surrounded by the domains of others, these formal and informal agreements act as constraints on their behavior, not only on what they do, but also on where they may refer patients when their own task is completed.

The domains of health agencies are largely determined throuth the interaction of economic and political forces in the organization's environment, and to survive and function, a health agency must gain both economic support and political acceptance in its environment. The domains of health organizations and professionals, then, are delineated primarily through the joint influence of support and control structures; of state legislatures, county councils, Community Chest or United Appeal Agencies, licensing boards, local and state medical societies, and numerous other organizations. Any attempt to reorganize health services necessarily also involves those organizations that support and control health organizations.[7]

A COMMUNITY CASE STUDY

In 1966, the Institute for the Study of Social Change at Purdue University began a longitudinal study of the organization of health services for tuberculosis control in the Calumet Region of Indiana.* The Calumet is Indiana's part of Chicago, three Northwestern Indiana counties that contain the world's second largest steel producing area, a population of 522,000, and two cities with more than 100,000 residents each. Four hundred sixty four private physicians and virtually all of the 158 health and welfare organizations in the area—three tuberculosis hospitals, seven local health departments, three tuberculosis associations, 11 general hospitals, 33 nursing homes, 44 township trustee poor relief offices, and 18 settlement houses and missions—were in some way involved in the elaborate process of tuberculosis control. In the Calumet, as throughout most of the United States, no single organization has the authority to coordinate the diverse activities of these organizations: detection, diagnosis, preventive care, therapy, medical supervision after hospitalization, and social welfare and economic aid. The relationships among the health units were determined by general agreements on organizational domains.

The American Medical Association and its constituent state and local societies have consistently and often successfully resisted the expansion of public health activities as invasions of the domain of private practice.[8] In most sections of the country, in fact, private physicians still have more expansive domains than any voluntary or public organization. Even in the area of tuberculosis control, which has been defined as a public health responsibility since the turn of the century, the private physician

* This study was supported by a research grant awarded by the Division of Community Health of the United States Public Health Service. The Study is reprinted in full in Robert L. Eichhorn and Jere A. Wysong, *Interagency Relations in the Provision of Health Services: Tuberculosis Control in a Metropolitan Region* (Lafayette, Ind., Institute for the Study of Social Change, Purdue University, 1968). The survey section of the study yielded information on 118 organizations and 226 physicians, although 52 questionnaires could not be used because they were incomplete.

234 : JERE A. WYSONG : ROBERT L. EICHHORN

has remained near the center of the referral system. In the Calumet both school health departments and tuberculosis associations routinely referred tuberculosis suspects to private physicians, rather than to public health departments or tuberculosis clinics. In 1967 the potential referrals for physicians included 94,000 school children who were tuberculin tested, and 45,000 people who were X-rayed. Except for the indigent who were served at public health clinics, all preventive care was rendered by private physicians, and admission to the tuberculosis hospital or adjacent clinic usually required a letter or phone call from the prospective patient's personal doctor. In general, Calumet physicians who were interviewed in the study defended these prerogatives and opposed any alteration in the referral system.* Eighty-one percent thought that people whose X-ray on a mobile unit bus was "suspicious" should be referred to their family doctor rather than to a health department or tuberculosis clinic. Fifty-six percent rejected the idea that *all* tuberculin testing, X-raying, record keeping, and treatment of tuberculosis should be done by one organization. And 55 percent believed that the federal government should not intervene in the resolution of local public health problems. The local medical societies' committees on school health services, public health, and communicable diseases generally worked to protect the majorities' attitude toward the sanctity of their domain.

The existence of well-defined and generally understood organizational domains is, of course, an important source of order in interorganizational relationships. Without some such agreements the health professional's problems in locating services for clients with specific needs would be almost insurmountable. At the same time, however, the existence of these agreements may be an im-

* Both private physicians and agency directors were asked the following questions, which provide the basis for Table I: 1) Private physicians can treat tuberculosis just as well as any other disease they encounter: a. agree; b. disagree. 2) When TB patients are discharged from the hospital, they should be placed under the supervision of: a. their family doctor; b. the local health department; c. the local TB Association; d. a TB clinic associated with the hospital. 3) It would be an improvement if ALL tuberculin testing, X-raying, recordkeeping, and treatment of TB were done by one organization: a. agree; b. disagree. 4) Public health problems should be solved by local agencies without the aid of the federal government: a. agree; b. disagree.

portant barrier in organizational innovation to meet changing health needs or to incorporate advances in medical knowledge into medical practice.

In the Calumet the Lake County Tuberculosis Hospital and Clinic adopted the Public Health Service's recommendation that all positive reactors receive prophylactic Isoniozid. Yet the area's private physicians clearly did not follow that policy in their own practice. A follow-up study on positive reactors who were referred to their private physicians by the region's largest school system indicated that only 40 percent of the reactors actually saw a doctor, and that 53 percent of those who did see a physician were told by their doctor that Isoniozid therapy was not necessary. On the basis of this study, the medical directors of the hospital and school system proposed to the public health committee of the local medical society that local health departments should assume the responsibility for both tuberculin testing and preventive therapy in school programs. After four months of deliberation on this proposal to reorganize health services, the committee rejected the proposal and left the task of preventive care to private physicians.

In the final analysis, the stability and survival of any society or portion of a society depends upon the continual affirmation of its legitimacy. Serious and widespread doubts about legitimacy are a prelude to social change and even to revolution. Among health professionals, the legitimacy of existing agreements on organizational domains is judged primarily in terms of whether they are thought to produce a high quality of care for those in need.

In the Calumet, as a result of the school survey and several meetings of public health personnel, the questioning was focused on whether private physicians were able to provide a high quality care for tuberculosis patients. In February 1967, 89 percent of the directors of 112 health and welfare agencies there agreed in a survey that private physicians could not treat tuberculosis so well as other diseases they encountered. As a result several major changes in organizational domains occurred. The Lake County Tuberculosis Hospital expanded its services to include out-patient facilities for post-hospital patients, and the two largest school systems in the area began routinely to refer all positive reactors to the hospital clinic. In addition, with the aid of a grant

TABLE 10.1: *Private Physicians' Attitudes toward Consolidation of Tuberculosis Control Activities**

	Uncritical Physicians		Critical Physicians	
	N	Percent	N	Percent
Favor placing discharged hospital patients under supervision of public health organization, rather than family doctor	(22)	43.1	(83)	65.4
Favor centralization of tuberculosis control activities in one organization	(18)	35.3	(62)	48.8
Do not oppose federal intervention in local health problems	(18)	35.3	(62)	48.8
Total N	(51)		(127)	

* This table is a summary of responses to three separate questions. The total number of respondents for each question are the same and only positive responses are reported here. The negative responses may be obtained by subtraction from the base figures (51 and 127).

from the Public Health Service, the hospital added a satellite tuberculosis clinic located in the region's largest city. In a climate of doubt about existing agreements on organizational domains, a tuberculosis hospital became a tuberculosis control center.

The skepticism of public health professionals was apparently contagious: many private physicians in the region began to doubt their own competence to treat tuberculosis. In the February, 1967 survey, 71 percent of them disagreed with the proposition that private physicians can treat tuberculosis as well as any other disease they encounter. Further, these reservations about their own competence were associated with a tendency to favor expansion of public health activities in the area of tuberculosis control.* As Table 10.1 indicates, the critical physicians were

* The questions listed above were answered by 178 of the 226 physicians. The responses of these physicians cannot be assumed to be completely representative of all doctors in the area, of course. On the other hand, a follow-up study of nonrespondents indicated that the study did include most physicians who had any experience with tuberculosis.

more likely than other doctors to approve placing discharged hospital patients under the supervision of a public health unit rather than a private physician and to centralize tuberculosis control activities in one organization. While the majority of physicians remained opposed to federal intervention in local health problems, those with doubts about the private physician's competence were somewhat less opposed. These doubts on the part of the area's doctors explain to some extent why there was little organized resistance from the local medical society to the hospitals expansion. Ultimately, any defense of an organizational or professional domain rests first on the conviction that the existing arrangements are right and necessary for the patient.

Because any reorganization of health services at the local or societal level necessarily involves alteration or disruption of the existing system of organizational domains, tradition and vested economic and organizational interests are significant barriers to reorganization. However, reorganization of health services also includes a critical evaluation of competence to provide high quality care, and in an era when quality care is intimately related to medical specialization and elaborate technology, those who have the knowledge and technology will claim that they have a legitimate right to treat the patient. Tuberculosis control is currently one of the relatively few areas where the public health sector can claim such a right with little dispute. The shape of the future depends in part at least on the extent to which public health organizations and professionals expand these claims in other areas.

ORGANIZATIONAL INTERESTS

The existence of agreements on organizational domains only determines the structure of the relationships between health units. It does not guarantee that such relations will occur between specific organizations, nor indicate what the content or frequency of the contacts will be. For example, a tuberculosis hospital is not obligated by law or tradition to seek help for clients or to engage in joint planning with another organization, but if it does, the existence of organizational domains indicates where it should seek help or counsel. In part, the factor that de-

termines whether health organizations actually do reach out to
other agencies and coordinate their own work with them is the
nature of their interests in clients. In general, when an organization's interest in clients is comprehensive and extended, an impe-
tus exists for developing interorganizational relationships. Lefton
and Rosengren distinguish between the longitudinal and lateral
interests of organizations, between an organization's interest in
the "biographical career" and "life space" of its clients.

> ". . . organizations have contrasting interests in their clients.
> Furthermore, these organizational interests in the 'client biogra-
> phy' may range from a highly truncated span of time, as for
> example, in the emergency room of a general hospital to an al-
> most indeterminate span of time as a long term psychiatric
> facility or a chronic illness hospital. There is, moreover, a second
> range of interests which considers the client not in terms of
> biographical time, but rather in terms of biographical space.
> That is, organizations may have an interest in only a limited
> aspect of the client as a person—as in the case of a short-term
> general hospital—whereas other organizations may have a more
> extended interest in who the client is as a product of and par-
> ticipant in society—as in the case of a psychiatric out-patient
> clinic.[9]

Organizational interest in clients varies in health units: interest may be limited to only those health problems that can be
legitimately treated by the organization or interest may extend beyond what the agency itself is able to do. Health and welfare organizations in the Calumet area displayed the entire range. The
three welfare departments, the tuberculosis hospitals, school
health departments, nursing homes, settlement houses, and missions were characterized as having a broad lateral interest in
clients—in their family relations, educational needs, psychological characteristics, and future plans, as well as their immediate
medical and economic problems. Private physicians, however,
were much more likely to confine their interests to only the medical problems of their patients, and the general hospitals and
township poor–relief offices were concerned only with the immediate problems of the poor and the sick.

In any large and elaborate complex of health organizations and professions the coordination and integration of services depends on the day-to-day contacts between organizations to seek help for patients and, on joint planning sessions. For Calumet organizations and physicians these contacts for help and planning were significantly influenced by the nature of their interest in clients. Organizations with narrow lateral or short-term longitudinal interests in clients were generally isolated from other community health organizations and professionals. Only 15 percent had contacts with many other organizations, although fifty-five percent with comprehensive and extended interests had both many short-term and many enduring relationships.* (See Table 10.2.) While contacts for planning were rare for all organizations, 37 percent of those with broad interests indicated more contacts with other organizations for planning purposes. Private physicians were less influenced by their view of patients than were the agencies, but lateral interests also significantly affected their relationships. (See Table 10.3.) Seventy percent of the doctors with narrow interests in patients had fewer than six contacts with other doctors and agencies to seek help for clients; only 35 percent of those with broader interests had so few contacts.

For the patient, the lack of coordination of health services has real and enduring consequences. Where agencies do not assist clients in contacting the organization to which they have been referred, for example, clients often do not complete the journey from one agency to another, but simply "disappear" in the maze of organizations. In the Calumet, however, the consequences of the lack of coordination of health services were most dramati-

* The lateral interests of organizations and physicians were operationally defined in terms of what they usually learn about their clients. Organizations or physicians that reported learning about fewer than three areas of the clients life space were classified as having a narrow interest; those with from three to five areas reported as having a medium lateral interest; and those with from six to eight areas reported as having a broad lateral interest. The question reads: In our work with clients, we usually learn about their: a. immediate medical problems; b. family relationships; c. other social relationships (e.g., work and neighborhood); d. economic problems; e. educational needs and experiences; f. psychological characteristics; g. plans and dreams.

TABLE 10.2: *Organizations Total Volume of Contacts with Other Organizations.*

| | To seek help | | | | | | To Plan | | | | | | Total | |
| | Low | | Medium | | High | | Low | | Medium | | High | | | |
LATERAL INTEREST	N	Percent	N	Percent	N	Percent	N	Percent	N	Percent	N	Percent	N	Percent
Narrow	(19)	70.4	(4)	14.8	(4)	14.8	(20)	74.1	(3)	11.1	(4)	14.8	(27)	100.0
Medium	(18)	38.3	(20)	42.6	(9)	19.1	(34)	72.3	(7)	14.9	(6)	12.8	(47)	100.0
Broad	(5)	13.1	(12)	31.6	(21)	55.3	(10)	26.4	(14)	36.8	(14)	36.8	(38)	100.0

TABLE 10.3: *Physicians' Total Volume of Contacts with Other Organizations*

| | To seek help | | | | | | To Plan | | | | | | Total | |
| | Low | | Medium | | High | | Low | | Medium | | High | | | |
LATERAL INTEREST	N	Percent	N	Percent	N	Percent	N	Percent	N	Percent	N	Percent	N	Percent
Narrow	(64)	70.3	(17)	18.7	(10)	11.0	(79)	86.8	(7)	7.7	(5)	5.5	(91)	100.0
Medium	(27)	45.8	(20)	33.9	(12)	20.3	(43)	72.9	(9)	15.3	(7)	11.8	(59)	100.0
Broad	(11)	35.5	(12)	38.7	(8)	25.8	(24)	77.4	(3)	9.7	(4)	12.9	(31)	100.0

cally apparent in the medical practice of private physicians. For example, the doctors' use of prophylactic drugs to treat TB was significantly influenced by their contact with the tuberculosis hospital. Only 37 of the private physicians in the survey reported any contact with tuberculosis hospitals for patient care planning. Of those without hospital contact, only 15 percent advised Isoniazid for tuberculous children. Yet 75 percent of those who engaged in planning with the hospital staff used the drug for the same problem.

Technical competence is absolutely essential to guarantee a high quality of medical care, but technical competence is not enough. In tuberculosis control—as in medical care in general—continuity and comprehensiveness of care are also crucial.[10] The data gathered in the Calumet area as well as in other areas of the United States, suggest that in the absence of coordinating councils or health and welfare exchanges, a partial integration of health services is achieved by those agencies that share broad and extended interests in their patients.* Yet is is also clear that the majority of agencies, professionals, and services are not integrated into a system of continuous and comprehensive care. Comprehensive care for patients can be implemented through increased contacts between organizations or expansion of the domain of an overall agency depending upon the legitimacy of the existing structure and based on broad and extended interests.

ALTERNATIVES FOR THE FUTURE

Relationships between the maze of health agencies and professionals in Calumet, as in the rest of the United States, are structured by agreements on organizational domains and motivated, in part, by interests in clients; but coordination of health services is only partially achieved. On the surface the solution seems rela-

* Levine and White found that hospitals with out-patient clinics had high rates of interaction with other agencies while those without clinics had low rates. They comment: "It may be that these two types of hospitals have different goals and that hospitals with clinics have a greater 'community' orientation and are more committed to the concept of 'comprehensive' care than are hospitals without clinics." See Levine and White, *op. cit.,* p. 592.

tively simple. Since interest in clients is a critical factor in the co-ordination of health services on the patient's behalf, the apparent solution is to educate health professionals toward the philosophy of comprehensive and continuous care and to provide coordinating councils or health and welfare exchanges to facilitate the exchange of patients, information, and plans. This should lead to the gradual and orderly coordination of health services without threatening the autonomy or interests of existing agencies and professional groups.

Here, however, the focus is on the coordination of existing health services and agencies based on the questionable assumption that the existing structure of health services is basically a sound one. It is not the product of a rational plan to control disease or serve the community but is instead, largely a reflection of the political divisions and powers in both the medical sector and the larger society. In most local communities the existing agreements on organizational domains are a product of the power and prestige of the private physician and his medical society vis-a-vis other health professionals. In most local areas, too, the geographical domains of public health departments or tuberculosis hospitals do not reflect either the distribution of the disease or the social organization of the larger community but rather the political subdivisions of township, city, county, and state.

One important measure for improvement in the delivery of health services, then, is the increasing consolidation of activities and powers in regional agencies that provide the entire range of basic health services. There are, of course, many attempts now being made to establish regional health districts or planning agencies. Unfortunately, most of these organizations do not have the power or resources to affect markedly the distribution of health services but are simply superstructures imposed on the existing organization of agencies and services; while the orientation of the agency is regional in nature, the region itself is usually determined by county and state boundaries rather than by the distribution of health problems or the social organization of the area. Finally, the existing regional agencies often confine their attention to one disease and are unable to deal effectively with the multiple health problems of the poor and the aged. Satellite clinics in ghetto areas that are limited to treatment of one disease such as tuberculosis are an improvement over the existing system, but their emphasis on one disease is incompatible with the interrelated health problems of ghetto populations. The major problems in the delivery of health services—particularly those in the urban ghetto—cannot be remedied until health planning is both regional in scope and comprehensive in service.

N O T E S

1. United States Department of Health, Education and Welfare, *Health Resources Statistics,* Public Health Service Publication No. 1509 (Washington, D.C., U.S. Government Printing Office, 1968), pp. 8–9.
2. *Ibid.,* p. 18 and p. 215; also see United States Department of Health, Education and Welfare, *Medical Groups in the United States, 1959,* Public Health Service Publication No. 1063 (Washington, D.C., U.S. Government Printing Office, 1963), pp. 9–10; Health Insurance Institute, *1967 Source Book of Health Insurance Data* (New York, Health Insurance Institute, 1967), pp. 46–47; United States Department of Health, Education and Welfare, *Directory of Local Health Units,* Public Health Service Publication No. 118 (Washington, D.C., U.S. Government Printing Office, 1966), Table I; American Medical Association, *Profiles in Planning* (Chicago, American Medical Association, 1965), p. 1.
3. See Avedis Donabedian and S. J. Axelrod, "Organizing Medical Care Programs to Meet Health Needs," *Annals of the American Academy of Political and Social Science,* 335 (September, 1961), 46–55; Walter Guzzardi, "What the Doctor Can't Order—but You Can," in W. Richard Scott and Edmund Volkart (eds.), *Medical Care: Readings in the Sociology of Medical Institutions* (New York, John Wiley and Sons, Inc., 1966); Herman and Anne Somers, *Doctors, Patients, and Health Insurance* (New York, Anchor Books, 1961); Harold Wilensky and Charles Lebeaux, "Conceptions of Social Welfare," in Mayer Zald (ed.), *Social Welfare Institutions: A Sociological Reader* (New York, John Wiley and Sons, Inc., 1965).
4. Somers and Somers, *op. cit.,* p. 93.
5. *Ibid.,* pp. 93–113.
6. Sol Levine and Paul White, "Exchange as a Conceptual Framework for the Study of Interorganizational Relations," *Administrative Science Quarterly,* 5 (March, 1961), 597.
7. See Ray Elling and Sandor Halebsky, "Organizational Differentiation and Support: A Conceptual Framework," *Administrative Science Quarterly,* 6 (Sept., 1961), 185–209.
8. Editors of the Yale Law Journal, "The American Medical Association: Power, Purpose, and Politics in Organized Medicine," in W.

Scott and E. Volkart (eds.), *Medical Care: Readings in the Sociology of Medical Institutions* (New York, John Wiley and Sons, Inc., 1966), p. 179.

9. Mark Lefton and William Rosengren, "Organizations and Clients: Lateral and Longitudinal Dimensions," *American Sociological Review,* 31 (December, 1966), 805.

10. Somers and Somers, *op. cit.,* pp. 28–37.

11 *The Local Health Center and the Regional Board*

RAY H. ELLING*

"Pure science" tends to be conservative with respect to the structure of society and the organization of health services. Edward S. Rogers takes sociology to task somewhat for not discovering "practical," finite things for public health personnel to manipulate. It is not particularly helpful, he says, "for social scientists to associate health and health services problems with such basic structural elements as social class, for "there is nothing very much that public health could be expected to do about the phenomenon of social stratification, or about 'social class' as a causative element. . ."[1]

Revision of a paper presented under the title, "Reorganizing the Health Services System, A Sociological Response to Edward S. Rogers." American Sociological Association Annual Meetings, San Francisco, September 1, 1969.

* Ph.D., Professor of Sociology and Head, Social Science Division, Department of Clinical Medicine and Health Care, School of Medicine, University of Connecticut. Currently on leave of absence as Chief, Behavioral Science Unit, Research Division, W.H.O. in Geneva.

245

Instead of shying away from basic change of social structure, the position is adopted here that we should study how human goals and actions develop and to do this we should employ descriptive studies of natural change situations, but in addition, we should design, set up, and evaluate significant efforts to change human goals and actions in desired directions—in short, study "what might be" as well as "what is" by attempting to create what might be and subjecting these attempts to systematic evaluation. This kind of effort will entail significant change in fundamental structures of society, including the class structure, if serious human problems associated with these structures are to be solved. The example of this kind of endeavor that follows illustrates the approach and should allow consideration of broad issues, problem-specific conceptual framework, and methodological issues. However, only certain aspects of these concerns can be covered here.

In an earlier paper, more attention was given the conditions supporting the successful design, enactment, and evaluation of planned change.[2] To develop any example of planned change, it is desirable to consider briefly the essential supportive conditions: (1) the change effort should be seen by its initiators and the ever enlarging circle of enactors as contributing to human well being in the short run as well as the long run; (2) a problem must exist and be recognized, that is, the initiators and relevant others must see a significant gap between ideals and realities; (3) those most concerned must admit to puzzlement about the best way to approach the ideal by altering undesirable realities or there will be no room for a departure from the usual; (4) adequate data on current relationships and promising theoretical formulations for reordering them should be in hand; (5) there must be a commitment to obtain rigorous measures over time in both experimental and control situations if theory is to be revised and knowledge gained about what happens and how it happens; and, finally, (6) the design- change- evaluation-effort must go on within a planning or societal framework that is responsive to the public as well as able to marshall the authority and support necessary to effect the desired change throughout the system designated in the design.

AN EXAMPLE OF PLANNED CHANGE

The Present Health System

A potential for generating movement is in part created by an analysis of problems or gaps in the existing system. This analysis also helps in formulating a theoretical solution. It is thus important to highlight several aspects of the present health system. (1) In spite of great and increasing expenditures for health, the problems of health services organization in this country are horendous, with only slow improvement or actual decline in indexes of effectiveness.[3] (2) Part of this picture seems attributable to a great number of already established, highly complex yet fractionated, and usually uncoordinated service organizations inappropriately involved in the prevention, treatment, and rehabilitation relevant to an individual and the population of which he or she is a member.[4] (3) Numerous network or planning organizations directed at the health services "establishment" to bring about comprehensiveness and coordination of services on a regional or areawide basis have failed for several reasons: competition (if not conflict) among themselves;[5] independent channels of organizational support and control structures; and striving of occupational groups in the health field to establish themselves with resultant "trained incapacities" and serious shortages or gaps in organization of health manpower on every hand.[7] (4) Both chronic disease and more specific acute health problems have been increasingly tied to environmental and general life conditions,[8] requiring that "public health. . .cross over into the new, uncharted territory of the molar, organismic administration of human affairs, or cease to be."[9]

Reorganizing the Periphery and the Center of the Region

It is the redesign of the interface between society and the health care system with which this example is concerned. We are especially concerned with the center of the regional health system and with the periphery where primary care is first entered. The most important and the most likely (possible or practical) place to begin the reorganization of health services is at the patient-population level, at the periphery of the system where persons first make contact for patient care. Possibly this should begin in "lower" class inner city areas. This strategy is adopted, first, because the most important problem in delivering health services can be confronted there (primary care for those in greatest need); second, it avoids the perhaps impossible political struggle of immediately and completely reorganizing the present back-up system, much of which is worth preserving. Finally, peripheral units such as proposed here can be expected to act as new concerting forces, bringing about a rational regionalization of the now fractionated and competing back-up structures, thus bringing about a more effective and efficient total health care system.

The establishment of regional health services planning boards is a second point of attack for rationalizing the present system. These central regional units will have several functions, but most important will be their dispersal of funds according to budgeted plans designed to cover all health services for the population of the region.

It should be clear that other levels of the health system are in need of redesign—national planning and coordinating structures, national financing mechanisms, preparation of health workers, and other service organizations. Still, these efforts will be more adequate if appropriately reorganized points of entry to the system and regional health boards are kept clearly in view.

Goals and Evaluation—The Dimensions of Good Health Care

If functioning well with respect to members of some geographically-located population, the health system should:

(a) Prevent disability through improving the quality of the environment and patterns of life.

(b) Increase the population's understanding of health problems and services and increase the understanding of health workers with respect to the real problems facing patients.

(c)   Achieve the patient's timely entry into care.

(d)   Generate satisfaction with care on the parts of both patients and providers.

(e)   Once the patient has entered the system, coordinate and provide care in a logical manner, according to the best current standards.

Each of these dimensions of care should be elaborated in a thorough discussion of effectiveness of care, a larger task than is possible here.[10] Since the last dimension may be more complex and difficult to measure, better understanding of it is suggested by realizing that it implies three questions: What is not done that should be done? What is done that should not be done? How do the appropriately performed services relate to one another? In addition, we must realize that an understanding of the patient as a person in a social environment (one environment being at home and another in the treatment setting) is essential if the patient's own contribution to the logic of the care process is to be made.

Although further elaboration of these dimensions of care would be desirable, the important points for present purposes are that they seem to suggest highly desirable thrusts, which are capable of measurement, for the system. In short, before–after (or during–later) and cross-population comparisons can be devised to "test," at least in a limited sense, the effectiveness of differently designed points or centers of first contact.[11]

Components of the Local Health Center and Their Functioning

A fully elaborated established theory of change would not only direct our attention to such broad categories as the control structure, the prestige-reward system, the division of labor and preparation for roles, physical setting and technology, information flow, and the group's ethos; it would fill in the specifics. But it may be that action will always precede theory, at least at the level of important detail. In any case, we are still at the stage where theoretical anticipations are minimal. Our abilities along these lines will grow out of the combination of actions and comparisons suggested here.

The overall character of the society may provide the real block to engaging in a planning approach of an experimental–feedback sort. Neither the advanced capitalistic society still espousing an ideology of individual enterprise, nor the doctrinaire communist society, nor the totalitarian society of the right may tolerate the approach suggested here. If so, we have done little other than call for a new society and a new sociology to go with it.

To achieve the goals identified earlier, particularly in a "lower" class inner city area (but possibly other areas as well), the following components of the local health center are proposed and their functions briefly identified.

COMMUNITY PARTICIPATION AND THE CONTROL STRUCTURE

This first component is pervasive in its effects. To help achieve an impact on the environment, increased sophistication of potential and actual recipients of care, patient satisfaction, as well as timely entry into care, a community organization component is included. This component should also contribute to the coordination and logical flow of the care process by encouraging the health worker to know the patient as a person in a social environment, thus allowing treatments appropriate to the patient's situation.

This component should also increase provider satisfaction over the long run by making preventive care and effective treatment more possible. Initially, guildlike ire and reluctance may be generated as heretofore exclusive prerogatives are shared. Discussing the South Bronx, Neighborhood Medical Care Demonstration (NMCD), which has been developed and directed by Harold Wise, Martin Cherkasky, writes:

> The providers of medical care no longer have the sole prerogative for decision-making and this is all to the good. Health planners cannot understand groups with problems and cultural determinants different from their own other than by engaging in the

most intimate collaborative planning and management of these joint health care enterprises. There have been over 150 meetings in the apartments of the people residing in the NMCD area, and we have begun that tortuous process necessary for building a sound relationship between our middle-class institutions and the ghetto. We have begun to understand this community, its priorities and needs. I do not have to tell you that this interrelationship is fraught with hazards and difficulties and frustrations almost beyond belief. There is only one point in favor of this process—it is essential.[12]

I want to emphasize that the fundamental aspect of this component is a well organized, hopefully representative group that shares significantly in the control, including the hiring and firing of personnel. It is possibly worth testing whether a citizen advisory component would be adequate. I hypothesize here that it will not be adequate. The basic theoretical reason for hypothesizing the importance of this component is that those in control play an important part in determining the norms by which people will be judged and receive self approbation. Positive reflexive self regard is important for appropriate participation in a social situation.[13]

If the population in the locale of concern is divided by distrust and numerous groups compete for person's identities and the power they can generate, this component will not be easy to establish.[14] The extent of this problem should be gauged through field work; this should determine the numbers of persons and size of budget devoted to community organization efforts. To develop this component, community organization personnel and health educators will be appropriate as long as they have avoided the "trained incapacities" Veblen so correctly identified with "professional" education.

The dialogue between citizen and health worker will generate a creative tension along a moving line between "lay" and "professional" competence.[15] It seems obvious that certain decisions such as hours of operation and locale of services fall primarily within the citizen realm, while others such as judgment of a physician's technical competence or use of resuscitation equipment or ordering of laboratory tests fall within the health workers' ken. With patience on both sides, a mutual increase in sophistication regarding health problems and their solution can be expected. The citizen will learn the true value and importance of well-founded expertise while exposing the ill-founded mystiques of some guildlike preserves (those health workers least certain of their knowledge base may be most uneasy about citizen-based control). The health worker will learn the abilities of citizens to recognize and contribute to the solution of health problems while exposing cultural and socioeconomic conditions that inhibit appropriate participation in the effective aspects of modern health care.

The local controlling group of citizens should evaluate achievements along the several dimensions of care identified above. This may be done through a research–evaluation component that feeds back general results, including the identification of problems in need of correction, to the staff and controlling body. The last dimension—the logic of the care process—covers those conditions, attitudes, and behaviors traditionally equated with the quality of care but is somewhat broader in conception in that patients as well as physicians and other health and welfare workers are seen as contributing (or not) to the logic of the care process. Certainly the medical expert should predominate in the panel or other evaluative procedure but it is not inappropriate to include lay persons as well as a range of health and welfare workers.

A final aspect of control can only be mentioned. As truly comprehensive regional health services planning and control structures are introduced, they should include citizen representatives from local health service center boards. This connection between periphery and regional center will contribute to the two-way flow of information and, once again, tend to orient the system toward the solution of problems existing at the point where patients first enter into care.

Beyond the control function, citizen participation should be elaborated as fully as the fundamental concerns and priorities of the population will allow. Health may not stand high. But it can be appropriately interpreted by community organizers and health educators as a sine qua non of other things. In short, if health is conceived as the ability to pursue a useful existence, then most other conditions—employment, housing, education, for example —are supportive of health or not. So conceived, health will have a high priority. This elaboration might take the form of citizen committees focused around health problems such as nutrition, lead poisoning, rat and vermin control, maternal and infant care, abortion and family planning. Some might focus around health service organization problems—preparation of health personnel and career opportunities; employee health programs; emergency services; the completeness, accessibility, and acceptability of services available in the locale and the region; communication across agency and professional boundaries, especially as regards the adequacy and use of records, including computerization; overcapitalization of major health facilities (for example beds and laboratories) versus getting care to the people through organized home care programs; screening programs. A legislative political action committee would be an appropriate extension.

Meeting rooms must be provided for this function, both in the service center and in satellite settings, depending on locale and population distribution.

THE PRESTIGE–REWARD SYSTEM

This complex topic, involving payments as well as other forms of reward, cannot be fully discussed here. It is important to hypothesize a few central conditions that will come as no surprise to students of medical care.

All services should be prepaid through public funds and available on request. If a comprehensive national system of prepayment comes into operation in the next few years, this condition will be met. Prepayment and avoidance of sudden and potentially sizable drain on the daily household budget is especially important for the poor but is a concern of all.

There are some difficult accounting problems to work out because of the shares due to back-up components (hospitals and other central treatment agencies, educational centers, and research groups); in general, reimbursement of the service center should be on a capitation basis for the target population, rather than on a fee-for-service basis. This will tend to orient and motivate toward prevention and rehabilitation, rather than limiting attention to acute care.

Staff, including physicians, should be salaried. This, again, will encourage a focus on the population and tend to avoid the "piece work," high turnover effects of entrepreneurial medicine.*

The physician closest to the front line of care (probably not a G.P., but a thoroughly trained general internist or general pediatrician in the case of children) whose focus is on coordinating the patient care process should receive a higher salary than backup specialists or administrative, teaching, or research physicians. This would tend to orient the system as a whole toward the periphery where care is entered and delivered, mitigating against the "boondocks" complex of much of the present system that shortchanges what should be the primary trust of the system: The delivery of good care to all members of the society.[16]

THE DIVISION OF LABOR AND PREPARATION OF PERSONNEL

Faced with shortages of appropriately prepared health manpower and the rigidities introduced by established occupational groups, enforced through licensure laws, accreditation criteria, and other means, we can do little more than suggest a principle to guide the health service center in this sphere: Persons with the *least* formal preparation suitable to performing a given task under adequate supervision should be assigned the task in question.[17] Computers and other machines should take over a number of tasks (and they will generate new ones). Patients generally have the least formal preparation of all, but can appropriately assume a wide range of preventive and other health tasks.

To bridge cultural gaps and expedite care through the bureaucratic back-up structures and help provide adequate discharge planning and follow-up, local residents should be employed and trained as community or family health workers. Provision must be made for further preparation and advancement when the interest and ability is shown.

---

* This hypothesized way of organizing payment of staff requires continuing careful evaluation. For counter evidence in a special situation, see C. A. Alexander, "The Effects of Change in Method of Paying Physicians: The Baltimore Experience," *American Journal of Public Health,* 57 (August, 1967), 1278–1289. For a broad overview of the problem, see the chapter by Roemer in this volume.

These workers should be assigned a number of dwelling units, perhaps 120 or so would not be too many for each team of two-family health workers to cover (using four persons per unit as an average), with the objective of contacting residents to develop a comprehensive health plan for each person. This may involve immunizations, eye glasses, corective surgery, etc. The diagnostic and other services of the system would be called upon as deemed appropriate by supervising nursing and physician personnel. Priority should be given to problems for which relatively firm knowledge and effective facilities and services are at hand.

A clinical–public health nurse who could move back and forth between the clinical environment and the community should supervise some four or six family health workers.

A well-prepared general internist (for adults) and pediatrician (for children) or a family practitioner (for both adults and children) should serve as the coordinator of the care process. This involves expert awareness of diagnostic, treatment, rehabilitative, and preventive possibilities available through the armamentarium of the region as well as an ability to relate in a humane way to the patient and his family. It is the coordinator of care who will be the architect of the person's health plan and provide supervision of progress toward its fulfilment. Depending upon the availability of physicians appropriately prepared and motivated to perform this crucial set of tasks, other persons or combinations of persons can be employed and prepared to serve the patient-care co-ordinating function.

Perhaps a single primary team would be composed of twelve family health workers, three clinical–public health nurses, an internist, and pediatrician. This group would cover a population of just under 4,000. A single health services center might include from one to six teams, depending on the population to be covered and access to the center.

Obviously, many specific functions will be performed by consultants and other specialists located in back-up structures (for example, hospitals, health departments), including those in surgery, laboratory medicine, obstetrics, and gynecology, psychiatry, dentistry, legal aid, social work, and so forth.

But the local center should include those in administration and record maintenance, well-child–play supervision (for which space and toys must be provided in the center), pharmacy, technicians, and possibly transportation. Housing and other problems with legal complications may be numerous enough to call for a lawyer as part of the local center staff. Community organizers and health educators were discussed above. Whether research and evaluation personnel should be included in each center or should be more centrally available is a matter to be decided by method and logistics. The probable best location would be with the semi-autonomous stance provided by a university-based health service research center responsive to the planning and service needs of the regional health services planning body.

Health personnel requiring more formal preparation should have curricula with equivalent elements or a common track so that those with the interest and ability can transfer from one set of functions to another (one occupational group to another) without loss of valuable months and years involved in starting preparation from the beginning. The mutual involvement of service agencies and community colleges and universities in a combination of on-the-job preparation and more formal work would be an important part of solving manpower problems of the region.

Regardless of the extent of formal preparation, it is hard to overemphasize the importance of practical, on-the-job training that will allow the student to integrate abstract material from several disciplines in the solution of concrete problems and teach the specifics of a set of tasks which are impossible to introduce in didactic or other classroom fashion.

PHYSICAL SETTING AND TECHNOLOGY

The key aspects in this sphere are effectiveness, accessibility, and attractiveness.

I am little able to comment on effectiveness. This concern applies mainly to often highly technical facilities and equipment as means to bring scientific knowledge to bear on the patient's problem. The more costly rarely utilized resources of this sort should be centralized and serve the region. Up-to-date facilities and equipment should be equally available to all persons throughout the region. If a given piece of equipment or service (for example, renal dialysis equipment as it first became available) is so costly that it cannot be provided to all, some decision body broadly representative of the population of the region should decide the receipt of this service on the basis of the person's wishes and social worth.

The peripheral service center should be located in the midst of the population to be served. This may involve a simple center or a center with satellites. Proximity to the population will prove particularly important in "lower" class inner city areas where the "life space" of many residents is largely organized around the neighborhood.

The service center should be connected with emergency and other acute back-up facilities by efficient transportation and communication means, including T.V.-telephones as these become available.

The center can be made attractive by incorporating ideas from citizens of the area and art works reflecting local cultural backgrounds and developments. Dingy or dilapidated facilities are not likely to be attractive regardless of the populations' cultures.

INFORMATION-FLOW

Some of the important ideas in this sphere include provision for continuing and other education, contribution to planning by all members of the system, incorporation in the care process of knowledge of the person in his sociocultural setting; maintenance of a problem-oriented data system, and maintenance of up-to-date patient records through the computer or other means. Time and space allow only a phrase or two in elaboration of these aspects. The most general notion involved is the two-way flow of information between periphery and back-up facilities.

Service of a specialized sort performed in the back-up facilities (at the center of the system) will be only as effective as allowed by knowledge of other procedures performed at the periphery and elsewhere in the system and knowledge of the person's social setting and prospects for flow-through and rehabilitation. Regionwide planning also requires information from the periphery regarding priority problems, concerns, and resources.

Suitable follow-through in the care process of a given patient at the periphery is dependent upon accurate and complete information on procedures performed in back-up facilities. Adequate care at the periphery generally is dependent upon the flow of

up-to-date information from the knowledge developing and
transmission components (generally the educational and research units such as the university health center).

For advice in emergency care and other consultation, access
to experts through T.V.-telephone or other means and a rapid
print-out of a patient's medical treatment record would be highly
desirable.

THE ETHOS

The health services center should be characterized by hopeful-
ness and a friendly humanitarian atmosphere.* There should be
a shared sense of direction toward prevention of disability and
improving the abilities of all persons in the population.

The cultures of the participating populations may contribute
to additional aspects of atmosphere. In many "lower" class,
urban ghetto areas, an air of informality and habit of direct
face-to-face exchange seem natural. In this same setting, success
in achieving the dimensions of care may be fostered by a readi-
ness to act in a present-oriented time perspective and in a general or unified way, rather than a future-oriented, highly specialized way.

THE REGIONAL HEALTH SERVICES PLANNING BOARD

Some of the components of the regional board have been suggested above—lay representation from local health center boards
to the regional health services planning body; a gradation of facilities from the more general at the periphery to the more special at the center; emphasis on in-service education; two-way
flow of information from periphery to center and return, with
emphasis on information reflecting gaps between ideals of care
and realities, especially as these are experienced by the patient at

* Sandra Blakeslee, "To Rural Negroes, Health Center is Hope,"
New York Times 119 (August 28, 1970) 34, an excellent description of
the Tufts Delta Comprehensive Community Health Center in North
Bolivar County, Mississippi. Started by Dr. Jack Geiger in 1965, the
center is now directed to a significant degree by local citizens. The center's
efforts have expanded beyond traditional medical concerns to the open-
ing of a brick factory, a canning factory, and cooperative farms so that
employment and living conditions in this extremely poor area would
improve.

the point of entry into care; and two-way flow of patients, personnel, and certain facilities and resources (for example, laboratory test materials and results, mobile special equipment). These components were explicitly recognized or implied in the first, largely enduring conception of a regionalized system.[19]

The planning, support, and control functions require brief special mention in recognition of the myriad independent agencies and programs to be coordinated on the American scene. (1) the planning function has to be provided for in terms of staff, budget, and space. Planning is a cost of the system but can be expected to contribute toward greater social benefit. (2) This planning function must be directly tied to the flow of influence in the system. Thus, the effective power structure of the region must be involved and effective "lower" class power blocks included if their needs and desires are to be adequately met. The planning must go on in relation to the flow of influence, not as a detached, purely "expert" function. (3) All support for capital expenditures, provision of services, preparation of personnel and research—whether from federal, state, local governmental or private sources—should flow to the region on a prepaid per capita basis through the regional health services planning body to agencies and programs throughout the region, including the local neighborhood health centers as described above. (Obviously, some research, training, and production of biologicals, etc. will be supported outside regional systems). Funds should be distributed in the region through a budget presentation and defense procedure. (4) The regional health services planning body should derive its authority through law as a public entity governed by a combination of directors, some publicly elected at large for specified terms (as is the case now for regional school boards) and some elected from local neighborhood health boards. (5) There should be a technical advisory board made up of health professionals and scientists appointed by the regional health services planning body. (6) In each region there should be a semi-autonomous health services research and evaluation center established under university auspices, financed in significant part through the regional health services planning body.

In terms of political theory, my faith is placed in a system of governance for the regional health services that combines some elements of decentralized populism, some of laissez faire individualism and some centralized public control with professional scientific advice. This strikes me as the most likely effective combination for the easily foreseeable future considering the highly fractionated character of the present system. Perhaps the heavier weight is placed on citizen control at the local level where health services are first experienced and the rest of the system is effectively brought to bear (or not). Room is assured for individual spontaneity and innovative group approaches through a focus on meeting problems at the periphery and through provision of special funds for innovation and demonstration. Public accountability is encouraged through election of local health center boards and election of the at-large members of the regional health services board. Central channeling of support and control through budget presentation and defense by local health centers, hospitals, schools for preparation of health workers, and so fourth, should allow some rationalization of the system through elimination of expensive duplications of items such as open heart surgery units, cobalt therapy equipment, beds, personnel. Such a structure should foster a recognition of priorities appropriate to the pursuit of the dimensions of good health care identified above. The research center could help in the evaluation of progress toward these central goals.

SUMMARY

Some potentially measurable objectives (the dimensions of care) and the general outlines of an organizational structure for achieving them have been proposed as a way of accepting Rogers' challenge to effectuate "the organismic administration of human affairs" as they apply to health. Health service centers and regional health services planning bodies organized along lines suggested here should be set up and receive systematic evaluation, including before–after and cross–situation comparisons with other forms of organization as to the extent to which the dimensions of care are achieved. Shortcomings in theory, design, and practice will thereby be identified, and reconceptualization, redesign, and more effective practice made possible. In this process, sociology and the social sciences generally will achieve a soundness and deserved recognition heretofore unrealized.

N O T E S

1. Edward S. Rogers, "Public Health Asks of Sociology . . . Can the health sciences resolve society's problems in the absence of a science of human values and goals?" Science 159 (2) (February 1968), 506–508.

2. R. Elling, "The Design, Institutionalization and Evaluation of Change in Colombian Health Services," in R. Badgley (ed.), *Social Science and Health Planning; Culture, Disease and Health Services in Columbia,* Part 2, The Milbank Memorial Fund Quarterly, 46 (April 1968), 258–273.

3. D. Rutstein, *The Coming Revolution in Medical Care* (Cambridge, Mass., MIT Press, 1967).

4. See the chapter by Wysong and Eichhorn in this volume. Also, M. I. Roemer and E. A. Wilson, *Organized Health Services in a County of the United States* (Washington, D.C., U.S. Public Health Services Publication 197, 1952).

5. C. Seipp, et al, *Coordination, Planning and Society, Part 1, Case Studies in Coordination;* University of Pittsburgh, Graduate School of Public Health, 1969, (reproduced).

6. Michael Aiken and Jerald Hage, "Organization Interdependence and Intra-Organizational Structure," *American Sociological Review* Vol. 6 (December 1968) 912–930. S. Levine and P. White "Exchange as a Conceptual Framework for the Study of Inter-organizational Relationships," *Admin. Science Quarterly* 5 (1961), 583–601.

7. A. Strauss, et al, "The Negotiated Order," in E. Freidson (ed.), *The Hospital in Modern Society* (New York, Macmillan, 1964). J. Walsh and R. Elling, "Professionalism and the Poor" *Journal of Health and Social Behavior* 9 (March 1968), 16–28.

8. A.M.M. Payne, "Innovation out of Unity," *The Milbank Memorial Fund Quarterly* 43 (October 1965), 17–30.

9. Rogers, *op. cit.*

10. A. Donabedian, "Evaluating the Quality of Medical Care," in D. Mainland (ed.), *Health Services Research* I, Part 2 of *The Milbank Memorial Fund Quarterly* 44 (July 1966), 166–203.

11. For a discussion of methods, see E. Suchman, *Evaluative Research* (New York, Russell Sage Foundation, 1967).

12. M. Cherkasky, "Medical Manpower Needs in Deprived Areas," *The Journal of Medical Education* 44 (February 1969), 126–131.

13. R. Elling, R. Whittemore and M. Green, "Patient Participation in a Pediatric Program," *Journal of Health and Human Behavior* 1 (Fall 1960), 183–191.

14. M. S. Davis and R. E. Transquada, "A Sociological Evaluation of

262 : RAY H. ELLING

the Watts Neighborhood Health Center," paper presented before
Medical Care Section, APHA, November 16, 1968, Detroit.

15. "Portent for Neighborhood Health Centers, Bronx Conflict Focussed
on Community Control," Hospital and University Edition of *Medical
Tribune and Medical News* 3 (May 5, 1969).

16. Dr. John G. Freymann, "The Community Hospital as a Major
Focus for Continuing Medical Education," *The Journal of American
Medical Association* 206 (3) (October 14, 1968), 615.

17. H. Fry with the collaboration of W. Shepard and R. Elling, *Education and Manpower for Community Health* (Pittsburgh, University of Pittsburgh Press, 1968), p. 95.

18. H. Wise, "The Family Health Worker," *American Journal of Public
Health* 58 (October 1968), 1828–1838.

19. Dawson of Penn. Report, Great Britain, Ministry of Health, Consultative Council on Medical and Allied Services, *Interim Report on
the Future Provision of Medical and Allied Services* (London, H. M.
Stationery Office), 1920.

12 Outwitting the "Developed" Nations

IVAN ILLICH*

It is now common to demand that the rich nations convert their war machine into a program for the development of the Third World. The poorer four fifths of humanity multiply unchecked while their per capita consumption actually declines. This population expansion and decrease of consumption threaten the industrialized nations, who may still, as a result, convert their defense budgets to the economic pacification of poor nations. And this in turn could produce irreversible despair, because the plows of the rich can do as much harm as their swords. US trucks can do more lasting damage than US tanks. It is easier to create mass demand for the former than for the latter. Only a minority needs heavy weapons, while a majority can become de-

Reprinted by permission of the author and *The New York Review of Books.* Copyright © 1969, The New York Review, from *The New York Review of Books* 13 (November 6, 1969), 20–24.

* Professor and Co-founder, Centro Intercultural de Documentacion, Guernavaca, Mexico.

263

pendent on unrealistic levels of supply for such productive machines as modern trucks. Once the Third World has become a mass market for the goods, products, and processes which are designed by the rich for themselves, the discrepancy between demand for these Western artifacts and the supply will increase indefinitely. The family car cannot drive the poor into the jet age, nor can a school system provide the poor with education, nor can the family icebox insure health food for them.

It is evident that only one man in a thousand in Latin America can afford a Cadillac, a heart operation, or a Ph.D. This restriction on the goals of development does not make us despair of the fate of the Third World, and the reason is simple. We have not yet come to conceive of a Cadillac as necessary for good transporation, or of a heart operation as normal healthy care, or of a Ph.D. as the prerequisite of an acceptable education. In fact, we recognize at once that the importation of Cadillacs should be heavily taxed in Peru, that an organ transplant clinic is a scandalous plaything to justify the concentration of more doctors in Bogotá, and that a Betatron is beyond the teaching facilities of the University of Sao Paolo.

Unfortunately, it is not held to be universally evident that the majority of Latin Americans—not only of our generation, but also of the next and the next again—cannot afford any kind of automobile, or any kind of hospitalization, or for that matter an elementary school education. We suppress our consciousness of this obvious reality because we hate to recognize the corner into which our imagination has been pushed. So persuasive is the power of the institutions we have created that they shape not only our preferences, but actually our sense of possibilities. We have forgotten how to speak about modern transportation that does not rely on automobiles and airplanes. Our conceptions of modern health care emphasize our ability to prolong the lives of the desperately ill. We have become unable to think of better education except in terms of more complex schools and of teachers trained for ever longer periods. Huge institutions producing costly services dominate the horizons of our inventiveness.

We have embodied our world view into our institutions and are now their prisoners. Factories, news media, hospitals, governments, and schools produce goods and services packaged to contain our view of the world. We—the rich—conceive of progress as the expansion of these establishments. We conceive of heightened mobility as luxury and safety packaged by General Motors or Boeing. We conceive of improving the general well-being as increasing the supply of doctors and hospitals, which package health along with protracted suffering. We have come to identify our need for further learning with the demand for ever longer confinement to classrooms. In other words, we have packaged education with custodial care, certification for jobs, and the right to vote, and wrapped them all together with indoctrination in the Christian, liberal, or communist virtues.

In less than a hundred years industrial society has molded patent solutions to basic human needs and converted us to the belief that man's needs were shaped by the Creator as demands for the products we have invented. This is as true for Russia and Japan as for the North Atlantic community. The consumer is trained for obsolescence, which means continuing loyalty toward the same producers who will give him the same basic packages in different quality or new wrappings.

Industrialized societies can provide such packages for personal consumption for most of their citizens, but this is no proof that these societies are sane, or economical, or that they promote life. The contrary is true. The more the citizen is trained in the consumption of packaged goods and services, the less effective he seems to become in shaping his environment. His energies and finances are consumed in procuring ever new models of his staples, and the environment becomes a by-product of his own consumption habits.

The design of the "package deals" of which I speak is the main cause of the high cost of satisfying basic needs. So long as every man "needs" his car, our cities must endure longer traffic jams and absurdly expensive remedies to relieve them. So long as health means maximum length of survival, our sick will get ever more extraordinary surgical interventions and the drugs required to deaden their consequent pain. So long as we want to use school to get children out of their parents' hair or to keep them off the street and out of the labor force, our young will be retained in endless schooling and will need ever-increasing incentives to endure the ordeal.

Rich nations now benevolently impose a straightjacket of traffic jams, hospital confinements, and classrooms on the poor nations, and by international agreement call this "development." The rich and schooled and old of the world try to share their dubious blessings by foisting their pre-packaged solutions on to the Third World. Traffic jams develop in São Paolo, while almost a million northeastern Brazilians flee the drought by walking 500 miles. Latin American doctors get training at the New York Hospital for Special Surgery, which they apply to only a few, while amoebic dysentery remains endemic in slums where 90 percent of the population live. A tiny minority gets advanced education in basic science in North America—not infrequently paid for by their own governments. If they return at all to Bolivia, they become second-rate teachers of pretentious subjects at La Pax or Cochibamba. The rich export outdated versions of their standard models.

The Alliance for Progress is a good example of benevolent production for underdevelopment. Contrary to its slogans, it did succeed—as an alliance for the progress of the consuming classes, and for the domestication of the Latin American masses. The Alliance has been a major step in modernizing the consumption patterns of the middle classes in South America by integrating them with the dominant culture of the North American metropolis. At the same time, the Alliance has modernized the aspirations of the majority of citizens and fixed their demands on unavailable products.

Each car which Brazil puts on the road denies fifty people good transportation by bus. Each merchandised refrigerator reduces the chance of building a community freezer. Every dollar spent in Latin America on doctors and hospitals costs a hundred lives, to adopt a phrase of Jorge de Ahumada, the brilliant Chilean economist. Had each dollar been spent on providing safe drinking water, a hundred lives could have been saved. Each dollar spent on schooling means more privileges for the few at the cost of the many; at best it increases the number of those who, before dropping out, have been taught that those who stay longer have earned the right to more power, wealth, and prestige. What such schooling does is to teach the schooled the superiority of the better schooled.

All Latin American countries are frantically intent on expanding their school systems. No country now spends less than the equivalent of 18 percent of tax-derived public income on education—which means schooling—and many countries spend almost double that. But even with these huge investments, no country yet succeeds in giving five full years of education to more than one third of its population; supply and demand for schooling grow geometrically apart. And what is true about schooling is equally true about the products of most institutions in the process of modernization in the Third World.

Continued technological refinements of products which are already established on the market frequently benefit the producer far more than the consumer. The more complex production processes tend to enable only the largest producer to continually replace outmoded models, and to focus the demand of the consumer on the marginal improvement of what he buys, no matter what the concomitant side effects: higher prices, diminished life span, less general usefulness, higher cost of repairs. Think of the multiple uses for a simple can opener, whereas an electric one, if it works at all, opens only some kinds of cans, and costs one hundred times as much.

This is equally true for a piece of agricultural machinery and for an academic degree. The midwestern farmer can become convinced of his need for a four-axle vehicle which can go 70 m.p.h. on the highways, has an electric windshield wiper and upholstered seats, and can be turned in for a new one within a year or two. Most of the world's farmers don't need such speed, nor have they ever met with such comfort, nor are they interested in obsolescence. They need low-priced transport, in a world where time is not money, where manual wipers suffice, and where a piece of heavy equipment should outlast a generation. Such a mechanical donkey requires entirely different engineering and design than one produced for the US market. This vehicle is not in production.

Most of South America needs paramedical workers who can function for indefinite periods without the supervision of an MD. Instead of establishing a process to train midwives and visiting healers who know how to use a very limited arsenal of medicines while working independently, Latin American universities estab-

lish every year a new school of specialized nursing or nursing administration to prepare professionals who can function only in a
hospital, and pharmacists who know how to sell increasingly
more dangerous drugs.

The world is reaching an impasse where two processes con-
verge: ever more men have fewer basic choices. The increase in
population is widely publicized and creates panic. The decrease
in fundamental choice causes anguish and is consistently over-
looked. The population explosion overwhelms the imagination,
but the progressive atrophy of social imagination is rationalized
as an increase of choice between brands. The two processes con-
verge in a dead end: the population explosion provides more
consumers for everything from food to contraceptives, while our
shrinking imagination can conceive of no other ways of satisfying
their demands except through the packages now on sale in the
admired societies.

I will focus successively on these two factors, since, in my
opinion, they form the two coordinates which together permit us
to define underdevelopment.

In most Third World countries, the population grows, and so
does the middle class. Income, consumption, and the well-being
of the middle class are all growing while the gap between this
class and the mass of people widens. Even where per capita consumption is rising, the majority of men have less food now than
in 1945, less actual care in sickness, less meaningful work, less
protection. This is partly a consequence of polarized consumption and partly caused by the breakdown of traditional family
and culture. More people suffer from hunger, pain, and expo-
sure in 1969 than they did at the end of World War II, not only
numerically, but also as a percentage of the world population.

These concrete consequences of underdevelopment are rampant; but underdevelopment is also a state of mind, and understanding it as a state of mind, or as a form of consciousness, is
the critical problem. Underdevelopment as a state of mind occurs when mass needs are converted to the demand for new
brands of packaged solutions which are forever beyond the
reach of the majority. Underdevelopment in this sense is rising
rapidly even in the countries where the supply of classrooms, cal-
ories, cars, and clinics is also rising. The ruling groups in these

countries build up services which have been designed for an affluent culture; once they have monopolized demand in this way, they can never satisfy majority needs.

Underdevelopment as a form of consciousness is an extreme result of what we can call in the language of both Marx and Freud *"Verdinglichung"* or reification. By reification I mean the hardening of the perception of real needs into the demand for mass manufactured products. I mean the translation of thirst into the need for a Coke. This kind of reification occurs in the manipulation of primary human needs by vast bureaucratic organizations which have succeeded in dominating the imagination of potential consumers.

Let me return to my example taken from the field of education. The intense promotion of schooling leads to so close an identification of school attendance and education that in everyday language the two terms are interchangeable. Once the imagination of an entire population has been "schooled," or indoctrinated to believe that school has a monopoly on formal education, then the illiterate can be taxed to provide free high school and university education for the children of the rich.

Underdevelopment is the result of rising levels of aspiration achieved through the intensive marketing of "patent" products. In this sense, the dynamic underdevelopment that is now taking place is the exact opposite of what I believe education to be: namely, the awakening awareness of new levels of human potential and the use of one's creative powers to foster human life. Underdevelopment, however, implies the surrender of social consciousness to pre-packaged solutions.

The process by which the marketing of "foreign" products increases underdevelopment is frequently understood in the most superficial ways. The same man who feels indignation at the sight of a Coca Cola plant in a Latin American slum often feels pride at the sight of a new normal school growing up alongside. He resents the evidence of a foreign "license" attached to a soft drink which he would like to see replaced by "Cola-Mex." But the same man is willing to impose schooling—at all costs—on his fellow citizens, and is unaware of the invisible license by which this institution is deeply enmeshed in the world market.

Some years ago I watched workmen putting up a sixty-foot

Coca Cola sign on a desert plain in the Mexquital. A serious drought and famine had just swept over the Mexican highland. My host, a poor Indian in Ixmiquilpan, had just offered his visitors a tiny tequila glass of the costly black sugar-water. When I recall this scene I still feel anger; but I feel much more incensed when I remember UNESCO meetings at which well-meaning and well-paid bureaucrats seriously discussed Latin American school curricula, and when I think of the speeches of enthusiastic liberals advocating the need for more schools.

The fraud perpetrated by the salesmen of schools is less obvious but much more fundamental than the self-satisfied salesmanship of the Coca-Cola or Ford representative, because the schoolman hooks his people on a much more demanding drug. Elementary school attendance is not a harmless luxury, but more like the coca chewing of the Andean Indian, which harnesses the worker to the boss.

The higher the dose of schooling an individual has received, the more depressing his experience of withdrawal. The seventh-grade dropout feels his inferiority much more acutely than the dropout from the third grade. The schools of the Third World administer their opium with much more effect than the churches of other epochs. As the mind of a society is progressively schooled, step by step its individuals lose their sense that it might be possible to live without being inferior to others. As the majority shifts from the land into the city, the hereditary inferiority of the peon is replaced by the inferiority of the school dropout who is held personally responsible for his failure. Schools rationalize the divine origin of social stratification with much more rigor than churches have ever done.

Until this day no Latin American country has declared youthful under-consumers of Coca-Cola or cars as lawbreakers, while all Latin American countries have passed laws which define the early dropout as a citizen who has not fulfilled his legal obligations. The Brazilian government recently almost doubled the number of years during which schooling is legally compulsory and free. From now on any Brazilian dropout under the age of sixteen will be faced during his lifetime with the reproach that he did not take advantage of a legally obligatory privilege. This law was passed in a country where not even the most optimistic could foresee the day when such levels of schooling would be provided for only 25 percent of the young. The adoption of international standards of schooling forever condemns most Latin Americans to marginality or exclusion from social life—in a word, underdevelopment.

The translation of social goals into levels of consumption is not limited to only a few countries. Across all frontiers of culture, ideology, and geography today, nations are moving toward the establishment of their own car factories, their own medical and normal schools—and most of these are, at best, poor imitations of foreign and largely North American models.

The Third World is in need of a profound revolution of its institutions. The revolutions of the last generation were overwhelmingly political. A new group of men with a new set of ideological justifications assumed power to administer fundamentally the same scholastic, medical, and market institutions in the interest of a new group of clients. Since the institutons have not radically changed, the new group of clients remains approximately the same size as that previously served. This appears clearly in the case of education. Per pupil costs of schooling are today comparable everywhere since the standards used to evaluate the quality of schooling tend to be internationally shared. Access to publicly financed education, considered as access to school, everywhere depends on per capita income. (Places like China and North Vietnam might be meaningful exceptions.)

Everywhere in the Third World modern institutions are grossly unproductive, with respect to the egalitarian purposes for which they are being reproduced. But so long as the social imagination of the majority has not been destroyed by its fixation on these institutions, there is more hope of planning an institutional revolution in the Third World than among the rich. Hence the urgency of the task of developing workable alternatives to "modern" solutions.

Underdevelopment is at the point of becoming chronic in many countries. The revolution of which I speak must begin to take place before this happens. Education again offers a good example: chronic educational underdevelopment occurs when the demand for schooling becomes so widespread that the total concentration of educational resources on the school system becomes a unanimous political demand. At this point the separation of education from schooling becomes impossible.

The only feasible answer to ever-increasing underdevelopment is a response to basic needs that is planned as a long-range goal for areas which will always have a different capital structure. It is easier to speak about alternatives to existing institutions, services, and products than to define them with precision. It is not my purpose either to paint a Utopia or to engage in scripting scenarios for an alternate future. We must be satisfied with examples indicating simple directions that research should take.

Some such examples have already been given. Buses are alternatives to a multitude of private cars. Vehicles designed for slow transportation on rough terrain are alternatives to standard trucks. Safe water is an alternative to high-priced surgery. Medical workers are an alternative to doctors and nurses. Community food storage is an alternative to expensive kitchen equipment. Other alternatives could be discussed by the dozen. Why not, for example, consider walking as a long-range alternative for locomotion by machine, and explore the demands which this would impose on the city planner? And why can't the building of shelters be standardized, elements be pre-cast, and each citizen be obliged to learn in a year of public service how to construct his own sanitary housing?

It is harder to speak about alternatives in education, partly because schools have recently so completely pre-empted the available educational resources of good will, imagination, and money. But even here we can indicate the direction in which research must be conducted.

At present, schooling is conceived as graded, curricular, class attendance by children, for about 1000 hours yearly during an uninterrupted succession of years. On the average, Latin American countries can provide each citizen with between eight and thirty months of this service. Why not instead, make one or two months a year obligatory for all citizens below the age of thirty?

Money is now spent largely on children, but an adult can be taught to read in one tenth the time and for one tenth the cost it takes to teach a child. In the case of the adult there is an immediate return on the investment, whether the main importance of his learning is seen in his new insight, political awareness, and willingness to assume responsibility for his family's size and future, or whether the emphasis is placed on increased productivity. There is a double return in the case of the adult, because not only can he contribute to the education of his children, but to that of other adults as well. In spite of these advantages, basic literacy programs have little or no support in Latin America, where schools have a first call on all public resources. Worse, these programs are actually ruthlessly suppressed in Brazil and elsewhere, where military support of the feudal or industrial oligarchy has thrown off its former benevolent disguise.

Another possibility is harder to define, because there is as yet no example to point to. We must therefore imagine the use of public resources for education distributed in such a way as to give every citizen a minimum chance. Education will become a political concern of the majority of voters only when each individual has a precise sense of the educational resources that are owing to him—and some idea of how to sue for them. Something like a universal G.I. Bill of Rights could be imagined, dividing the public resources assigned to education by the number of children who are legally of school age, and making sure that a child who did not take advantage of his credit at the age of seven, eight, or nine would have the accumulated benefits at his disposal at age ten.

What could the pitiful education credit which a Latin American Republic could offer to its children provide? Almost all of the basic supply of books, pictures, blocks, games, and toys that are totally absent from the homes of the really poor, but enable a middle-class child to learn the alphabet, the colors, shapes, and other classes of objects and experiences which insure his educational progress. The choice between these things and schools is obvious. Unfortunately, the poor, for whom alone the choice is real, never get to exercise this choice.

Defining alternatives to the products and institutions which now pre-empt the field is difficult, not only, as I have been trying to show, because these products and institutions shape our conception of reality itself, but also because the construction of new possibilities requires a concentration of will and intelligence in a higher degree than ordinarily occurs by chance. This concentration of will and intelligence on the solution of particular problems regardless of their nature we have become accustomed over the last century to call research.

I must make clear, however, what kind of research I am talking about. I am not talking about basic research either in physics, engineering, genetics, medicine, or learning. The work of such men as Crick, Piaget, and Gell-Mann must continue to enlarge our horizons in other fields of science. The labs and libraries and specially trained collaborators these men need cause them to congregate in the few research capitals of the world. Their research can provide the basis for new work on practically any product.

I am not speaking here of the billions of dollars annually spent on applied research, for this money is largely spent by existing institutions on the perfection and marketing of their own products. Applied research is money spent on making planes faster and airports safer; on making medicines more specific and powerful and doctors capable of handling their deadly side-effects; on packaging more learning into classrooms; on methods to administer large bureaucracies. This is the kind of research for which some kind of counterfoil must somehow be developed if we are to have any chance to come up with basic alternatives to the automobile, the hospital, and the school, and any of the many other so-called "evidently necessary implements for modern life."

I have in mind a different, and peculiarly difficult, kind of research, which has been largely neglected up to now, for obvious reasons. I am calling for research on alternatives to the products which now dominate the market; to hospitals and the profession dedicated to keeping the sick alive; to schools and the packaging process which refuses education to those who are not of the right age, who have not gone through the right curriculum, who have not sat in a classroom a sufficient number of successive hours, who will not pay for their learning with submission to custodial care, screening, and certification or with indoctrination in the values of the dominant elite.

This counter-research on fundamental alternatives to current pre-packaged solutions is the element most critically needed if the poor nations are to have a livable future. Such counter-research is distinct from most of the work done in the name of the "year 2000," because most of that work seeks radical changes in social patterns through adjustments in the organization of an already advanced technology. The counter-research of which I speak must take as one of its assumptions the continued lack of capital in the Third World.

The difficulties of such research are obvious. The researcher must first of all doubt what is obvious to every eye. Second, he must persuade those who have the power of decision to act against their own short-run interests or bring pressure on them to do so. And, finally, he must survive as an individual in a world he is attempting to change fundamentally so that his fellows among the privileged minority see him as a destroyer of the very ground on which all of us stand. He knows that if he should succeed in the interest of the poor, technologically advanced societies still might envy the "poor" who adopt this vision.

There is a normal course for those who make development policies, whether they live in North or South America, in Russia or Israel. It is to define development and to set its goals in ways with which they are familiar, which they are accustomed to use in order to satisfy their own needs, and which permit them to work through the institutions over which they have power or control. This formula has failed, and must fail. There is not enough money in the world for development to succeed along these lines, not even in the combined arms and space budgets of the super-powers.

An analogous course is followed by those who are trying to make political revolutions, especially in the Third World. Usually they promise to make the familiar privileges of the present elites, such as schooling, hospital care, etc., accessible to all citizens; and they base this vain promise on the belief that a change in political regime will permit them to sufficiently enlarge the institutions which produce these privileges. The promise and appeal of the revolutionary are therefore just as threatened by the counter-research I propose as is the market of the now dominant producers.

In Vietnam a people on bicycles and armed with sharpened bamboo sticks have brought to a standstill the most advanced machinery for research and production ever devised. We must seek survival in a Third World in which human ingenuity can peacefully outwit machined might. The only way to reverse the disastrous trend to increasing underdevelopment, hard as it is, is to learn to laugh at accepted solutions in order to change the demands which make them then necessary. Only free men can change their minds and be surprised; and while no men are completely free, some are freer than others.

For Further Reading

Abel-Smith, Brian, *An International Study of Health Expenditure and its Relevance for Health Planning*. Geneva, World Health Organization, Public Health Papers, No. 32, 1967.

Administrative Science Qaurterly Special Issue on Organizations and Social Development, 12 (December, 1968.)

Aiken, Michael, and Jerald Hage, "Organization Interdependence and Intraorganizational Structure," *Amer. Sociological Rev.*, 6 (Dec., 1968) 912–920.

Anderson, Nancy N., *Comprehensive Health Planning in the States: A Study and Critical Analysis*. Minneapolis, Institute for Interdisciplinary Studies, American Rehabilitation Foundation, 1968 (Processed).

Badgley, Robin F., ed., "Social Science and Health Planinng, Culture, Disease and Health Services in Columbia," Part 2, *The Millbank Memorial Fund Quarterly*, 46 (April, 1968).

John Bryant, *Health and the Developing World* Ithaca, New York: Cornell University Press, 1969.

Cumming, Elaine, *Systems of Social Regulation*. New York, Atherton, 1968.

Elling, Ray H., "The Hospital Support Game in Urban Center" in Eliot Friedson (ed.), *The Hospital in Modern Society*. New York, Macmillan (Free Press), 1968.

277

————, "The Design and Evaluation of Planned Change in Health Reorganizations," in A. Shostak (ed.), *Sociology in Action*. Homewood, Ill., Dorsey Press, 1964, pp. 292–302.

Friedmann, John, "A Conceptual Model for the Analysis of Planning Behavior," *Administrative Science Quarterly,* 12 (September, 1967).

Kahn, Alfred J., *Theory and Practice of Social Planning*. New York, Russell Sage Foundation, 1969.

Levine, Sol, and Paul White, "The Community of Health Organizations," in Howard E. Freeman, Sol Levine and Leo G. Reeder, eds., *Handbook of Medical Sociology*. Englewood Cliffs, N.J., Prentice-Hall, Inc., 1963.

Litwak, Eugene, and Lydia F. Hylton, *Interorganizational-Analysis: A Hypothesis on Coordinating Agencies. Admin. Science Quarterly,* 6 (March, 1962) 395–420.

Mechanic, David, "Problems in the Future Organization of Medical Practice," *Law and Contemporary Problems.* 35 (1970).

Miller, S. M., "Solving the Urban Dilemma in Health Care: More Poverty, Greater Demand for Public Services, Reduced Financial Resources, and Fragmentation of Services," in *New Directions in Public Policy for Health Care, Bulletin of the New York Academy of Medicine.* 42 (Dec., 1966), 1150–1156. Also, Edmund D. Pellegrino, "Regionalization: An Integrated Effort of Medical School, Community, and Practicing Physician," pp. 1193–1200.

Mott, Basil J. F., *Anatomy of a Coordinating Council*. Pittsburgh, University of Pittsburgh Press, 1968.

Newman, Edward, and Harold W. Demone, "Policy Paper: A New Look at Public Planning for Human Services," *Journal of Health and Social Behavior,* 10 (June, 1969), 142–149.

Roemer, Milton I., and Ethel A. Wilson, *Organized Health Services in a County of the United States*. Washington, U.S. Public Health Service, Publication No. 197, 1952.

————, "A Coordinated Health Service and the Problem of Priorities," *Israel Journal of Medicine,* 1 (July, 1965), 643–647.

Schwartz, Jerome L., *Medical Plans and Health Care: Consumer Participation in Policy Making with a Special Section Section on Medicare*. Springfield, Ill., Charles C. Thomas, 1968.

Seipp, Conrad, ed., *Health Care for the Community, Selected Papers of Dr. John B. Grant*. Baltimore, The Johns Hopkins Press, 1963.

Seipp, Conrad, et. al., *Coordination, Planning and Society,* Part 1, Cases in Coordination: Six Studies of State Mental Retardation Planning. Pittsburgh, Graduate School of Public Health, 1968 (Processed).

————, *Medical Schools and Hospitals, Interdependence for Education and Service*. Evanston, Ill., Association of American Medical Colleges, 1965.

Somers, Anne R., "Some Basic Determinants of Medical Care and Health Policy," in William L. Kissick, ed., *Dimensions and Determinants of Health Policy,* Part 2, *The Millbank Memorial Fund Quarterly,* 46 (January, 1968), 13–31.

Stoeckle, John D., and Lucy M. Candib, "The Neighborhood Health Center—Reform Ideas of Yesterday and Today," *New Eng. Jrl of Medicine,* 280 (June 19, 1969), 11.

Index

P3